The
Van Sweringens
of Cleveland

THE WESTERN RESERVE HISTORICAL SOCIETY
Cleveland

The Van Sweringens of Cleveland

THE BIOGRAPHY OF AN EMPIRE

Ian S. Haberman

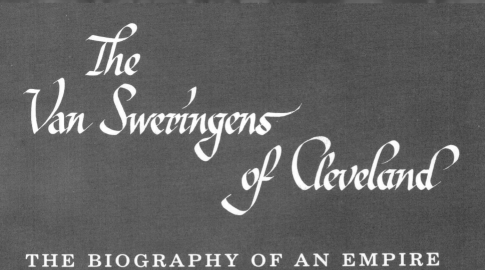

Publication of this book has been partially underwritten by a generous and deeply appreciated grant from Chessie System, Inc.

The further support of the Shaker Historical Museum is an additional and appreciated courtesy.

This is publication number 148 of
The Western Reserve Historical Society.

Library of Congress Cataloging in Publication Data

Haberman, Ian S.   1945-
    The Van Sweringens of Cleveland.

    Bibliography: p.
    Includes index.
    1. Van Sweringen, Mantis James, 1881-1935. 2. Van Sweringen, Oris Paxton, 1879-1936. 3. Erie Railroad—History. 4. Businessmen—United States—Biography. I. Title.
HE2754.V25H27   385'.902'2 [B]   79-21855
ISBN 0-911704-20-5

To C. H. Cramer

Contents

Foreword

In each generation, a few men appear who become great builders. They are men with vision, energy, and a willingness to risk. The progress of civilization often depends upon the dreams of men of this type, men who possess indomitable courage and a willingness to undertake great risks.

Such men were the Van Sweringen brothers. Beginning as newsboys, they dreamed of beautiful suburbs where farms still existed. When their suburbs needed transportation, they dreamed of fast commuter trains to the heart of Cleveland. When a railroad blocked their way, they bought the railroad. Railroad ownership brought forth the vision of a great railroad system; and, with risking, borrowing, and building, a dream of a better rail service from the Atlantic to the West. Time has proven that this dream was a very practical and necessary one.

As successful builders, the Van Sweringen brothers became powerful and wealthy; as leaders of national fame, they brought prestige to Cleveland. Not too many of us are alive today who remember the Van Sweringens and their inspiring leadership in civic affairs; yet the impact of their successful operations has left landmarks of significance such as the Terminal Tower, Shaker Heights, and Shaker Square.

Many builders who bring progress and change live to old age with fame and respect. However, some are plagued with unforeseen catastrophes such as war and depression which upset America's steady growth and which are tragic for such men. Unfortunately, the great depression struck at the peak of the Van Sweringens' success. Values on which progress was built collapsed and the empire fell. Yet memories of their achievements live on, while around us significant landmarks stand as lasting reminders of their accomplishments.

Until this publication, the dramatic story of the Van Sweringen empire had not been told. We are much indebted to Dr. Haberman whose laborious searches have unearthed this fascinating story. It represents a major contribution to Cleveland and to national history.

Our Society has a very special reason to rejoice in publishing a book about the Van Sweringens. They were Trustees of the Society who provided substantial funds to acquire some 1,700 books that filled important gaps on our library shelves.

Frederick C. Crawford
Chairman of the Board
The Western Reserve Historical Society

Preface

In the opening lines of his biography of the utility magnate, Forrest McDonald asks: "Do you remember Samuel Insull?" He provides his own answer: "Chances are you do if you are an American over forty, or have taken a course in recent American history." A similar question could be asked about O. P. and M. J. Van Sweringen, and while those born before 1930 could probably answer in the affirmative, it is doubtful whether more than a few students would be so knowledgeable. Even if someone had heard about the brothers, he or she would find it none too easy to find out more about them. Beyond an occasional chapter here or there, little is easily available in print. Indeed, a recent history of American railroads—John F. Stover's *The Life and Decline of the American Railroad*—does not even mention the Vans. It is hoped that this study will help in filling that void.

Why should one want to fill the void anyway? It is primarily to enlighten the public on the Vans' achievements, how and why they succeeded where they did—and where, how, and why they failed where they did. The underlying assumption is that there is value and utility in the public knowing how public plans and policies have been affected by the plans, hopes, and visions of two boys from small towns in Ohio.

The fabric of the Van Sweringen story must be woven from many historical threads. The economic collapse of the 1930s occasioned several investigations into the alleged abuses of "big business." One of the most important, Senator Burton K. Wheeler's probe into the railroads of the eastern United States, produced a comprehensive report in 1941 entitled *The Van Sweringen Corporate System: A Study in Holding Company Financing*. O. P. Van Sweringen died only weeks before this investigation began its hearings and never had the opportunity to "tell his own story" to the committee; to a limited degree, it was told for him by business associates and corporate records. This evidence is supplemented by the record of the brothers' involvement with the Interstate Commerce Commission. The ICC's decisions on the Vans' various applications are easily obtained; the transcripts, exhibits, and letters behind those decisions are to be found in great bulk at the commission's office in Washington, D. C. Summaries of the testimony in these cases are to be found in the balanced accounts in *Railway Age*, a journal invaluable for any study of the history of railroads.

This investigation of the Van Sweringens does not deal with matters of corporate organization or with the process of decision-making as practiced within the Vans' corporate household, nor is it more than an approximation of what the Vans "really were like." Rather, this is an attempt, on the basis of documents now available, to provide the story of how—from the most modest of beginnings—they built an empire that brought them fame, fortune, and ultimately ruin. It is the biography of an empire.

During the course of the several years required to complete this study of the Van Sweringens, I have received considerable assistance from many people. I now have the pleasure of thanking them for being so kind.

This book is based on sources, and many of those sources stand on shelves and sit in boxes in various libraries. To the men and women at Freiberger and Sears Libraries of Case Western Reserve University, the Cleveland Public Library, the Western Reserve Historical Society, the Shaker Historical Museum, the Cleveland Municipal Library at City Hall, the Robert Frost Library at Amherst College, and the New York Public Library I owe an immeasurable debt of gratitude. Special mention must be made of the legion service provided me by the staff of the Interstate Commerce Commission in Washington, D. C.

It would be impossible to mention by name the many friends and colleagues who supported, cajoled, urged, needled, and pushed me on to produce this book. They know who they are. To them I offer my thanks. I must recognize Professor James Friguglietti and David S. Levenson who read every word and offered needed suggestions for improvement.

Dean C. H. Cramer, to whom this book is dedicated and under whose tutelage this study of the Van Sweringens began, is the model advisor—critical, vigorous, demanding, patient, kind, and sympathetic. He has served as a source of inspiration for thousands of students at Case Western Reserve University; I include myself in that multitude.

The
Van Sweringens
of Cleveland

I

How It All Began

It took the Van Sweringen family over two hundred years to travel the four thousand miles between Beemsterdam, Holland, and Cleveland, Ohio. After Clevelanders became well acquainted with two of Gerret van Sweringen's illustrious descendants, many citizens of the city insisted that their lives would have been much better off had that Dutch nobleman never left Holland. But set sail from Amsterdam he did, on December 21, 1656. Only twenty years old, Gerret van Sweringen secured employment on the Dutch West India Company's ship *Prince Maurice*, then carrying immigrants and supplies to the Dutch colony of New Amstel (now New Castle, Delaware) on the Delaware River. When his ship reached its destination on April 16, 1657, he liked what he saw and decided to stay.

Gerret van Sweringen married Barbarrah de Barrette, a native of Valenciennes, France, in 1659. Trade, land cultivation, and appointments as sheriff, commissary, and member of the council at New Amstel brought him wealth and importance. When the New

3

Netherland colony passed to the British in 1664, he publicly broke his sword across his knee and renounced his allegiance to the Dutch. In 1669 he moved to Maryland. Discovering that only British subjects could own land there, he and his family became naturalized British citizens. The change in government had very little effect on the family's fortunes. Within a short time, Gerret van Sweringen rose to a position of prominence as an "innholder" and landowner, and later as an alderman of the city of St. Mary's and sheriff of St. Mary's County. His son Thomas fathered four sons of his own, thus ensuring the line's continuance. One branch of this family tree is of particular importance. It began with Thomas' son Van Swearingen (1692-1801); then came Van's son Thomas (1737- ?), who moved to Juniata County, Pennsylvania; next, Thomas' son Samuel (1760-1834); then Samuel's son Thomas (1805-1855); and finally, Thomas' son James. All became well-to-do farmers or property owners holding prominent places in their communities—all, that is, except James.[1]

James Tower Sweringen[2] was born in Bealetown (now Honey Grove), Pennsylvania, in 1832. At first he sought fortune in the Pennsylvania oil fields; later he moved to Ohio. At the outbreak of the Civil War, he joined the 4th Ohio Volunteers, seeing action at the Battle of Spotsylvania Court House in May, 1864, where he was wounded. At the end of the war, he returned to Pennsylvania and, in 1867, married Jennie Curtis. Within seven years, she had borne him four children: Herbert C., Maude Alene (who died in infancy), Carrie B., and Edith E. Some time between 1875 and 1878 the family moved back to Ohio, settling in the town of Wooster, sixty miles south of Cleveland.[3]

James Sweringen's Civil War injuries prevented him from returning to the oil fields or engaging in the hard manual labor which farming demanded. Rather, he had to limit himself to a succession of odd jobs in an attempt to support his wife and several children. Not in the best of health herself, Jennie Sweringen, "a woman of more than ordinary intelligence and refinement," gave her husband "loyal and active help . . . in the struggle to rear their family." The family remained desperately poor, always living in rented quarters, always moving from town to town. Once, when they had no place to live, they were taken in by the Paxton Downings of Wooster, who let them stay in a combination shop and summer house. Shortly thereafter their fifth child, Oris Paxton, was born on April 24, 1879, in Chippewa Township, Wooster—the "Paxton" representing an expression of thanks to the Downing family. Two years later, on July 8, 1881, Mantis James was born at Rogue's Hollow, also near Wooster.[4]

A year after Mantis' birth the Sweringens moved again, first to Wadsworth and then to Geneva, Ohio, about forty-five miles east of Cleveland. Tragedy struck the overburdened family on January 18, 1886, when Jennie Sweringen, who "for three years past had been slowly wasting away, being most of the time a great sufferer," died of consumption at the age of forty-one. In 1890 or 1891, the family moved to Cleveland, settling in the Doan (now East 105th Street) -Cedar Avenue area. James Sweringen found occasional employment as a watchman, engineer, and advertiser, but rarely did these jobs last as long as a year. Herbert worked at the Cleveland Storage Company and became the family's chief source of financial support, while Carrie, the older of the two surviving daughters, assumed the role of mother and took charge of the care of Oris and Mantis.[5]

The physical characteristics and mental habits that distinguished these two brothers as adults became noticeable quite early in their lives. The two shy boys were inseparable—Oris, the dark-complexioned, the thinker, physically slow and inactive but with a clear mind; Mantis, the light-skinned, the doer, quick and alert. An early acquaintance recalled that "O. P. was always more serious and wanted to work at something constructive, while Mantis and I were fooling around the farm. Oris did lots of things to help my mother and seemed to enjoy that more than playing ball or doing things that Mantis and I were doing." Actually, they complemented each other well; Mantis made the snowballs, Oris threw them. As Congregationalists, they had been brought up to observe the Sabbath strictly; even whistling on Sunday was not permitted. Their mother and sisters taught them neatness and good taste, while they learned thrift and enterprise from their father, primarily because he lacked them. Both first attended Bolton School, located at East 89th Street and Carnegie Avenue, then transferred to the Fairmount School on East 107th Street. Although their formal education ended with the eighth grade, the brothers continued to read widely, and out of this came a broad, if somewhat disorganized, taste for many things.[6]

Oris and Mantis, or O. P. and M. J., as they were generally known, started earning money by delivering the morning and evening editions of the Cleveland *Leader* along routes that took them up Woodland Hill Pike and onto the lands originally settled and cultivated by Shakers. At other times, they carted groceries, tended cattle, lit street lamps, and operated a bicycle shop on Bond (now East 6th) Street. In 1896 or 1897, Herbert, then a bookkeeper with the Bradley Fertilizer Company, persuaded O. P. to accept an offer of a clerkship with the same firm at a salary of $15 per week. M. J. had an egg-and-butter business for a short time but gave it up to join his two older brothers at the chemical company. In 1901 Herbert and O. P. left the company and became stone dealers, opening their own business, the Pioneer Stone Company. O. P. served as its president, Herbert as secretary-treasurer. M. J. also quit the Bradley firm to work for the Morreau Gas Fixture Manufacturing Company as a billing clerk. Within a year, however, the stone business had closed and O. P. and M. J. had formed the Prospect Storage and Cartage Company. Although this enterprise lasted less than a year, the brothers felt little disappointment at its demise. They now had the opportunity to succumb to a temptation that had long enticed them.[7]

While still in his teens, O. P. had decided that at the age of twenty-one he would enter the real-estate business. When he did, M. J. joined him. Their early real-estate ventures were conducted only on a part-time basis but were successful. Twenty-four hours after receiving an option on a house on Carnegie Avenue, they sold the property and made a $100 profit. A few weeks later they repeated this same operation. When the brothers decided to enter real estate on a full-time basis, they turned their attention to the new suburb of Lakewood, west of Cleveland. Here they met failure, and a foreclosure judgment was entered against them. This inconvenience did not stop the Vans; during the two years in which the judgment stood they continued to do business under their sisters' names.[8]

Their father died in 1903. Herbert joined the Cleveland-Cliffs Iron Company as a bookkeeper and from that point, it appears, had little involvement with his younger brothers' business affairs. Besides dealing in real estate, O. P. found another occupation. This was in March, 1905, during the trial of Cassie L. Chadwick, the lady who bilked hundreds of thousands of dollars from conservative bankers by claiming Andrew Carnegie as her father. For the duration of the proceedings, her possessions were attached, and O. P. was hired, at the rate of $5 per day, to guard them. After this episode, he went to Texas, where he tried to obtain options on a telephone line. This trip seems to have been the only time O. P. and M. J. were separated by such a distance and for a considerable length of time. When O. P. returned to Cleveland, the two resumed selling real estate. This time, however, they shifted their interests to Cleveland's east side, specifically to North Park Boulevard in Cleveland Heights, where they began subdividing properties for large residences. Success there led them to expand their venture to Fairmount Boulevard. For $3,000, one-third borrowed for the down payment with the rest to be paid in installments, the Vans purchased some acreage along Fairmount. Again the aim was the same—to provide luxurious housing for the well-to-do. Here too they met with considerable success, and this impelled them to enlarge their real-estate activities still further. A large tract of land formerly owned by a group of Shakers now attracted their attention.[9]

This area had been surveyed in 1796 and found to be well stocked with timber, grapevines, howling wolves, Indians, bees, and honey. Another thirteen years passed before the first brave souls settled there and the initial log cabin was built. In 1822 the "North Union Society of the Millenium Church of United Believers"—familiarly called the Shakers—established a colony on the property of a Western Reserve land grant inherited by a member of the sect. Though situated on a plateau some four hundred feet above Lake Erie, the colony received the name "The Valley of God's Pleasure" because of the lowlands surrounding Doan Brook, which flowed through the territory. This stream became the Shakers' source of power and sustenance: they dammed it, creating the Shaker Lakes, and used the water to power their sawmill, gristmill, and woolen mill. In addition to cultivating their extensive farm lands, the Shakers manufactured furniture, grew herbs, packaged seeds, and spun cloth.[10]

As practiced at North Union, Shakerism meant a close, disciplined, and orderly form of existence with celibacy, communism, and a religious service of singing, dancing, "quaking," and oral confession as its most obvious external manifestations. The prime sources for new members were converts and orphaned children whom the Shakers took in and raised as their own. At its peak, Shaker membership reached three hundred, but by the mid 1880s this figure had dropped precipitously. The Shakers were fighting a losing battle for survival. Indeed, the religion itself proved to be its own worst enemy.[11]

Throughout the various Shaker colonies, young people no longer felt compelled to suppress normal sexual urges, and they began fleeing the communities in droves. As one Shaker diarist observed, "Fifteen of our young people have gone to the world in less than two weeks," and an Elder predicted, "Youth shall ever be our burden." North Union did not escape this trend. "The Valley of God's Pleasure" also faced serious economic problems. A declining population and a loss of strong young people forced the Shakers to hire outside labor for the heavier farming and manufacturing tasks. This added expense came at a time when the demand for Shaker homemade products, in competition with mass-produced goods, was falling off drastically. Finally, lawsuits and unscrupulous businessmen further depleted the colony's meager treasury. In 1888 Elder James Prescott, the head of North Union, died, and the sect's governing Elders decided to disband the colony. Only twenty-seven aged Shakers remained. Admitting their attempt to create a lasting utopia a failure, they too left the community and joined other Shaker colonies in the East.[12]

On October 24, 1889, the North Union Society was dissolved; within three years a group of Clevelanders purchased the properties. Henry Avery, one of the businessmen involved, described how Shaker Heights got its name:

> One night at a dinner at my home on Granger Street, now East 19th Street, Laurence Lamb said, "What shall we call this property?" Different names were suggested by the different ones, and my wife

spoke up and said "Why don't you call it Shaker Heights, after the Shakers, and because it is high up on the hills." It was so decided that that was the name the allotment should bear. . . .

The Shaker Heights Land Company now set about to develop the properties. As a first step, a better network of roads had to be built to make the Heights more accessible. The Land Company suggested that if the landowners in the Cedar Glen area would donate a portion of the land from Cedar Road to Coventry Road along Doan Brook for park and road purposes, it would do the same from Coventry Road east. Agreement was reached between the parties involved, and, aided by a liberal donation from John D. Rockefeller, the Park Commission of Cleveland laid out and developed North Park, South Park, and East Boulevards. But rather than develop the land any further, the company sold its 1,400 acres for $316,000 to a syndicate of Buffalo capitalists headed by W. H. Gratwick and J. J. Albright. Shaker Heights was now opened for settlement, and, initially at least, the times seemed ripe for the creation of a successful real-estate development. The syndicate laid out lots, provided another boulevard, and secured the services of several land agents to get the property on the market. But the financial depression of the 1890s dampened hopes for quick profits from the sale of real estate. Gratwick, Albright, and their associates would have to wait for better days to return to Cleveland before the city's wealthier citizens would risk building palatial estates in a relatively uncharted hinterland.[13]

They did not have to wait long, for by the turn of the century prosperity had returned to Cleveland. Shipping, shipbuilding, manufacturing, coal, steel, and oil provided many Clevelanders with money to spend on luxury housing. Even so, Gratwick and Albright had had enough of trying to sell land that had grown over with weeds and brush and the appraised value of which had fallen to $240,000. They were not at all optimistic about the situation. O. P. and M. J. Van Sweringen were; they saw great possibilities for the future. In late 1905 the brothers met with O. C. Ringle, the land agent for Gratwick and his associates, and obtained and then sold a few of the lots Ringle had on his hands. Shortly thereafter, and at Ringle's urging, they travelled to Buffalo to see if a complete arrangement could be set up.[14]

The Vans met with Gratwick and asked for an option to sell a number of the Shaker Heights plots. They did not come to Buffalo "hat in hand." Certain that they could succeed where others failed, they pressed for the acceptance of two key demands. First, they insisted that if they succeeded in disposing of the land within a specified period of time, they would be guaranteed a second option for the sale of twice as much land. Second, not wanting to put any of their own money behind their plan, the brothers proposed to sell the land first and then pay the Buffalo syndicate from the proceeds. Gratwick and his fellow investors realized that nothing would be lost and all could be gained from such an arrangement; they accepted the brothers' offer.[15]

All that was needed to turn Shaker Heights into a profitable real-estate development was vision, energy, and courage. The Vans possessed all three. They had already demonstrated their abilities as real-estate salesmen on the Fairmount Boulevard development, and their reputation for fairness and honesty brought them the support of wealthy and influential Cleveland businessmen (the stigma of the Lakewood foreclosure judgment having long since disappeared). But ability would go for nought unless the brothers had something people wanted to buy.[16]

The barriers of Lake Erie to the north and the industrial district to the south combined with a rapid influx of immigrants moving into the older residential areas of the city to force wealthy Clevelanders to search for new land suitable for high-quality residential living. To the well-to-do and those with sufficient credit to act well-to-do, the Vans offered the idea of a superior suburban village, ideally located in relation to downtown Cleveland. They easily disposed of the first block of optioned land and soon returned for more, fulfilling each succeeding sales contract in the same way. After they had sold about two hundred acres, it became apparent to the brothers that this tedious and time-consuming procedure prevented them from operating at their maximum. They decided to buy the entire twelve hundred acres still held by the Buffalo-based Shaker Heights Land Company. Actually, the Vans did not purchase this acreage; instead, they organized a syndicate of Cleveland businessmen, including bankers J. R. Nutt and Charles

Lee Road from Fairmount, looking south (ca. 1900-1905)

"The Valley of God's Pleasure"
The abandoned Shaker Village in 1898

Lower Shaker Lake (1904)

Moreland Circle, looking southeast—the site of Shaker Square (ca. 1927-1928)

Bradley, securities dealers Warren S. Hayden and Otto Miller, and several others, to buy the land for them. They continued to follow this same pattern during the three decades spanning the growth of their corporate empire. Thus it was from their development of Shaker Heights that they first learned how to convince others to provide them with the financial backing needed for their expansion plans.[17]

When the Vans began, Shaker Heights consisted of little more than brambles, weeds, and brush. The streets had deteriorated into impassable and unusable lanes, while the long-deserted Shaker dams, mills, and communal buildings lay in ruins. Within a few years the brothers cleared the land, repaired what merited saving, made improvements to restore and enhance the natural charm and beauty of the area, and created (as one commentator observed) "the fashionable residence locality of the city." They succeeded because, as a piece of promotional literature phrased it, "Most communities just happen; the best are always planned." Ten years of careful planning preceded the formal opening of Shaker Heights for public sale.[18]

"There had been no instance in the history of American real estate development," one architectural authority wrote, "where any man or set of men had set such a definite plan for the development of so large a piece of property along such rigidly controlled lines as the Van Sweringens set for the development of the Shaker farm tract." The keystone of their plan was the accommodation of houses of different price levels on the same tract of land without the destruction of the value of the more expensive homes. This was accomplished by abandoning the traditional "gridiron" scheme of straight streets and rectangular blocks in favor of the novel "curvilinear" style of street design. This fundamental plan for the physical layout of Shaker Heights provided for through traffic along straight, wide thoroughfares running east and west—Fairmount, Shaker, South Moreland (now Van Aken), Kinsman (now Chagrin), South Woodland—and along other roads running north and south—Coventry, Lee, Warrensville Center, Green, and Richmond. Within this system of main thoroughfares, curved "inside" streets divided the properties into the different price sections. In addition, these "inside" streets were laid out in conformity to the natural topography of the land, thereby providing home sites which would be esthetically pleasing, distant from heavy traffic, and serviceable in terms of providing outlets for storm water.[19] The plan was imaginative, useful, and practical. While the traditional real-estate community may have scoffed at the Vans' idea of putting 180-to-200-foot-wide boulevards through the Heights, that same idea immediately struck the fancy of Cleveland's house-hunting wealthy. And that was what mattered most. O. P. once recalled that he and his brother had been told "gently but unmistakably that it was nonsense . . . [to give] away land that might as well be sold." But as it turned out, he noted, those same lands became "more profitable to us than if we had sold them as lots."

Thoughtful planning explains only part of the Vans' triumph. Another important factor was their skill in selecting the right men for the job at hand, a talent the brothers would use to considerable advantage throughout their careers. In this instance, the designation of the F. A. Pease Engineering Company to do all the work relating to drawing surveys, mapping subplots, and designing and improving streets, plus that firm's skill in translating the brothers' visions into concrete reality, looms large as a vital element in the ultimate success of Shaker Heights.[20]

The first section of Shaker Heights to be surveyed, platted, and readied for sale by the Vans was the area roughly bounded by North Park Boulevard and Coventry, South Woodland, and Warrensville Center Roads. Next came the area directly south of the first development, extending the settlement to Kinsman (Chagrin) Road, and then the tract of land between Warrensville Center and Green Roads. Finally, the brothers began, but never finished, the "Shaker Country Estates," 4,000 acres lying east of Green Road, between Fairmount and South Moreland (Van Aken) Boulevards, and stretching as far as the Chagrin River. To sell these properties, the Vans established the Van Sweringen Company, the vehicle that was to be used for practically all of the realty transactions relating to Shaker Heights from 1913 until several years after the brothers' deaths. They realized that a variety of sales methods would be both a necessity and a valuable asset in getting the Shaker development started. "My idea," one of them explained, "is to build a few high-priced homes and offer them so much less than cost to the people of the right sort that they will be irresistible. In that way we'll get the place pioneered." One innovation consisted of selling small blocks of Shaker Heights property at the moderate price of $25 a front foot while guaranteeing to repurchase any particular plot of land from a dissatisfied buyer if the value of the land had risen to $30 a foot. However, most original sales were made not to individuals but rather to syndicates. These groups purchased or underwrote sections of land which would be subdivided into home sites and later sold to individuals, usually under the auspices of the Van Sweringen Company itself or its adjunct, the Green-Cadwallader-Long Company. When they wholesaled lots in such a manner, the Vans insisted there be no fewer than ten persons in any given syndicate, reasoning that a number of lots owned by ten or more men, each one of them having a circle of acquaintances, would sell far more rapidly than one-tenth the same number of lots owned by one man.[21]

On July 31, 1916, Green-Cadwallader-Long opened the Shaker Heights allotment for public sale. The time had come for making a community out of plots of land. But it would not be just any community. Stringent restrictions regulated the architecture of houses, their relation to street lines, the appropriateness of their color schemes, their resale, the construction of multi-family dwellings, the placement of business districts—all, as the Vans said in one piece of promotional literature, to "safeguard home communities [so] that you can select your neighborhood now and safely plan for generations." "Shaker Village Standards" meant several things. Conservative architectural designs, usually in Colonial, English, or French styles, had to be in accord with rigid specifications as to the "proper" kinds and colors of sash, shutters, doors, chimneys, fly-screens, roof, mortar, balconies, stucco, shingles, and stonework. All had to receive the approval of the village's Architectural Board. The re-sale of Shaker Heights houses was limited to those buyers approved by the Van Sweringen Company or by a majority of the owners of adjoining lots. These deed restrictions were to be imposed for ninety-nine years in order to insure against the encroachment of "undesirable" improvements and residents, both of which, the Vans held, would depreciate the value of Shaker residential property. Until after World War II such "undesirables" included Jews, Roman Catholics, and blacks.[22]

No apartment houses might be built in Shaker Heights. However, recognizing the rights of apartment lovers, the Vans placed the corporate boundary of the suburb at Coventry Road so they could build, west of Coventry, the stately Moreland Courts complex and other apartment buildings. (The restriction against apartment houses was removed after World War II.) While insisting that industrial enterprises had no place in a strictly residential area, the brothers realized that sections of Shaker Heights had to be set aside to provide for the shopping needs of Shaker residents. Therefore, business districts were situated at the intersections of main streets and at sufficient intervals so as to avoid the need for travelling too great a distance in order to shop. The most pleasing—and yet the most revolutionary—design of all was placed at Moreland Circle at the junction of Shaker and South Moreland Boulevards. With its fine shops, restaurants, bank, and theatre, Shaker Square was said to be the nation's first fully planned and integrated shopping center. Philip L. Small and Charles Bacon Rowley designed it in uniform Georgian architecture, thereby giving the development the appearance of a quaint English village. When Shaker Square opened in 1929, it contained twelve stores and office buildings; it had cost $1,000,000, exclusive of land, to complete. During the first year of operation, the volume of business at the Square was $200,000. As Shaker Square was about to celebrate the fiftieth anniversary of its founding, its owners could note with pride that the shopping center continues to meet many of the needs of Shaker Heights residents.[23]

Despite—or more likely because of—these strict regulations, the village boomed. Statistics tell part of the story. Shaker's population of 200 in 1911 grew to 1,600 in 1920 and to 18,000 in 1930. By 1923 some 60 miles of improved streets with sidewalks, sewers, and utility connections had been laid down; twelve years later this figure rose to 161 miles. The lands comprising Shaker Heights had been appraised for taxation purposes at $240,000 in 1900, but this figure swelled to

$2,525,800 in 1910, $11,805,810 in 1920, and $29,282,000 in 1923. This increase of 7,200 percent in land values over the short time span of twenty-three years led the Cuyahoga County Auditor to report, "It is doubtful if there is another taxing district in the entire world which has made such phenomenal increases in land values during this period." He continued, "It is a very conspicuous example of what may be accomplished by constructive real estate development and reflects great credit upon the promoters thereof." When other interests began to consume a greater share of their time, the Vans entrusted the future development of Shaker Heights to one of their closest friends and business associates, Benjamin L. Jenks, who became president of the Van Sweringen Company. Under his careful scrutiny, Shaker continued to grow at an astounding rate; for example, on the $30,000,000 worth of land sold from 1922 through 1935, over 4,500 building permits were issued and more than $67,500,000 worth of construction was completed. Jenks made certain that it was all in complete accord with the basic aims and principles the Van Sweringens had set down for developing what they expected to be *the* perfect suburban community.[24]

But houses, businesses, and streets alone do not make a community. A municipal government, schools, cultural and recreational centers, and a rapid transit had to be provided for the Vans' total plan to be fully realized. In 1905 and 1906 governmental control over the Shaker settlement, previously divided among Warrensville, East Cleveland, and Newburgh Townships, was unified when it became a part of the Village of Cleveland Heights. In August, 1911, these lands, and other tracts adjacent to them, were detached from Cleveland Heights and consolidated to form the Township of Shaker Heights; O. P. Van Sweringen and two associates acted as trustees of the Township. This interim measure served as a prelude to the establishment of the Incorporated Village of Shaker Heights on October 27, 1911. Shortly afterwards, the land between East 128th Street and the Baldwin Reservoir was separated from Shaker Heights and made a part of Cleveland. In later years the suburb attained its present legal boundaries by the transfer of lands from Warrensville Township, East View, Beachwood, and Idlewood (now University Heights). First John

Mitchell and then Ford M. Clapp served as mayor of the fledgling community. In 1915 William J. Van Aken, a realty associate of the brothers, was elected mayor. Along with Benjamin Jenks, he shaped much of the future development of Shaker Heights. By 1929 $12,000,000 worth of bonds had been issued for municipal improvements, including several million dollars for schools.[25]

From the beginning, the task of providing a superior education for the children of Shaker Heights residents remained an overriding concern of the Vans. One of the brothers once stated that if necessary they would "provide big automobile vans to take the children of our settlers to the nearest school and deliver them back home again each noon and evening"—until the needed schools had been built in Shaker itself. For the first two years of its existence, Shaker Heights conducted classes in a building that also served as the city hall and housed the engineering offices of the Van Sweringen Company at Shaker Boulevard and Lee Road. Eventually, the village erected the Southington School as the first of many instructional facilities. The Vans also aided the school board in a survey of future educational needs of Shaker Heights and in the acquisition of land needed for the construction of eight new public and three private schools. By 1923 the brothers could boast of an investment of almost two million dollars in property and equipment devoted to education; they could promise that "the present schools will be supplemented by others, until there is practically one for each square mile of Village area." In 1924, to ensure a complete program of educational opportunities from grammar school through college, the brothers offered a 300-acre tract as a site for the proposed "greater university of Cleveland" to be formed by the merger of the Case School of Applied Science and Western Reserve University. The institutions did not merge at that time and declined to accept the gift. However, the site did become the home of the Hathaway Brown School for Girls, while the Vans' efforts to get St. Ignatius College (now John Carroll University) to move from downtown Cleveland to the vicinity of Shaker Heights also met with success.[26]

Shaker residents could choose from a variety of recreational facilities. The Vans were convinced that the establishment and the successful operation of golf courses were essential to the proper development of the Shaker Heights they envisioned. Therefore, they deeded territory around the upper Shaker Lake to the Shaker Country Club and were similarly instrumental in the founding of the Canterbury and Pepper Pike Country Clubs. Other activities available to Shaker Heights included the Troop A Riding Club, the Cleveland Tennis Club, the Shaker Lakes Canoe Club, and "three hundred acres of parks . . . filled with birds and affording breathing space for Shaker residents." The Coit-Lyceum "course of attractions," among other programs, contributed to the cultural life of Shaker Heights; the season of 1921-1922 included such guests as Pitt Parker, a cartoonist-humorist, Mrs. Breed, a reader, Burnel R. Ford, an electric wizard, and Charles C. Gorst, a bird man.[27]

The beautiful homes, the restrictions, the stores, the parks, and the clubs led Lord Rothermere, the English newspaper tycoon, to call Shaker Heights "the finest residential district in the world." Even the Van Sweringens' severest critics have praised their development of the community. One stated quite clearly: "I think you will find few suburbs in our country more sweetly planned, or so well cared for." Another lauded the "thriving suburb . . . which they had so skillfully and ambitiously engineered." But all of their planning and restrictions and beautiful homes would have gone for nought if there had been no rapid transit to take the inhabitants of Shaker Heights to their offices in downtown Cleveland. The rapid transit remains the chief reason for the success of Shaker Heights.[28]

II

The Vans Buy a Railroad

W<small>ILLIAM</small> J. V<small>AN</small> A<small>KEN</small>, the long-time (1916–1952) mayor of Shaker Heights, once referred to the Shaker Rapid Transit as "the lifeline" without which the "miracles" of the suburb would never have occurred. From the outset, O. P. and M. J. Van Sweringen knew that the success or failure of their model community would ultimately depend upon the village's transportation facilities to downtown Cleveland.[1]

The experience gained from their earlier real-estate development along Fairmount Boulevard taught them that "population follows transportation" and gave them a sharp understanding of commuters' needs that shaped much of their future involvement in real estate and railroads. In 1905, in the days of unpaved streets when nearly everyone travelled by trolley, the Vans had faced a very real problem: to prospective homeowners, would the physical desirability and beauty of the Fairmount Boulevard development outweigh its location some two to three miles beyond the nearest stop of one of the Cleveland Railway Company's streetcar lines? To meet this need for added transportation, the brothers proposed that a spur to the railway's "Heights" line be built. Only when they had agreed to pay a monthly addition to the fares collected did John J. Stanley, the hard-nosed president of the transit company, consent to build the desired extension. By 1907 service was being provided along the "Shaker Lakes" or "Fairmount Boulevard" line which ran out Euclid Avenue, up Cedar Hill, then via Cedar Road to Fairmount and out Fairmount to Lee Road.[2]

When the Vans' real-estate interests shifted to Shaker Heights, the necessity of providing sufficient rapid-transit service for future Shaker residents proved to be an immediate and pressing reality. O. P. Van Sweringen later recalled that "it was impossible to do anything with the property in any material way without car service." He soon returned to President Stanley's office with a request for another extension. But Stanley hedged, stating that he would extend the line once the brothers had populated the area. After some dickering, Stanley did agree to build the extension from the Fairmount Boulevard line south on Coventry Road into one small section of Shaker Heights—but only after the Vans had consented to provide the extension's right-of-way and pay part of its cost.[3]

However, with more than four-fifths of the Shaker Heights territory still lacking any trolley service, this extension could in no way meet the expected demand for quick public transportation. In fact, sales of real estate in that part of Shaker lagged and the Vans realized that the chief reason for this was the section's lack of a rapid-transit link to downtown Cleveland. O. P. paid a third visit to Stanley, now carrying a proposal that Cleveland Railway build another extension through this larger portion of Shaker Heights. This time Stanley flatly refused. Since the building of the other line, he maintained, it had become evident that extensions of local streetcar lines were "bleeders instead of feeders" to a traction system. Even if the brothers gave him the whole line built and ready for operation, Stanley asserted, he would not accept it. Part of the problem stemmed from an anti-trolley climate resulting from the battle then raging between Cleveland Mayor Tom L. Johnson, the protagonist of the three-cent fare, and the city's traction interests. The Vans appeared to be stymied. Here was enough acreage to supply homes for a community of 25,000 people, but to have Shaker Heights serve those for whom it was planned, a way had to be found to bring the development closer to Cleveland. A solution was discovered in 1909 when the Van Sweringens decided to build their own rapid transit from Shaker Heights to downtown Cleveland. This decision proved to be a turning point for the careers of these hitherto unknown young men, for Cleveland, and, eventually, for the history of American railroading.[4]

Having determined to go into the rapid-transit business, the Vans now searched for the best possible route for their proposed line. The brothers, following an established habit, spent hours consulting various government topographical maps. (Referring to their interest in maps, O. P. once explained to a friend, "My favorite authors are Rand and McNally.") A seemingly insignificant thin black line caught their attention. Their eyes had fastened upon a ravine that led from the one-time heart of downtown Cleveland to Shaker Heights. Most Clevelanders saw this gully, along what was called Kingsbury Run, as a hindrance to central-city expansion southward, and O. P. Van Sweringen himself called it "more or less a tin can disposal plant." But a careful study made it apparent that this site could provide the ideal right-of-way for the Vans' rapid transit.[5]

"Here," wrote one of the Vans' public-relations men, "was a great inclined runway almost to the heart of Cleveland, wonderfully adapted to traction service; a remarkable excavation arranged by nature, which, with good engineering skill, could be utilized for rapid travel, bringing Shaker Heights within *fifteen minutes of the office*, yet keeping it *six to eight miles from the city smoke*." Over a period of several years, the brothers obtained many of the properties comprising Kingsbury Run, as well as four acres downtown at Public Square for a proposed terminal to serve the half-dozen interurban lines entering Cleveland. On July 18, 1911, they organized the Cleveland and Youngstown Railroad Company (C. & Y.) to construct a four-track electric railway to take passengers from Cleveland through Shaker Heights, Chagrin Falls, Garrettsville, Leavittsburg, Warren, Niles, and Girard, and on into Youngstown. The proposal met a generally favorable reception in Cleveland. In October of the same year, when the C. & Y. filed an application with the Cleveland City Council for a franchise to build the line, business interests received the news enthusiastically and the *Plain Dealer* "welcomed" the project as an "aid in the solution of the city's pressing transportation problem." Within a year's time, the city council had granted the C. & Y. request "without debate or opposition."[6]

City approval secured, the Vans now had to find a way to pay for the project. True, the brothers had done well in their initial real-estate ventures, but most of their profits had been plowed back into other land enterprises. They themselves did not have the several million dollars needed to build the C. &. Y. alone; however, they soon discovered a friend at the New York Central Railroad.[7]

In 1913 the Van Sweringen brothers sought to acquire a piece of farmland adjoining their properties in Shaker Heights. They approached the owner, a dynamic, charming former Clevelander named Alfred H. Smith, senior vice-president of the New York Central. During one of Smith's trips to Cleveland, O. P. and Smith met and "closed the deal in less than three minutes." Those three fateful minutes marked the beginning of a close working relationship between the Van Sweringens and Smith that would change the course of the brothers' lives. Smith introduced them to the world of railroading—and altruism on his part had nothing to do with it.[8]

Smith's New York Central lines were having problems in Cleveland. Three Central roads passed through the city: the all-important Cleveland, Cincinnati, Chicago and St. Louis (the "Big Four"), the Lake Shore and Michigan Southern (the "Lake Shore"), and the all-but-forgotten New York, Chicago and St. Louis (the "Nickel Plate"). The Nickel Plate had a terminal at Broadway and East 9th Street, while the Lake Shore and Big Four, until 1905, shared the lakefront Union Station with the Pennsylvania Railroad. Built in 1865, this depot had become, by the turn of the century, decrepit and a bottleneck unable to serve a city that had seen a ninefold increase in population during the years 1860 to 1900.[9]

To relieve some of the pressure and congestion on its lake front lines, the Central built the twenty-mile-long Cleveland Short Line Railway between 1906 and 1912. When completed, it took freight traffic not bound for or originating in Cleveland south around the city, thereby freeing the lakefront trackage for passenger trains and local freight. But this too soon proved inadequate. From 1904 to 1909 Cleveland experienced a tremendous industrial boom. During that period the number of industrial establishments grew by 33 percent, the amount of capital invested in Cleveland industries increased by 45 percent, and the total value of products manufactured in the city leaped by 58 percent. Its location alone prevented the Short Line from giving the Central lines much help in servicing Cleveland's industrial needs. In addition, new commercial and industrial sections were developing south of the city, while the Central's principal freight terminals were still located close to Lake Erie on the north. This situation alone might not have been disastrous for the Central, but at the same time a new, well-located terminal the Pennsylvania had built in 1905 enabled that line to take away a considerable amount of business. Also, the Central's freight terminals, even with their unfavorable location, were already being taxed to capacity—at a time when the demand for freight facilities was increasing at a rate of 7 percent a year. An extra twenty cents per ton which the cartage interests charged the Central lines to haul freight from the lakefront did not help matters either. These conditions were thoroughly familiar to Alfred H. Smith when he had that first meeting with the Vans.[10]

After agreeing to sell the farm to the Vans, Smith asked O. P. for a tour of the Cleveland & Youngstown's property on Kingsbury Run. "I hadn't the slightest idea what was in his mind," O. P. later recounted, but he "gladly" complied with the request:

I took him to this place which was in Kingsbury Run near 37th Street. He stood and looked the territory over for a few minutes, asked about the elevations and grades, . . . looked toward town studying the territory along Broadway and Pittsburg Avenues, and then asked if in my judgment a block of land in the latter region could be assembled cheaply, giving me an idea of the dimensions of the property he would want. I agreed to plat and tabulate it and make an estimate of its cost. He then wanted to know whether our right of way, the Cleveland & Youngstown, was wide enough so he could have room for two tracks. . . .

It now became apparent to O. P. Van Sweringen what Smith had in mind. Smith believed he had found a way to improve the Central's situation in Cleveland. By using a portion of the C. & Y.'s right-of-way in Kingsbury Run, he could provide the freight facilities the Central lines needed.[11]

Negotiations between the Vans and the New York Central began early in 1913 and ended on August 5 of that year. Several important provisions of the agreement stand out. First, the brothers agreed to give half of their C. & Y. right-of-way to the New York Central, retaining the other half for their rapid transit. Second, the C. & Y. would not only lay track for the rapid-transit line from Shaker Heights to downtown Cleveland, but would also build a freight terminal at the intersection of East 15th Street and Broadway and Orange Avenues, and a make-up and assembling yard at East 40th Street in Kingsbury Run. Third, and most significant, the necessary money for purchasing additional land and for constructing the various facilities would be supplied by the New York Central. Once again, the Vans had found a way to carry out their plans—this time for a rapid transit for Shaker Heights—with capital provided by someone else.[12]

When the Vans applied for city council approval of their freight terminal project, council was not nearly as unanimous as it had been four years earlier when the initial C. & Y. grant had been authorized. Councilman Alex Bernstein led the fight by introducing twelve crippling amendments to the proposed ordinance; all failed, and the measure subsequently passed, 19 to 6. However, enough signatures were gathered from opponents of the project to put the ordinance to a referendum vote.

Opposition to the project came from several sources. The Citizens' Referendum League, for example, objected to the ordinance "on the ground that it is closing too many streets where its freight terminal is to be established." The Broadway Improvement Association challenged the project for severing "direct communication of the members of the association with their churches, with the schools of their children and with a district which has hitherto been a source of much valuable trade to them." But the chief reason for the antagonism of Councilman Bernstein and others lay in their suspicion that the New York Central—a dirty word to many in Cleveland—had encouraged the project mainly to get out of its agreement to participate in building a union depot on the lakefront. During the council debate on the matter, the Vans neither admitted nor denied the Central's involvement in their freight terminal project. As O. P. wrote to Mayor Newton D. Baker, in a letter transmitted to city council, "the high level freight yard of the Cleveland & Youngstown Railroad will be used by various railroads, and . . . the New York Central is one of those railroads." Nothing was said of the Central-C. & Y. financial arrangements. Despite these questions, the ordinance received approval at the general election on November 2, 1915, by a vote of 62,836 to 23,631.[13]

Largely under the direction of W. E. Pease, the Vans' chief engineer, construction of the Shaker Rapid began, and within a short time considerable progress had been made in establishing grades, laying road foundations, building bridges, and letting out contracts for structural steel and rails. By 1914 C. & Y. tracks reached East 34th Street, but at this juncture they hit a snag in the form of the dilapidated Nickel Plate railroad. Typically, the Vans succeeded in turning a possible disaster into their own good fortune.[14]

Unknown to the Vans, the Nickel Plate was planning to expand its own Kingsbury Run freight facilities and had already purchased some land there—land that the Vans would need not only to complete their rapid-transit line but also for their interurban terminal. When they found the Nickel Plate comfortably ensconced in the path of their project, the brothers realized they had two options: either seek a costly rearrangement of their real-estate/rapid-transit plans for downtown Cleveland, or come to terms with the Nickel Plate's owners for joint use of that line's lands and facilities. Initial discussion followed this second option and focused on a Van proposal to provide the Nickel Plate with an entry into the freight facilities they were going to build, in exchange for the C. & Y.'s use of the Nickel Plate right-of-way from 34th Street into downtown Cleveland. "We saw," O. P. later recounted, "that if we could arrange with the Nickel Plate it would save a good many hundreds of thousands, if not into the millions, by enabling us to get through and at the same time giving them high level freight facilities." To the brothers, William H. Canniff, the popular and efficient president of the Nickel Plate, seemed moderately encouraging; still, in terms of practical results, little came of these discussions. Late in 1914, however, the situation changed appreciably, primarily as a result of a Department of Justice anti-trust investigation into the relationship between the Nickel Plate and its parent company, the New York Central.[15]

The Nickel Plate had been a part of William Vanderbilt's New York Central lines since the 1880s. Initially built by some enterprising promoters as a 523-mile blackmail road to parallel and compete with the Central's Buffalo-to-Chicago Lake Shore and Michigan Southern, the Nickel Plate soon proved equal to—if not better than—the Lake Shore. When that road's profits dipped, and when it appeared that the Central's arch-rival, Jay Gould, might purchase the Nickel Plate, the Vanderbilt forces succumbed to the pressure and by 1887 controlled the Nickel Plate. Now the New York Central system could decide whether to feed or starve the line—and for nearly all of the years it owned the road, the Central did little to nurture the Nickel Plate. When the Vans became involved with the road, it had fallen into such disrepute that some called it an "aging streak of rust" and Cleveland Mayor Newton D. Baker claimed that it ran "just frequently enough to be dangerous."[16]

While the United States Department of Justice showed only a minimal concern for the Nickel Plate's physical attributes and cared little about the line's timetable, it did express certain doubts as to the legality of the Central's control of the Nickel Plate, especially in view of the recently enacted Clayton Anti-Trust Act. Soon thereafter a rumor began to circulate that the Central would be quite willing to sell its not-quite-so-nickel-plated orphan. The Vans knew that the successful completion of their rapid-transit/real-estate project would require either the Nickel Plate's tracks and right-of-way or an expenditure of much time and upwards of a million dollars for additional land and construction. They also knew that the Central did not relish the thought of allowing the road to fall into the hands of any of its competitors, the

Lackawanna, the Pennsylvania, or any other unfriendly railroad. Therefore, claiming that the Nickel Plate "dovetailed" with their overall plans, and believing that it, with the terminal project, would make "a valuable development" for the city of Cleveland, the Van Sweringen brothers decided to buy the railroad.[17]

In mid-February, 1915, O.P. Van Sweringen wrote to Alfred H. Smith, now president of the Central system, asking what it would cost to purchase the Nickel Plate. Smith's reply was: "$9,000,000." Nothing came of this inquiry immediately. Ten months later, however, Smith began in earnest to determine what might realistically be asked for the Central's Nickel Plate interest. This action came only one week after U.S. Attorney General Thomas W. Gregory informed Smith that the New York Central's control of both the Nickel Plate and the Lake Shore and Michigan Southern constituted "a combination of naturally competitive lines of interstate transportation," and therefore violated the Clayton Anti-Trust Act. On January 31, 1916, Smith wrote to the Vans asking for "any information . . . as to the possibilities regarding the matter of taking over the railroad that you were considering." The Vans' first definite offer for control of the Nickel Plate came on February 4, but was not acceptable to the Central; their second proposal, made on February 17, met with the Central's approval. For $8,500,000, the brothers would receive 62,400 common, 25,032 first preferred, and 62,750 second preferred shares in a 523-mile railroad capitalized at close to $60,000,000; they also obtained first call on vast acreages of choice land on both the east and west sides of Cleveland. They agreed to pay $2,000,000 down and give ten notes of $650,000 each for the balance; the first note was payable in five years and the remaining ones were due in successive years after that.[18]

To consummate the deal, the Vans first had to come up with the $2,000,000 in cash for the down payment, a "hard enough" task for two brothers who did not have $2,000,000 in the bank. Their obvious alternative was to borrow the money, and by July 3, 1916, they had successfully negotiated a $2,100,000 loan from Cleveland's Guardian Savings and Trust Company, pledging as collateral their equity in the Nickel Plate shares along with several thousand shares of Terminal

Properties Company, a recently organized consolidation of a number of their real-estate projects. With this down payment in hand, they completed the purchase of the Nickel Plate shares two days later, on July 5.[19]

The Vans had to find a method for paying the interest, and later the principal, on the $650,000 notes due the Central, as well as for repaying the Guardian loan. Here they turned to the corporate device of the "holding company," a mechanism which they would use with considerable skill in the years to come.[20] On December 4, 1916, they formed the Nickel Plate Securities Corporation for refinancing the Nickel Plate purchase. To this holding company the Vans transferred their right, title, and interest in the agreement of July 5 with the New York Central together with all of the capital stock of the Nickel Plate described in that agreement, and their stock in another newly created enterprise, the Cleveland Terminal Company. In exchange for this, the Nickel Plate Securities Corporation gave the Vans all of its common stock (250,000 shares worth $12,500,000 in which was vested the exclusive voting power), assumed all of the brothers' obligations incurred in the agreement of July 5, and agreed to accept responsibility for repaying $2,074,787 the brothers still owed the Guardian Savings and Trust. Within two weeks, 20,100 shares of Nickel Plate Securities preferred had been sold, bringing $2,010,000 into the corporation's treasury; a conveniently timed Nickel Plate first-preferred dividend fattened that same treasury by an additional $210,455. On January 3, 1917, the Guardian loan was settled and the first note to the New York Central paid.[21]

Reaction was favorable to the Vans' purchase of the Nickel Plate and what it meant for their terminal plans. The Cleveland *Plain Dealer* called it "a boon and the realization of a dream of years," while the *Cleveland News* lauded the brothers for "doing MORE FOR CLEVELAND than they are for themselves." Later commentators would find much to criticize in the brothers' financial methods; one complained about the "shoestring" that had "never . . . been more skillfully looped around the throats of varied, cumulative enterprises," while another called their "perfection and abuse" of the holding company and "use of other people's money in banks" a "betrayal of Cleveland." In 1916, however, there was hardly a raised eyebrow and, with everything done openly and aboveboard, none would have been expected.[22]

Ingenious financing was only one half of the Van Sweringen technique. The other half was able operation, and here the Vans followed one of their long-standing business practices: they hired one of the best railroad men in the United States to run their new acquisition. "Chunky, compact, sparing of word and quick of deed," John J. Bernet was, according to one author, "an authentic railroad hero of the most popular type." Bernet was born in Erie County, New York, on February 9, 1868. After attending public schools, he found employment first as an office boy, then as a blacksmith, and in 1889 as a telegrapher for the Lake Shore and Michigan Southern. He received successive promotions to train dispatcher, trainmaster, assistant division superintendent, division superintendent, and assistant general superintendent. In 1911 he was appointed assistant to the vice-president, and later assistant vice-president of the Central Lines west of Buffalo, with headquarters in Chicago. In 1915, with the consolidation of the New York Central and Hudson River and the Lake Shore and Michigan Southern Railroads into the New York Central, Bernet became resident vice-president in Chicago for the consolidated lines.[23]

When M. J. Van Sweringen announced the appointment of Bernet as president of the Nickel Plate, he asked the reporters gathered to "please tell the public that Mr. Bernet will really operate the Nickel Plate using his own ideas as to how to build it up. He's a first class railroad man, and nobody will interfere with him." Producing as he did, there never was any need to. In the future, Bernet would hold the post of chief operating officer for the Vans' railroad empire; for the present, however, this shining light in the Central's galaxy of topnotch operating men, whom many had considered to be Smith's hand-picked successor for the top post at the New York Central, had a huge task ahead—to make that "aging streak of rust" into a railroad.[24]

Guided by three simple principles—economy, sound equipment, and new business—Bernet turned the Nickel Plate into a profitable road. He was convinced that passenger traffic would barely pay its own way, if at all. For that reason he did not attempt to compete with his old employer for that branch of the railroad business. The Nickel Plate had travelled 91,472,607 passenger miles during the year ending December 31, 1914; by the end of 1921, this figure had fallen to 43,083,509 and passenger receipts constituted only 7 percent of the road's total revenues. Not the passenger trade but freight traffic in coal and high-grade manufactures made money for railroads. To this type of business Bernet gave his greatest attention. He converted the one-track line into a two-track road, lengthened sidings and strengthened bridges to accommodate heavier freight, bought locomotives that really pulled, built new stations, shops, and engine houses, and created a new *esprit de corps* among Nickel Plate employees. Within four years' time, Bernet had plated the Nickel Plate with gold. In 1916 the road's operating revenue was $23,969 a mile; by 1920 Bernet had increased it to $44,867 a mile. When he took charge of the line its average trainload was 355 tons; in four years he had raised it to 771 tons. Per freight mile earnings had been $1.82 in 1915; in 1919 they were $6.32. Traffic expenses in 1915 reached $1,075 per mile; they fell to $604 per mile by 1919. And while gross income increased more than 100 percent during the same period, a rise of only 25 percent in operating expenses accommodated the new business. In such ways, the Nickel Plate strengthened its treasury; by 1919 the road's finances were in such good shape as to warrant the declaration of a 5 percent dividend on its common stock.[25]

The Nickel Plate purchase occupies a significant place in Van Sweringen history. For one thing, it brought the brothers into the steam railroad business, the basis for their future growth. Also, it marked their financial "coming-of-age," for the methods they used to pay for their latest acquisition exemplified the techniques they subsequently perfected in the 1920s when they became the largest individual owners of railroads in the United States, controlling some 30,000 miles of track worth over $3 billion. Its immediate importance, however, lay elsewhere. With the Nickel Plate guided by the firm hand of John J. Bernet, the Vans now returned to the source of their initial encounter with the road: their plans for a rapid-transit line to Shaker Heights.[26]

Purchase of the Nickel Plate stock gave the Vans the green light to resume construction of the Shaker Rapid. However, World War I, with its building restrictions, high prices, and shortages of material, caused numerous construction delays so that actual operations did not start until April 11, 1920. Initially, the Rapid took its passengers from Public Square through Kingsbury Run to Shaker Square, a distance of 6 ⅛ miles. At Shaker Square, the line divided (as it still does) into two surface branches, one extending 2 ⅞ miles over South Moreland (now Van Aken) Boulevard as far as Lynnfield Road, the other extending 2 ⅝ miles over Shaker Boulevard as far as Courtland Boulevard. To eliminate unnecessary delays, the Vans built the line without grade crossings between downtown and Shaker Square, and with grade crossings every one-third mile on the Shaker and South Moreland branches. They lengthened the Shaker branch to Warrensville Center Road in 1928 and to Green Road in 1937, and the South Moreland branch to Warrensville Center Road in 1932. All of these plans worked, for when completed the Rapid did what it was supposed to do; it took Shaker residents, including those living at the end of the line, downtown in less than thirty minutes. At the same time an unusual and profitable situation developed on the Shaker system. Running through a territory whose residents clamored for domestic help, the Rapid carried maids and gardeners eastward in the morning, providing a counterbalance to the inbound traffic and thus making it one of the few transportation systems able to collect fares in both directions during rush hours. In addition, the Vans had plans to construct business or community centers at the various Rapid stops in Shaker, in order to derive some income from the concessions. None was ever constructed during their lifetimes, however.[27]

When it first began operations, the Shaker Rapid used the Cleveland Railway Company's tracks to move its cars from East 34th Street to Public Square. This route was a circuitous one, crossing many city streets and occasionally leading to traffic delays. The Vans soon saw construction of their own tracks and a hasty completion of their terminal project as immediate necessities—and it was upon these undertakings that their attention now focused.[28]

III

A Towering Achievement

The story of how the Van Sweringen brothers gave Cleveland its most notable landmark—the Terminal Tower—begins thirteen years before O. P. Van Sweringen was born. On November 10, 1866, Amasa Stone, one of Cleveland's leading citizens and president of the Cleveland, Columbus & Cincinnati Railroad, hosted a brilliant banquet. At its conclusion he dedicated the city's new Union Depot. Located at the edge of Lake Erie just east of the mouth of the Cuyahoga River, this 603-foot-long structure of Berea stone had been constructed at a cost of $475,000, making it what many considered the finest railroad station west of New York City. The Cleveland *Leader* forecast in grandiloquent terms that "the massive walls of this incomparable structure will stand while Time endures, and though Cleveland should increase ten-fold in population, still will its ample accommodations be sufficient for the ten thousand travelers who would daily enter its portals."[1]

Thirty years later, however, this one-time city showplace

provided Clevelanders with only the minimum in terminal facilities and
had become a soot-covered eyesore that caused civic-minded citizens
much embarrassment. One enterprising but furious advertising man,
Charles Bryan, erected a huge billboard near the station directed at
those New York Central and Pennsylvania passengers using the
facility: "DON'T JUDGE THIS TOWN BY THIS DEPOT." Nor, he
might have added, by *any* of the city's train depots, since those of the
Nickel Plate, Baltimore & Ohio, Erie, and Wheeling & Lake Erie lines
were just as shabby and unsightly, their only virtue being a secluded
location in the Cuyahoga River Valley southwest of the Public Square.[2]

Public demands for the Union Depot's replacement grew louder
until a solution seemed in sight. For several years prior to the turn of the
century, Clevelanders engaged in a search for the best way to provide
federal, county, and city authorities with some new and desperately
needed downtown facilities. A variety of factors—most notably the
success of the famous grouping of buildings at the Chicago World's Fair
of 1893—encouraged plans for constructing a federal building, a city
hall, a county court house, and a public library on a single site and with
a uniform style of architecture. Inspired by the Chicago example, the
Cleveland Architectural Club held a competition for "proposed
arrangements of the public buildings in a comprehensive group." No
specific project emerged from this exercise, but one positive result was a
broadened enthusiasm for the concept of a "grouping" of public
buildings: the Public Library board, the Cleveland chapter of the
American Institute of Architects, and the Chamber of Commerce,
among many others, soon endorsed the idea. Supporters of a "group
plan" launched a broad campaign to convince the public of the
desirability and feasibility of such a proposal. Under this pressure the
Ohio legislature passed the necessary laws creating a commission of
three architects charged with the task of devising a "group plan" of
public buildings for Cleveland. In June, 1902, Mayor Tom L. Johnson
appointed the first members of the Group Plan Commission: Daniel H.
Burnham, the famed planner of the "White City" at the Chicago Fair of
1893, along with John H. Carrère and Arnold W. Brunner, both experts
in the design of public buildings.[3]

After several months of study, the commissioners released a *Report* which recommended that the public buildings be constructed on a site bounded on the north by Lake Erie, on the south by Superior Avenue, on the east by Erie Street (now East 9th Street), and on the west by Seneca Street (now West 3rd). This area of the city had once been a prime residential neighborhood but, by the beginning of the twentieth century, had deteriorated into a slum. Building on this site had two advantages: first, the needed land could be acquired at a comparatively low cost, and second, a run-down section of Cleveland could be cleared. Moreover, by 1903 construction of an imposing "United States Post-Office, Custom House, and Court House" on Superior Avenue had already begun.[4]

The blueprints included included this Federal Building, a County Building, a City Hall, and a Public Library flanking the four corners of a broad mall that would form the main axis of the group of buildings and would lead from the lakefront to Superior. The Public Library would be to the east of the Federal Building on Superior, with the space between forming the south entrance to the mall. At the northern limit of the mall, at the end of a stately colonnade between the County Building and the City Hall, was to be located the entrance to a proposed Union Station. Here on the lakefront a dignified entrance to the city would greet travellers.[5]

Within a few years the City Hall, County Court House, and Federal Building had been built; the Library was not erected until the mid-1920s. However, a long-standing land dispute between the city and three railroads threatened plans for the proposed union depot on the lakefront. The origins of this controversy can be traced to 1849, when the Cleveland City Council "sold" for $15,000 a plot of land on "Bath Street" to predecessor-companies of the Cleveland, Cincinnati, Chicago & St. Louis, the Lake Shore & Michigan Southern, and the Pennsylvania railroads. Located on the lakefront between Water Street (now West 9th) and the Cuyahoga River, this tract initially contained six or seven acres; using land-fill, the railroads enlarged the strip so that by the early 1890s it comprised over fifty acres crowded with trackage, engines, water tanks, turntables, and a station. This was fine for the railroads, but to city officials it represented a loss of fifty choice acres of harbor space needed for shipping; as a result, in 1893 Cleveland went to court to recover the land. For over twenty years, this continuing litigation effectively prevented the development of a friendly, working relationship between the city and the railroads. While the suit was in the courts, no agreement on a new depot was possible. Eventually, the courts decided in favor of the city by holding that the city council had only *leased* the Bath Street property to the railroads in question and that the city still maintained the "right, title and interest in and control over the property." Forced to deal with a landlord who wanted to evict them from an area on which they had constructed several million dollars worth of facilities, the railroads now became quite willing, even anxious, to talk with the city about a new lakefront depot and an agreement allowing them to remain on Bath Street.[6]

Mayor Newton D. Baker, hoping for a true union station that would serve *all* the steam railroads entering the city, not simply the Central's lines and the Pennsylvania, extended invitations to the Erie, Wheeling & Lake Erie, Baltimore & Ohio, and Nickel Plate roads to join the negotiations. But these four lines came into the city from the south— unlike the other roads which entered along the lakefront—and therefore they declined the offer on the grounds that they could not afford constructing the new trackage needed to bring them in along the lake. Discussions began in 1913 between Mayor Baker, Alfred H. Smith of the New York Central, and J. J. Turner of the Pennsylvania.[7]

An all-encompassing accord was reached on August 12, 1915. The city agreed to release its rights to the Bath Street tract in exchange for an equivalent amount of filled land east of East 9th Street. In addition, the railroads consented to buy a piece of land between West 3rd and East 9th Streets, at a cost of some $1,000,000, for the site of the depot on the lakefront. These provisions were embodied in Ordinance No. 37901-A, the so-called "1915 Union Depot Ordinance." Passed first by the Cleveland City Council, it was subsequently approved by the Cleveland electorate at the general election in November, 1915, by a vote of 68,357 to 17,153, receiving the "very great approval" that the *Plain Dealer* had believed the measure deserved. Steps were taken immediately to complete architectural plans for the depot, acquire the needed property, and start construction. But American entry into World War I, with its resulting shortages of men, materials, and money, quickly halted work on the project. Ultimately this killed the Union Depot on the lakefront by setting in motion a series of events which subsequently gave the Van Sweringen brothers the opportunity to turn what they had once envisioned as a small interurban station on Public Square into a huge union depot at the same location.[8]

The Vans had developed these plans for a depot over several years. In 1909, while obtaining the land needed to construct the rapid transit to suburban Shaker Heights, they had purchased four acres at Public Square for the line's downtown terminus. By the time of the Cleveland & Youngstown's incorporation in 1911, talk revolved around plans for a full-size terminal designed to accommodate all of the electric interurbans that came into the Square as well as all of the trolleys that radiated from it; later the four steam railroads that came into the city from the south and had declined to join the project on the lakefront—the Baltimore & Ohio, Wheeling & Lake Erie, Erie, and Nickel Plate roads— received invitations to join the enterprise. With their purchase of the Nickel Plate in July, 1916, the Vans further stimulated the project by arranging for their own engineers to meet with counterparts from the Wheeling & Lake Erie and Erie railroads for the purpose of developing specific plans for a depot. This group worked together for several months, producing a report in March, 1917, that called for the joint construction of a stub-end depot (as opposed to a through station) adjacent to Public Square; subsequently the B. & O. asked to join the project on a tenant basis.[9]

But just as America's entry into World War I halted the plan for a lakefront depot, so too did it hamper progress on the Vans' proposed depot at Public Square. Agreements had just been reached among the various railroads involved in the brothers' project when, on January 1, 1918, the United States Railroad Administration (U.S.R.A.) came into existence, and the government gained control of the railroads. With U.S.R.A. approval now required for the capital expenditures involved in such a large-scale project, the Vans quickly submitted their plans to

John Skelton Williams, its Director of the Division of Finance. On February 20 Williams informed them that "the Director General [William G. McAdoo] will not object to some appropriate plan for financing the terminal proposition" and asked them to "submit in detail the specific plan which you think should be adopted." Just prior to the Vans' submission of those detailed plans, the Regional Director for the Eastern Division requested a meeting with O. P. to discuss railroad congestion in Cleveland. Out of this encounter was to come still another proposal for a union depot, this one to be built not on the lakefront but on Public Square, and to be used by *all* steam railroads that entered the city.[10]

"Chaotic" was the only way to describe the situation in which American railroads found themselves in early 1918; during the previous year they had gone through an operational crisis when suddenly confronted with the demands of war. Statistics on freight-car supply clearly demonstrate this. In 1915 there were 300,000 more freight cars than loadings, but in 1917 the nation's shippers produced loadings for 100,000 to 150,000 more freight cars than the railroads possessed. In 1916 English and French war orders were beginning to create traffic congestion on eastern trunk lines and in terminals; within a year, war exports had increased so much that car shortages and terminal congestion constituted dangerous problems. Cleveland, which served as the gateway to the East for traffic through Chicago, St. Louis, and Cincinnati, became a severe bottleneck. Solving this problem was the task assigned to the U.S.R.A.'s Regional Director for the Eastern Division, the Vans' old friend, Alfred H. Smith. In searching for a solution, Smith confronted two basic facts: first, the New York Central and Pennsylvania railroads' passenger traffic constituted a full 30 percent of the total lakefront traffic, and, second, the bulk of Cleveland's industries devoted to manufacturing war materials were located along the tracks of these two railroads. Smith reasoned that the shift of passenger trains off the lakefront and onto tracks that would lead into a depot closer to the center of the city, possibly at Public Square, would automatically free the lakefront trackage and terminals for freight and considerably increase the freight capacity of those facilities. This was the substance of the suggestion that Smith made to O. P. Van Sweringen during their meeting. As O. P. later recalled it:

> He [Smith] said to me: ". . . In short, I want to relieve the freight situation, which is congested out there: I want to open up the through ways, and I had in mind that the solution was to put the passenger business on those tracks and leave the facilities that now exist exclusively for the use of freight facilities or for the freight business. The freight business can't be moved; you can't change those facilities; they are tied to industries." "Well," I said, "Just how will you get in the union station on the lakefront?" I presumed that hadn't occurred to him. He said—he hesitated a moment and then he said: "Is your station that you are proposing over on the square large enough?" and I told him that I thought it might be, but I called his attention to the fact that as it was then designed, it was a so-called stub-end station, as applied to other railroads, and would involve a back-up movement for perhaps a train length from the main right-of-way. He replied that that was not desireable [*sic*], he wouldn't stand for that on such trains as limited trains, and then he suggested to me the idea . . . "Can't you turn your tracks around and make a through station of it, building a new bridge across the Cuyahoga Valley and getting out through the west?"

As a "citizen of Cleveland . . . [whose] future depends upon the success of Cleveland," O. P. told Smith he "would be very glad to try it."[11]

Compared with the plan for a terminal on the lakefront, the proposed terminal on Public Square had its weaknesses: cost would be higher; the hilly site meant steeper approaches and grades, as well as sharply curved entrances; it threatened to increase the concentration of traffic at the Square; it would reverse the trend of Cleveland's business development out Euclid Avenue; and it violated the "Group Plan" in which the city had invested so much. But the Public Square plan also had its strengths. For one, shifting the passenger traffic off the lakefront would leave that trackage free for through freight and local industrial traffic, thus meeting Smith's request. Beyond that, there were clear advantages for Clevelanders in general and the train-travelling public in particular: though the project would cost more, its large size and central location would enable all of the steam railroads, as well as all interurban and rapid-transit lines, to use it. Thus it would serve as the true union terminal the lakefront station could never be. It could provide better commuter service by removing the interurbans from city streets, putting them on tracks alongside steam railroad rights-of-way, and cutting their average running time by thirty minutes. Finally, if the new depot violated the published "Group Plan," it also proposed to eliminate the slum south of Public Square, putting in its place "a magnificent architectural development, involving perhaps in its ultimate cost an expenditure of $50,000,000." O. P. Van Sweringen, rarely the master of overstatement, said, "I regard this situation of a union terminal proposed on the Public Square as the greatest improvement Cleveland has ever had to consider."[12]

In late May, 1918, despite an initial lack of enthusiasm in Cleveland for the idea, the Vans convened a group of engineers from each of the city's steam railroads to discuss Smith's suggestion for consolidating all of Cleveland's passenger stations into a single union-passenger terminal. By August this committee concluded that "the proposed plan [is] feasible from a physical standpoint." The Vans then organized the Cleveland Union Terminals Company as the corporate instrument for executing it. Negotiations between the company and the railroads resulted in a proposed contract which provided for the Vans' sale of Terminals Company stock to the railroads; in addition, the railroads would either advance the monies needed or guarantee the bonds the terminal company would have to issue in order to pay for constructing the terminal. The contract stipulated that even after they had sold the stock, the Vans would remain involved in the project by receiving proxies to vote the shares of the Terminals Company at their own discretion during the period of construction.[13]

While the committee of engineers continued to consider such details as cost, routing of trains, track layout, warehouse and freighthouse development, and the possibility of congestion, plans had advanced sufficiently to allow the Vans, in September, 1918, to bring before the Cleveland City Council an ordinance authorizing the Cleveland Union Terminals Company to build the proposed terminal. Between September 11 and October 22, 1918, council met fifteen times to discuss the proposal. O. P. Van Sweringen and his aide, John L.

Cannon, president of the Terminals Company, responded to numerous questions. How urgent a measure was it? Did it destroy the "Group Plan" in which the city had invested millions? What would be done about smoke? When would the lines be electrified? Would congestion increase on Public Square? Who would pay for the project? Should there be a time limit on construction? Did city council have any jurisdiction over rates? Finally, on October 23, 1918, after two months of such sharp questioning, the council voted 21 to 2 to approve Initiated Ordinance No. 47814 and set January 6, 1919, as the date for the public to vote on the measure.[14]

Initially, Cleveland's newspapers gave very little coverage to the debates in council. Instead they devoted most space to reports of the impending peace in Europe and the influenza epidemic at home. A few weeks before the referendum, however, the project became a controversial issue. Newspaper advertisements of the Terminals Company proclaimed that it would employ "thousands of workers and returning soldiers," add "millions of dollars to the tax duplicate of the City" thus "lighten[ing] the load that the taxpayers are now carrying," and "greatly lessen . . . pedestrian surface traffic in the Public Square." Its critics, such as the "Citizens Committee," urged Clevelanders to vote "NO" on the project, calling it a monopoly that would cost the city millions and "SOMETHING OF A NEW YEAR'S PRESENT TO PICK UP ON ELECTION DAY." The newspapers now rallied behind the project. The *Plain Dealer* called it "one of the biggest public improvements ever submitted to the approval of the people of Cleveland," while the *News* had "no hesitancy in urging a favorable vote upon every citizen who has the interest and welfare of his home city at heart." Several days before the special election a "spirited debate," lasting over two hours, was held at Gray's Armory between William H. Boyd, who defended the proposal, and Councilman E. H. Krueger and former Judge R. M. Morgan, who attacked it. When the votes in the referendum were finally counted, Clevelanders had approved the plan 30,731 to 19,859.[15]

Following passage of the ordinance, the Vans began discussing with the railroads involved such specific details as cost and terms for using the terminal. Although a more expensive venture than the contemplated lakefront depot, the Public Square project received approval by the New York Central and the Big Four in November, 1919. Negotiations with the Pennsylvania did not go as smoothly, however. Citing "the salient and striking advantages of the Lake Front site . . . over the public square site," available at a much lower price, the Pennsylvania announced that it would not join the project on the Square.[16]

Clevelanders reacted with indignation and defiance. "The Pennsylvania railroad cannot bulldoze the citizens of Cleveland," stormed Councilman James J. McGinty, while the *News* suggested that "Cleveland can get along without the Pennsylvania as comfortably as the Pennsylvania can get along without Cleveland which is very comfortable indeed." The Pennsylvania's decision not to participate in the Public Square project also led the normally taciturn O.P. Van Sweringen to affirm: "We believe that the union station should be built whether it is used by the Pennsylvania Railroad or not. . . . At the next meeting of the City Council we will request proper action by the Council which will permit us to go forward immediately with the building of this station." Further legislation from council was necessary because the ordinance as passed in January, 1919, stipulated that unless the Central, Big Four, *and* Pennsylvania joined the project the ordinance would become null and void. Thus the possibility existed that *no* terminal would be built; a solution had to be found, and quickly. On December 17 Councilman McGinty, the Vans' champion in city council, introduced Emergency Ordinance No. 51011, which was designed to amend the Ordinance of 1919 by requiring that only two of the three railroads signal their intentions to use the depot. With the New York Central and its subsidiary, the Big Four, already in favor of the Public Square depot, this seemed a very neat solution to the problem.[17]

However, to many this was an incorrect interpretation of the City Charter and a misuse of the legislative device of "emergency legislation." The Civic League of Cleveland wrote city council asking it to defeat the proposed ordinance and study the entire proposition further. The Chamber of Commerce also urged that the measure be rejected and insisted that "this ordinance is of too great importance to be the subject of emergency legislation." Council itself was willing to consider the measure as an "emergency" only if the council clerk could determine whether any of the other Cleveland railroads, besides the Central and Big Four, would be interested in joining the project. Since no satisfactory replies came of the clerk's inquiry, the ordinance was defeated on December 29, 1919, when it received 17 yea votes and 9 nays—one vote shy of the two-thirds needed to pass a piece of emergency legislation.[18]

Reaction came swiftly. The Builders' Exchange and the Cleveland Building Trades Council, among many others, vehemently protested the council's decision. John L. Cannon, president of the Terminals Company, suggested quite plainly that "apparently the Public Square station is dead." The next day, December 30, Mayor Harry L. Davis made what he called "one last attempt to pass the legislation so vital to the growth and progress of the city." He called a special meeting of the city council and announced that he had met with representatives of the B. & O., Wheeling & Lake Erie, Nickel Plate, and Erie railroads who had assured him that "if the ordinance passed they had reason to believe they would enter the depot and be part of the contract." After this plea from the mayor, the council voted again. This time the measure was approved, 19 to 6. A five-minute ovation ensued, and a very pleased O.P. Van Sweringen declared: "We are going to make good with the people of Cleveland and build them the much needed depot. . . . We mean business."[19]

But the terminal was not to be built as quickly as O.P. would have liked. On July 11, 1920, the Esch-Cummins Act (Transportation Act of 1920) became effective; it required the brothers to seek Interstate Commerce Commission approval of the plans they had worked out between the Terminals Company and the railroads. In February, 1921, the New York Central, Big Four, and Nickel Plate roads made a joint application to the ICC for "Certificates of Public Convenience" to build and use the proposed terminal and for authority to purchase the corporate stock of the Cleveland Union Terminals Company. During the proceedings which opened in Washington on April 19, the commissioners heard a great deal of testimony and received numerous letters from supporters and critics of the plan. Professor A. R. Hatton of Western Reserve University insisted that "the chief motive of the promoters of the station on the square has been that of a gigantic land speculation rather than transportation," while Cleveland Mayor W. S. FitzGerald stated that "the proposed improvement is a very much needed one for the City and for the railroads." Obviously a bitter struggle was in the offing.[20]

Leading the attack against the project almost single-handedly was Peter Witt, the man Mayor Baker had appointed street railway commissioner of Cleveland in 1912. Although his education had ended at the fifth grade, Witt ably countered the arguments offered by F. J. Jerome and H. D. Howe, the railroads' distinguished legal counsel, and those of former Mayor Baker, now counsel to the Van Sweringens. He took up the battle for two reasons. Witt held no one in higher regard than his late mentor, Mayor Tom L. Johnson. Because of his loyalty and affection for Johnson, as well as his own conviction about the rightness of the idea, he clung tenaciously to Johnson's "group plan" with its proposed union depot on the lakefront. Even more important, he viewed the Vans' entire project as a scheme whereby "representatives of special privilege" and "malefactors and conspirators against the welfare of the common people and the city" could make themselves a lot of money. While Baker waxed "eloquent" over the new proposal that would "enormously improve" both freight and passenger service to Cleveland, Witt "with a finger pointing and eyes blazing" denounced the entire proposition as "fraudulent" and warned the commission against a "grab." When the ICC voted, with only one dissent, to dismiss the application, it was obvious that the former traction commissioner had been persuasive indeed; virtually all of the reasons cited for denying the request had been advanced by Peter Witt.[21]

The commissioners did not quarrel with the need for a new terminal in Cleveland. They did question whether "the project for which the people voted is . . . in all respects the project which is now under consideration," and pointed to "evidence of a sharp division in both public and expert opinion" on the question of its site. Beyond these issues, the commissioners expressed great reservations over the financial arrangements connected with the proposal. They objected strongly to the "unusual provision" authorizing O. P. Van Sweringen "until completion and tender of a portion of the union passenger terminal to the Railroads . . . , to vote the stock of the Cleveland Union Terminals at any general or special meeting of the stockholders of said company for the election of Directors." The ICC found such an arrangement, which meant that control of a project the railroads would be financing would not be theirs, was unjustifiably favorable to the project's promoters, the Vans. It was also skeptical about the prospects of the interurbans paying an annual rental of $850,000 for use of the terminal. At that time the interurbans were not financially healthy and a plan under which they would receive some income from the terminal's stores, restaurants, and the parcel room seemed tenuous and insubstantial. Finally, the Vans' proposal for control of the terminal's "air rights" seemed of doubtful propriety to the commission. The depot plan called for development of the site on two levels, with two terminals for steam railroads and electric interurbans on the lower level and various office buildings on the upper level. The Vans designated this upper level as "air rights"; its development was to be carried forward by one of their companies, the Cleveland Terminals Building Company. The ICC was not "persuaded that the reservation of 'air rights' in the hands of private interests is in accordance with sound public policy."[22]

Refusing to accept defeat and imbued with a "we've just begun to fight" attitude, the Van Sweringens and their friends filed for a rehearing before the ICC and mounted an intense campaign for a different decision. On August 26, 1921, the commission granted their request for a rehearing and directed Commissioner Johnston B. Campbell to hold it in Cleveland. During the week of September 20 Campbell heard testimony from the city's leading business, civic, political, and social organizations—all of which demonstrated solid support for the project. Expressions of approval came from the Democratic and Republican County Executive Committees, and from the Chamber of Industry, the Chamber of Commerce, the Cleveland Federation of Labor, the Kiwanis Clubs of Cleveland and Lakewood, several Knights of Columbus councils, and the Veterans of Foreign Wars. Even the Administrator of the Catholic Diocese of Cleveland expressed his support: "Catholicism and civic progress are synonymous, and if we stood quietly by and let the adverse decision of your body pass without a vigorous protest, we would feel that we were not keeping step with the policy of progressiveness that we have always maintained in other civic matters."[23]

Beyond this "sentiment" testimony, as Commissioner Campbell called it, more substantial evidence supporting a terminal on Public Square came from a variety of reasonably qualified sources. For one thing, a depot on the lakefront would not be a *union* depot. G. A. Paquette and P. A. Hayes of the Big Four testified that routing the B. & O., the Erie, and the Wheeling & Lake Erie over Big Four tracks would be a physical and operational impossibility. "Such a plan," said Hayes, "would add to burdens from which we are now seeking relief." Representatives of the B. & O. and the Erie argued that a lakefront station would slow down their running time, add to congestion on tracks already overloaded, and increase operating costs. Both called the Public Square project "feasible and desirable"; in fact, Ralph M. Beglem, general manager of the western lines of the B. & O., stated that "if the station were located on the Mall, I don't think the B. & O. would use it." Six of the seven steam railroads entering Cleveland preferred Public Square to the lakefront. Chances for the construction of Cleveland's desperately needed union terminal were greatest if that terminal were located on Public Square.[24]

Another point stressed throughout the rehearing was that rapid-transit and interurban lines would use the terminal. W. H. Boyd, one of the Vans' lawyers, introduced a document signed by officials of all seven interurban companies indicating their willingness "to avail themselves of the opportunity to use the proposed Public Square passenger station." Bringing these lines into the terminal on rights-of-way adjacent to the steam railroad tracks would remove interurban cars from city streets, cut running time, and relieve street congestion in the downtown area—all positive results. To allay any fears that the interurbans would not be able to pay the $850,000 rental, evidence was

ntry Station,
r Village

field Station,
r Village

land Station,
r Village

Rapid Transit Railway

The southeast corner of Public Square, site of the Cleveland Union Terminal and Tower

An early rendering of the Cleveland Union Terminal

Downtown Cleveland and the Terminal Tower, from the northeast

"Sentinel of the Night" by John C. Moddejonge

presented claiming their profits from concessions in the proposed depot alone would produce an income of almost $850,000.[25]

Throughout the week of testimony Peter Witt continued to damn the entire project and engage in verbal "tilts" filled with "sarcasm and asperity." Witt's cross-examination of one witness "furnished a cross-fire of personalities and passages so sharp" that Commissioner Campbell once peremptorily brought the proceedings to a halt. When Attorney Boyd declined to make public the estimated cost of property still to be bought, Witt retorted, "That is the trouble with your entire transaction. . . . It was born in the dark, carried through the political sewers of the city and involves intricacies that are a shame and a disgrace to the railroads participating in it." Newton D. Baker replied dryly that "those who know Mr. Witt and his oratorical efforts are aware that his habitual assumption of virtue to himself and vice to everybody else is chronic."[26]

This time, Witt's effort failed. After receiving the additional testimony, the ICC reversed its previous decision and on December 6, 1921, voted its approval of the Vans' Union Terminal project. "In approaching this problem," Commissioner Campbell wrote for the majority, "care must be taken to consider the city of Cleveland not only from the standpoint of local convenience and needs, but as a gateway through which passes a huge volume of through traffic, both freight and passenger." Campbell called Cleveland "the congesting point of this great highway of national transportation" and cited estimates of a 27 percent increase in industrial growth within five years. He foresaw "the time . . . when local traffic and switching will be of such volume as to make Cleveland a point of constant restriction or blockage of through traffic, unless the facilities are enlarged." To the ICC, the Vans' proposed plan, with "the great advantage of completely segregating the passenger movement through the city, thus leaving the full capacity of the lakefront tracks and of the Cleveland Short Line available for freight movements only," seemed to be feasible, not unduly costly, and in the public interest. In a stinging dissent three times the length of the majority report, Commissioner Joseph B. Eastman reached the exact opposite conclusion, arguing that railroad congestion in Cleveland could be relieved effectually and with a "much smaller expenditure of capital" by adoption of the Mall plan. Subsequently, he referred to the project as a "wholly unnecessary opportunity for great private profit . . . bestowed upon the Van Sweringens." It was not the last time the fiercely independent Eastman would lock horns with the Vans.[27]

Before and during the commission's deliberations on the Union Terminal proposition, the Vans sought the financial backing they would need to pay for the project when and if the ICC gave its approval. Initially, they sought a bond offering of $10,000,000. Acknowledging that the Cleveland banks upon which they had depended in the past were too small to provide the large-scale financing required, they held discussions with representatives of various New York banking houses, but these negotiations came to naught. The price the banks offered for the bonds, coupled with a proposal that the Vans give them part of the "air rights," led the brothers to look elsewhere.

Their old ally Alfred H. Smith suggested they contact the New York Central's bankers, J. P. Morgan & Company. Following this advice they eventually reached an agreement with the Morgan, and in June, 1922, the first series of bonds was issued. Although the Vans could not turn over the bulk of terminal financing to Cleveland banks, they saw to it that the recently formed Union Trust Company, in which their close friends J. R. Nutt, C. L. Bradley, and J. J. Sherwin held the top executive positions and the Cleveland-based securities firm of Hayden, Miller & Company, headed by their old associates William S. Hayden and Otto Miller, received 15 and 10 percent respectively of the issue. From June, 1922, until March, 1930, $60,000,000 worth of Cleveland Union Terminal bonds were offered for sale through a syndicate consisting of J. P. Morgan & Company, National City Company, First National Bank, Union Trust Company, Chase National Bank, and Hayden, Miller & Company. As in their smaller promotions prior to the terminal proposition, the Vans had succeeded in attracting investors willing to provide the money required to carry out a project that cost more than they themselves could pay.[28]

At last, construction of the Union Terminal could begin. Before anything could be erected, however, thirty-five of Cleveland's most corrupt, squalid, crime-ridden, and poverty-filled acres had to be razed. Under the direction of "the world's greatest wrecker," W. H. Suloff, 2,200 buildings on that site were demolished, and the 15,000 people who lived there were relocated. In addition to eliminating many of the city's meanest eyesores, Suloff oversaw the destruction of a number of historic buildings: two hosteleries, the Forest City and American Houses; two breweries, Diebolt's and Gehring's; the Central Police Station; and Stein's Cafe. Portions of three cemeteries had to be bought and the *corpi delecti* removed to different burial grounds. The first spade of earth for the foundation was turned on a rainy day in September, 1923. In less than ten years, this site would be covered with steel and limestone worth almost $200,000,000.[29]

Working on a commission from the Vans, the Chicago architectural firm of Graham, Anderson, Probst & White created a veritable "city-within-a-city" that included the terminal as well as office buildings, a hotel, and shops. On one side of the terminal, directly on Public Square, the Vans erected the Cleveland Hotel; on the other side they built an $8 million wing to house a department store—and purchased the Higbee Company to fill it. A new "street on stilts" was constructed to the south of the terminal; on it the Vans placed three eighteen-story office buildings: the Midland Bank Building, the Medical Arts Building, and the Builders' Exchange-Terminal Garage Building —all linked to one another and the terminal by a series of passageways.

The main terminal facilities, exclusive of the baggage and express spaces, cab stand, and auxiliary equipment, occupied a central structure approximately 640 feet long and 340 feet wide that contained one large central public space for the accommodation of steam railroad passengers and two smaller side concourses for the use of traction passengers. The layout provided ultimately for the construction of twenty-three platforms and thirty-four tracks. As part of the total project, many grade crossings were eliminated and highway bridges built. A 3,400-foot-long viaduct spanned the Cuyahoga River and Valley, and numerous streets had to be laid in the terminal area.

As a center of commerce the station provided shoppers with "Cleveland's most beautiful dining room" (The Oak Room) as well as a drug store, haberdashery, women's shop, gift shop, bookstore, food store, pastry shop, newsstand, toy shop, and barber shop—in addition to a fifty-two-story tower of offices rising 708 feet directly overhead. The interior of the terminal was a visual delight: lavish use of space, lofty arches, a monumental portico (153 feet long, 36 feet wide, and 47 feet high), colorful murals (by artist Jules Guerin, illustrating the four elements of Water, Air, Earth, and Fire, with a central panel representing Industry and Commerce), and rich Botticino marble. The complex as a whole, however, disappointed one of America's leading architectural critics, Henry-Russell Hitchcock, who wrote that "the Union Station Tower is said to be the second tallest in the world, but does not seem to rank so high in design"; he called it "an obvious bid for publicity."[30]

It did not disappoint any of the 2,500 distinguished guests who attended a luncheon on June 28, 1930, marking the official opening of the terminal, nor did it disappoint the two men most responsible for its construction, the same duo who had declined for reasons of modesty to attend that luncheon—O. P. and M. J. Van Sweringen.[31]

It is doubtful if many of the luncheon guests either knew or worried about the perilous state of railroad passenger traffic in the United States, a situation that would have a profound effect on the fortunes of the Union Terminal. While this country's population increased almost 15 percent during the 1920s, total railroad passenger mileage fell during the same period by nearly 45 percent, the number of railroad tickets sold by 44 percent, and the amount of rail passenger revenue by 42 percent. In 1922 Clevelanders could choose from among ninety-four passenger trains that left the city daily; in 1930 that choice had narrowed to eighty-five and by 1932 to seventy-eight. Even during World War II no more than sixty-three passenger trains passed through Cleveland. Additional trains continued to be eliminated so that the early 1970s saw only eight trains serving the city. By the late 1970s Clevelanders could go west to Chicago at 7:30 in the morning or east to New York or Boston after 11 o'clock at night. And that was it. Only two passenger trains for a metropolitan area of nearly two million—and those two AMTRAK trains do not use the Union Terminal but rather stop at a shiny hut on a narrow strip of land between Cleveland's City Hall and Memorial Shoreway. Just as passenger trains made less and less use of the Union Terminal so too did the interurban and rapid-transit platforms sit unused for years. In fact—as had been predicted by some—all the interurbans went bankrupt before the terminal opened; in 1930 only the Shaker Rapid Transit entered the depot. It would take another twenty-five years—and the inauguration of rapid-transit service between the east and west sides of the city—for cars of the Cleveland Transit System to use the terminal. The automobile, buses, airplanes, and interstate highways, as well as labor, the government, and the policies of the railroads themselves—all had taken their toll. But this was still in the future.[32]

In June, 1930, the *Plain Dealer* hailed the day:

> The terminal Project's official opening inaugurates a new epoch, an epoch to be marked by modern outlying railroad stations, by widespread rapid transit into Cleveland and by a healthy development not only in Cleveland proper and in its suburbs, but also in the scores of cities and towns scattered over a widely extending Cleveland-centered radius—Cleveland now becomes more closely linked with these cities and towns, once seemingly far away, but now forming a vital part of that great, growing district known as the "New Cleveland Trade Empire."

From The Greenbrier Suite, their offices on the thirty-sixth floor, the Vans could watch all this happen and direct an empire which had grown considerably larger since they had first decided to build a terminal.[33]

IV

Back to Railroads

In DESCRIBING the Van Sweringens' initial success in railroading, *Railway Age* noted that "the Nickel Plate is not favored with anything particularly noteworthy in the way of facilities . . . [and] its unusually favorable operating results have been secured in spite of, rather than because of, the character of its physical plant." Its exclusively main-line mileage, high average rate of miles travelled per car per day, high traffic density, the efficiency with which it handled fast freight, and "its apparent ability to handle almost any volume of business turned over to it by connections"—all of these factors distinguished the Nickel Plate's operation in the early years of Van Sweringen ownership and resulted in a marked increase in the road's earnings. During the years 1914 to 1920 the total operating revenues of the Nickel Plate rose impressively from $11,294,971 to $28,655,764, and its corporate income climbed from a deficit of $183,881 to a profit of $2,498,635.[1]

The brothers' progress in turning the Nickel Plate into a money-maker heightened their interest in railroad development and emboldened them in charting a course for the future. "We had seen what was possible . . . with the Nickel Plate," O. P. said later, "and we believed it could be done with other railroads of like character." The consolidation section of the recently passed Esch-Cummins Transportation Act of 1920, he added, "appealed to us as a further constructive opportunity consistent with public policy."[2]

With the ultimate objective of "assuring the profitable and efficient operation" of American railroads, this section of the act directed the Interstate Commerce Commission to "prepare and adopt a plan for the consolidation of the railway properties of the continental United States into a limited number of systems." This signaled a fundamental shift in American policy, which had, since 1890, discouraged such combinations. The framers of the measure now assumed that consolidation, not intense competition, would bring the simplified rate-making, increased investor support of railroad securities, and greater operational economies that spelled profits.[3]

Following this mandate, the ICC engaged Professor William Z. Ripley, a distinguished transportation expert at Harvard University, to prepare a tentative plan of consolidation. Ripley began his work in September, 1920, guided by several criteria: competition between systems had to be preserved as fully as possible, existing routes of trade were to be maintained where profitable, and earning power of the railroads would be equalized. Before writing his report, Ripley devoted almost five months to research, correspondence, and interviews with executives of the nation's railroads. In November he wrote to the Vans asking for their suggestions on a consolidation of railroads in the "eastern region," the area that included the principal trunk lines between Chicago and the Atlantic seaboard. The Vans in turn asked their trusted friend Alfred H. Smith for advice. Smith replied vaguely:

> You might merely say to him [Ripley] that the Nickel Plate's future, you believe, would best be provided for by having a connection with all lines diverging from Buffalo on the east because of the fact that you gather from many lines in the west which deliver business having variable destinations in the east . . . , that you have

opinions reaching into the coal districts . . . , and that you also believe there are other possibilities for the Nickel Plate extending into Michigan. . . . "[4]

In their response to Ripley the Vans proposed a system that adhered to Smith's outline—but where Smith had made general recommendations, the brothers presented a definite map. Following Smith's advice, they sought to acquire the Lehigh Valley and the Lackawanna, both successful lines between Buffalo and New York City. For entrance into the Pittsburgh industrial district and passage through it to the eastern coal regions, the brothers selected the Wheeling & Lake Erie, the Pittsburgh & West Virginia, and the Western Maryland. They also put in claims for the Pere Marquette (a Michigan line) and the Cincinnati Northern, the latter to serve as an entrance into the South. Going beyond Smith's suggestions, the Vans asked for the Toledo, St. Louis & Western, which would finally connect the Nickel Plate with St. Louis, and the Lake Erie & Western, which would bring their road to Peoria, Illinois—both cities important gateways to the West.[5]

Underlying these proposals was a fundamental assumption the validity of which the Vans continued to emphasize for many years. In drafting a plan that "would fit all our conditions best and still preserve the alliance of weak and strong railroads, trends of traffic, natural interchanges and other things . . . , " the Vans held that "there should not be more than four systems in the eastern region." But Ripley recommended in his report of January, 1921, that two hundred of America's railroads be grouped into nineteen systems, including five in the eastern region. The ICC subsequently agreed to this when it issued its tentative plan of consolidation later that year. The commissioners concluded that the East already contained the nuclei of three systems in the Pennsylvania, the New York Central, and the Baltimore & Ohio; they acknowledged the difficulty of creating two strong systems with sufficient feeder lines, branch lines, and terminals out of the most important remaining lines—the Erie, Nickel Plate, Wabash, Lehigh Valley, and Lackawanna. But they also thought that combining all of these into one system would result in considerable duplication of facilities as well as parallel trackage in several instances and would produce "a heterogeneous aggregation altogether surpassing the possibility of efficient management." Ripley therefore suggested Erie-Wabash-Lehigh Valley and Nickel Plate-Lackawanna combinations. The ICC modified this proposal into Erie-Lackawanna-Wabash and Nickel Plate-Lehigh Valley systems; more specifically, it proposed that the Vans' Nickel Plate become the backbone of a system including the Lehigh Valley, the Toledo, St. Louis & Western, the Lake Erie & Western, the Wheeling & Lake Erie, the Pittsburgh & West Virginia, and the Bessemer & Lake Erie. The commission's proposal was quite generous, but it was not exactly what the brothers had wanted.[6]

While this issue of four or five systems continued to be debated, the Vans reached a separate conclusion. "The variation between the commission's plan and Dr. Ripley's plan," O.P. later said, "simultaneously published by this commission indicated . . . that there was no sacredness to the tentative groupings as made." With that as a basis, the Vans set out to collect the railroads they wanted, justifying those purchases, when it seemed opportune, by pointing to the ICC's tentative report.[7]

"To get Western business our tracks should penetrate the West," John J. Bernet told the Vans. The Toledo, St. Louis and Western, or "Clover Leaf," which in 1920 represented a consolidation of many "first roads" that had been constructed during the last decades of the nineteenth century, was one road that could provide the opening the brothers wanted. It carried cargoes of lumber, grain, and livestock from the fertile agricultural expanses of northwestern Ohio, central Indiana, and Illinois on 454 miles of track that stretched from Toledo to St. Louis. The line offered two distinct advantages for the Nickel Plate, a road with which it connected at Continental, Ohio, and one which it resembled since both were basically stems with few "feeders" or branch lines. First, it finally gave the New York, Chicago & St. Louis Railroad direct access to the western terminus in its name and the substantial volume of business that moved between the Buffalo and St. Louis gateways. Second, the Clover Leaf's joint ownership, with the Grand

Trunk Western Railroad, of the Detroit & Toledo Shore Line, assured the Vans access to Detroit for a share of the traffic that originated in that city, most notably at the Ford Motor Company plant. A reading of the line's recent financial history also told the Vans that this was a desirable bargain.[8]

By February, 1922, the brothers had concluded negotiations which led to their purchase of the Clover Leaf.[9] As O. P. later commented, "Our majority control . . . cost us, in round numbers, $3,500,000, and consisted of 60,500 shares of common and 39,890 shares of 4 percent preferred stock, both having voting power." On March 8 the taciturn O. P. did not change his style when he announced,

> I see no reason for not giving the public an outline of the facts. Briefly, the interests I represent have acquired the majority shares of what is known as the Clover Leaf railroad. This road, jointly with the Grand Trunk Western railroad, owns the stock of the Detroit & Toledo Shore Line railroad, which runs from Toledo into Detroit.
> Negotiations have been pending for about thirty days. The deal is consummated. I guess this is the first announcement. The management and operation of the Clover Leaf is unchanged. Walter L. Ross of Toledo, who is president, remains in full charge as heretofore. That's all there is to say.

This statement brought a favorable response from *Railway Age*, which suggested that the position of both roads in the "highly competitive territory" they served would be "considerably improved." It went on to predict that "if the expected happens the Nickel Plate-Clover Leaf route will become one of the leaders in the St. Louis-Buffalo fast-freight business."[10]

Ownership of over 700 miles of Lake Erie & Western (L.E.&W.) track, the Vans thought, would also increase their importance in the fast-freight business. This road's 412-mile-long main line struck out southwest from Sandusky, crossing the Nickel Plate at Fostoria, Ohio, and the Clover Leaf at Frankfort, Indiana, and passing through the heart of Indiana and the fertile central region of Illinois, terminating in Peoria. Two branch lines had been constructed in Indiana: one extended north 159 miles from Indianapolis to Michigan City, crossing the main line at Tipton and the Nickel Plate at Argos, while the other branch ran from Connersville in the southern part of the state, through Muncie, where it connected with the main trackage, and on to Fort Wayne, where it met the Nickel Plate. It was a logical and valuable purchase. First, although the L.E.&W. alone was relatively limited in scope, connections with the Nickel Plate would give agricultural and manufacturing areas of Ohio, Indiana, and Illinois a direct route into Cleveland, one of the primary markets for much of what the area produced. Second, a connection with the Peoria gateway permitted an interchange with several western roads at that point instead of at Chicago. This avoided Chicago's congestion and heavy terminal charges while at the same time providing a more direct entrance to the West and Southwest for goods coming from the railroad lines in the East and Northeast. Finally, as O. P. later noted, "the [Interstate Commerce] commission's suggestion in its tentative plan to segregate the Lake Erie and Western Railroad from the New York Central and to group it with the Nickel Plate provided the basis for an argument with the Central people that they should also dispose of this property."[11]

As in the case of the Nickel Plate of earlier years, majority stock control of the Lake Erie & Western rested with the New York Central. The fact that the L.E. & W. paralleled much N.Y.C. trackage had led the Central to purchase the line in 1899 for $5,760,000 and to integrate it with the Lake Shore & Michigan Southern. But the road had not made money for the Central: it paid its last dividend on preferred stock in 1907 and never paid one on common. In late 1921, after conferring with their mentor, President Smith of the Central system, the brothers began negotiating with A. H. Harris, the vice-president in charge of the N.Y.C.'s finances, for purchase of the majority control of the L.E. & W. By January 11, 1922, agreement had been reached. For $3,000,000— $500,000 in cash and five promissory notes totalling $2,500,000—the Vans secured 59,300 shares of preferred and 59,400 shares of common stock and successfully relieved the New York Central of property for which it had paid almost twice that amount twenty-three years earlier.[12]

Just as with the Clover Leaf purchase, reaction to the Vans' latest coup was favorable. F. K. Baer, traffic commissioner of the Cleveland Chamber of Commerce, called it "a splendid move and one which will undoubtedly result in great good to Cleveland." Several Cleveland railroad men, according to the *Plain Dealer*, "said its importance to Cleveland from a traffic standpoint could hardly be overestimated" and indicated "that it was but natural for the 'clear-headed' Van Sweringens to grab a good thing when they saw it."[13]

Both purchases—of the Clover Leaf and of the Lake Erie & Western—were financed identically and both involved intimately the use of a new Van Sweringen holding company, the Vaness Company. Vaness, O. P. would later testify, "was originally designed as our own personal basket . . . to hold and to own securities and other assets that principally surrounded the ownership of O. P. and M. J. Van Sweringen." For more than a dozen years, Vaness remained the capstone of the pyramid of Van Sweringen companies. "Above it was only the partnership of O. P. and M. J. Van Sweringen," one report noted, "and this was a comparatively inactive entity while Vaness bought and sold, borrowed and lent, and in general lived dangerous-ly."[14]

Until January, 1922, when the Delaware-chartered Vaness was born, the Nickel Plate Securities Corporation had remained the center of Van Sweringen affairs. For two reasons its replacement was a necessity. First, the company, by its very name, was too closely associated with only one railroad, and this at a time when the brothers were negotiating for control of two additional railroads. Second, and probably decisive, a new company gave the Vans a chance to eliminate a number of shareholders in the securities corporation, limit the number of participants in their new endeavors, and select several new associates for the future. Specifically, as one memorandum phrased it:

> Certain interrelated but diverse projects of great extent and potentiality carrying heavy obligations moral and financial, both public and private in character, have been far advanced chiefly by the genius and energy of two projectors. Cherishing their fine purpose, recognizing their obligations and realizing the fraility of human tenure, the projectors desire now to associate with themselves four other trustworthy and capable men, wholehearted-ly in sympathy with their purpose, who will systematically aid in the administration of affairs and assure for a long period the

carrying forward of the projects in the spirit of the purpose of the projectors without danger due to the disability of any individual.

What this meant was that the Vans and four others—Otto Miller, Warren S. Hayden, C. L. Bradley, and J. R. Nutt, all considered the most dependable, closest, and useful of the brothers' friends—exchanged their various securities in the Van Sweringen Company, the Nickel Plate Securities Corporation, the Terminal Properties Company, the Cleveland Traction Terminals Company, and the Cleveland Hotel for shares in Vaness.[15]

On January 10, 1922, the day after the company was incorporated, its entire issue of 162,500 shares of no-par-value common was sold to O. P. and M. J. Van Sweringen in exchange for 195,825 common shares of the Nickel Plate Securities Corporation having a par value of $9,791,250 and 93 shares of the Cleveland Traction Terminals Company worth $9,300. The Vans kept 97,500 shares each, distributing 16,250 each to Nutt, Bradley, Hayden, and Miller. In addition, 50,000 shares of non-voting preferred were authorized. To ensure Vaness a permanent and stable government and the Vans' continued control of the company, "geared up against death and other contingencies," another accord stipulated:

> This Agreement shall inure to the benefit of and be binding upon the heirs, executors, administrators, successors and assigns of the respective parties. The acceptance of Certificates issued hereunder shall constitute the recipient of such Certificates parties hereto for all purposes as fully as though they had signed this Agreement or a duplicate thereof. . . .

This, in effect, gave the brothers control of Vaness even if they sold their interest in it, an arrangement that could only be changed by a private agreement with their successors. Thus, through this "ingenious device," as one commentator called it, "the brothers had erected a holding company whose control could not be wrested from them and through which, consequently, control of their other enterprises was more firmly secured." The usefulness of Vaness was soon demonstrated in their purchases of the Clover Leaf and Lake Erie & Western railroads.[16]

According to O. P., "It was not especially difficult at this stage in our undertakings to provide $1,250,000, the necessary initial cash for both these railroads." This was quite a change from the "hard enough" days in 1916 when the brothers had to produce $2,000,000 for a down payment on the Nickel Plate! Obviously their success both in converting the Nickel Plate into a profitable line and in promoting the Terminal project had increased their credit and credibility. In six short years the Vans had grown from two local businessmen to entrepreneurs of importance in the railroad and finance communities.[17]

On February 25, 1922, the Vans organized the Clover Leaf Company "for the purpose of acquiring the controlling interest in the capital stock of the Toledo, St. Louis and Western Railroad Company." Actually, several days before the Clover Leaf Company was created, the brothers secured control of the Clover Leaf railroad by using nearly $800,000 which Vaness had borrowed from Cleveland's Union Trust Company. Vaness received all 35,000 shares of common stock issued by the Clover Leaf Company. Eventually, in June, 1922, the Vans transferred the controlling shares of the Clover Leaf railroad to the Clover Leaf Company.[18]

On March 11, 1922, the brothers incorporated the Western Company "for the purpose of acquiring control of the Lake Erie and Western Railroad Company and as an aid in financing the purchase of the majority of its outstanding capital stock." It was authorized to issue 35,000 shares of no-par-value common stock and 35,000 shares of preferred at a par value of $100 per share. On April 26, 1922, the Western Company purchased the controlling shares of L.E. & W. from the New York Central for the agreed-upon sum of $3,000,000. Just as in the Clover Leaf purchase, the initial cash payment came as a loan to the Western Company from Vaness, which had borrowed a like amount form the Union Trust Company. Western gave to Vaness as security a pledge of its equity in the shares involved, as well as the entire 35,000 shares of common stock.[19]

The Clover Leaf and Lake Erie & Western transactions were "monotonously alike." As one report noted,

the amounts involved were nearly the same; the purpose of the acquisitions was the same; the same method of financing was used in both. A new company was set up in both instances; the new companies were Delaware corporations; 35,000 shares of the common stock of each company—all of the stock—was issued to Vaness. The officers and directors of the two companies were the same. O.P. and M. J. Van Sweringen, J. R. Nutt, C. L. Bradley, Otto Miller, Charles Stage, Warren Hayden, William Pinkett, John Murphy, Darwin Barrett, and B. L. Jenks as officers and/or directors carried out the corporate rituals as required in the mechanical life of the new subsidiary corporations.[20]

The Vans now owned three railroads: the New York, Chicago & St. Louis ("Nickel Plate"), the Lake Erie & Western, and the Toledo, St. Louis & Western ("Clover Leaf"). Almost immediately, the brothers put John J. Bernet in charge. Improvements including facilities for interchange of traffic between the two new acquisitions and the Nickel Plate, larger equipment, and a higher grade of maintenance, as well as more efficient handling of trains and traffic, resulted in enormous gains in operating revenue and net income. And while individually these "small Midwestern railroads" were not physically impressive, as a group they constituted a respectable system comparable in mileage, equipment, and finances to such lines as the Lehigh Valley and the Wabash. In fact, the relationship between the lines was so close that a virtual consolidation had been effected. It became even closer on July 1, 1922, when the Nickel Plate and the Lake Erie & Western signed a contract stipulating that the Nickel Plate

should operate, manage and control the railroads and properties of both companies, and that all receipts, income, expenses, disbursements, and charges should be divided between the two companies on the same basis . . . as such income and expenses would have been received and paid under separate operation and management.

But in 1922 this alone did not make a real "system." In the minds of the owners, who had increased their indebtedness considerably by acquiring the roads, a real consolidation meant reduced debts as well as economies in operation and general administration.[21]

Unified control offered several advantages to these railroaders. One Van associate predicted that consolidation would "enable the roads to compete more effectively with the larger systems serving the same territory." According to John Bernet, the public would benefit from "expedited traffic, the elimination of transfer from one line to another and standardization of operating practices." This would be in addition to economies resulting from "uniform interline way bills" and new accounting procedures already adopted. Furthermore, Bernet explained, "closer touch with shippers," the elimination of "duplication of solicitation," and other economies that would come from unified control might mean "we may be able to reduce our operating ratio by 1 per cent."[22]

The Vans' lawyers—chief among them, W. A. Colston, previously director of the ICC's Bureau of Finance—supervised the process of consolidation. First, the directors of the lines involved received a proposal to consolidate their companies into one corporation to be called the New York, Chicago & St. Louis Railroad Company. The agreement and articles of consolidation provided that the new corporation have an authorized capital stock of $105,500,000, consisting of 458,800 shares of 6 percent cumulative non-voting preferred stock and 596,200 shares of common. Of these, 327,200 shares of the preferred stock and 462,479 shares of common were to be exchanged for the stock of the constituent companies at certain fixed ratios; the remainder was to be held in the company's treasury. At the time this proposal was made, thirteen directors had seats on the board of the Nickel Plate, eleven on the Clover Leaf's, and nine on the Lake Erie & Western's. Eight of these directors, O. P. and M. J. Van Sweringen, W. A. Colston, Otto Miller, J. R. Nutt, C. L. Bradley, J. J. Bernet, and John Sherwin, sat on the boards of all three companies. Not surprisingly—and, in fact, with "ease and rapidity"—the boards approved the proposal on December 28, 1922. During the following March and April a majority of the stockholders of each company also voted approval of the proposal—again not a difficult accomplishment as the Vans controlled a majority of the outstanding stock of each company.[23]

Now the Vans had to face the ICC and a potential problem. The Transportation Act of 1920 authorized the commission to sanction only those railroad mergers that conformed to its plan of consolidation—but in 1923 no final plan existed. Did this mean the brothers had to wait for one before they could unify their lines? Rather than delay the consolidation, the Vans and their lawyers decided not to seek the ICC's permission to merge their lines. Instead, after the proposal received stockholders' acceptance, it was submitted to and subsequently approved by the appropriate regulatory agencies in the states through which each railroad passed. Then, claiming that the consolidation had already been consummated under state laws, the New York, Chicago & St. Louis Railroad Company asked the ICC, *not* for approval of the merger, but simply for authority to issue the $105,500,000 worth of stock and for the certificate of public convenience and necessity needed to acquire and operate the five railroads.[24]

However, as *Railway Age* noted, by using this method, the Vans tried to avoid—but only succeeded in raising—several questions. Could a consolidation of non-competing lines authorized under state laws be carried out without the approval of the commission? Could this be done prior to the formulation of its final consolidation plan? Had Congress intended complete control of consolidations to rest with the commission? Counsel Colston, in a brief filed with the ICC, held that "to assert that the Interstate Commerce Commission, by refusing a proper certificate of convenience and necessity, by withholding authority to issue securities, or in any other way, may nullify or destroy a consolidation, or any other incorporation, under state laws, would be to usurp for the Commission a power which Congress itself does not possess." However, the ICC's own examiner, E. H. Boles, recommended the request be denied on the grounds that Congress had intended "that complete control of consolidations should be in [the] hand [of the ICC]." Colston referred to this "assumption" as "pure hypothesis . . . and more moonshine." Commissioner Joseph B. Eastman agreed with

Boles, insisting that approval would reduce "to a state of helpless futility . . . our power to administer successfully what the authors of the transportation act, 1920, deemed to be one of its most constructive and important provisions." But Eastman could obtain the support of only two other commissioners, and on June 18, 1923, the ICC, by a vote of 7 to 3, approved the Nickel Plate's application.[25]

Several factors shaped the majority's decision: the lack of opposition; the approval and active support of the states of New York, Ohio, Indiana, Pennsylvania, and Illinois; the fact that "the constituent companies are included in the Nickel Plate-Lehigh Valley system in the grouping of roads under the tentative plan of consolidation"; and their belief that the proposed stock issue was in the public interest. Finally, since Congress had rejected the concept of compulsory consolidation when it wrote the Transportation Act of 1920, the majority did not feel it "should conclude that the Congress intended to prevent voluntary consolidations under available State laws in order thereby to force consolidation under such general plan as we may ultimately adopt." In order to quiet the dissenters' fears the commission let it be known that "nothing in this report shall be construed as restricting the commission in its action with respect to the promulgation of a complete consolidation plan."[26]

Consolidation approved, the Vans could now unmortgage most of their purchases of the preceding seven years. The first step involved exchanging old shares for new. The formula for the exchange of stock provided that each 100 shares of a constituent company's stock be converted into new stock as follows:

For 100 Shares of	New Preferred	New Common
Nickel Plate first preferred	100	
Nickel Plate second preferred	100	
Nickel Plate common		100
Lake Erie & Western preferred	50	40
Lake Erie & Western common		45
Clover Leaf preferred	65	
Clover Leaf common		85

Prior to the exchange, the total number of outstanding shares of the constituent companies of the new Nickel Plate equaled 789,679 shares; with the exchange of shares, this total dropped to 604,840 and consisted of 320,640 voting common and 284,200 non-voting preferred. Of this, the Vans had 189,809.6 shares of common, or 59 percent of the total, which meant control of the company. Their preferred holdings, 161,160.5 shares, were a marketable commodity, and with their debts now standing at slightly more than $21,000,000, sale of these preferred shares held out the opportunity to liquidate that debt.[27]

Negotiations with an underwriting syndicate composed of the Guaranty Company of New York (a subsidiary of the Guaranty Trust Company of that city), Lee, Higginson & Company of Boston and New York, and Cleveland's Union Trust Company and Hayden, Miller were concluded in October, 1923. This syndicate agreed to purchase 150,000 shares of Nickel Plate preferred at a price of $81.50 per share for a total of $12,225,000. Vaness' account at Guaranty Trust was credited with this sum and a loan of $7,900,000. Using these funds Guaranty Trust liquidated nearly all of the debts incurred by the Vans and their companies in the Nickel Plate, Clover Leaf, and Lake Erie & Western purchases. A month later, Guaranty Trust bought an additional 38,285.5 shares of Nickel Plate preferred, further cutting the Van Sweringen debt to $3,500,000. By the end of 1923, their total indebtedness had been sliced to less than $2,000,000. In January, 1924, the Vans stopped disposing of Nickel Plate preferred; their 160,340 shares of common stock, or 53.095 percent of the total, gave them control of the consolidated Nickel Plate. These shares cost the brothers $3,896,980.66—but since the Vans and their companies had received dividends during the period 1917-1923 totalling $6,709,522, control of the new Nickel Plate had, in effect, cost them nothing. To the contrary, they had paid off their debts and made $3,000,000 on the deal![28]

Financial wizardry was always only half of the Van Sweringen technique—sound management was the other. On July 1, 1923, the "new" Nickel Plate officially began operations as a consolidated system. Three weeks earlier, John Bernet, president of the company, had announced plans to spend over $11,000,000 for new cars, locomotives, and improvements of yards and trackage, all designed to put the Nickel Plate "in a position to give the best possible service." Three new freight trains began operation, two for carrying meat from Kansas City to Buffalo and points east, and one for transporting livestock and perishables from Indianapolis to Buffalo. Such steps succeeded in getting the Vans new business. "Western shippers love success," wrote one correspondent, "so Van Sweringen management, with active solicitation for business, has been followed by a flood of routing orders. Service plus aggressiveness, banking associates say, is the sole reason for the increase in Van Sweringen rail traffic and earnings." And profits did increase: in 1921 the Nickel Plate's operating revenue stood at $27,030,663, its total operating expenses at $20,613,594, and its net corporate income at $3,169,072; by 1923, the first year of the consolidation, operating revenues had risen to $57,469,689, operating expenses to $43,938,162, and net corporate income to $6,331,342.[29]

The years 1922 and 1923 mark the end of one phase of the Van Sweringens' careers. During this period the Vans purchased the Clover Leaf and Lake Erie & Western railroads, formed a "new" Nickel Plate, and negotiated the retirement of a series of debts incurred while establishing firm control of a 1,700-mile railroad system. "The question now arises," observed *Railway Age*, "as to how much farther the Van Sweringen plan will be carried, if it is to be carried farther." Obviously, for the Nickel Plate to become a system comparable in size and stature to such principal trunk lines as the New York Central, the Pennsylvania, and the Baltimore & Ohio railroads, acquisition of an outlet to the Atlantic was imperative. Convinced of their skill as railroad entrepreneurs and free of financial obligations, the Vans could now devote their energies to fulfilling this need for an Atlantic outlet. The fact that Henry E. Huntington wished to dispose of his controlling bloc of shares in the Chesapeake & Ohio only helped the situation.[30]

V

A Greater Nickel Plate

Even before the consolidation of the Nickel Plate, Lake Erie & Western, and Clover Leaf had been legally authorized, the Vans were already looking for new properties to add to their collection of railroads. Alfred H. Smith had told them to extend their interests into Michigan to capture a part of the booming automobile industry traffic, and into Virginia and West Virginia for a share of the soft-coal traffic. Financial analysts and railroad experts pointed to a lack of on-line sources of freight revenue and the absence of an outlet to the Atlantic seaboard as weaknesses in the Van Sweringen system. Taking such advice and criticism seriously, the Vans built a railroad empire that soon ranked with the biggest and the best.[1]

"We need new industries along the Nickel Plate," said John J. Bernet, president of the road, "but they won't come in until we can supply them with steam coal." As one possible answer to this problem, the Vans looked to the coal-carrying Chesapeake & Ohio (C. & O.). The C. & O.'s 2,551 miles of track ran from Newport News in the Virginia tidewater region to Richmond, Louisville, and Cincinnati, with branches north and south throughout the New River, Kanawha, Elkhorn, and Logan bituminous coal regions of West Virginia, Kentucky, and Virginia. Its ownership of 80.35 percent of the stock of the 345-mile Hocking Valley Railroad (H.V.), combined with its trackage rights over the Norfolk & Western's Scioto Valley line from Portsmouth to Valley Crossing, Ohio, gave the C. & O. access to the H.V.'s extensive terminal facilities at Toledo, the busiest coal terminal on the Great Lakes; its wholly owned subsidiary, the Chesapeake & Ohio of Indiana, brought the line from Cincinnati into Chicago.[2]

The years 1909 to 1920 had been a period of continual expansion, improvement, and modernization of facilities for the C. & O., one which saw a further exploitation of coal as the line's primary source of traffic. After World War I, the "Pocahontas" coal carriers—the C. & O., the Norfolk & Western, and the Virginian—shared the prosperity non-union coal producers were reaping as a result of lower wage rates and easily and cheaply mined coal seams. The C. & O., about 75 percent of whose revenue tonnage came from this bituminous coal, found 1922 a "fairly prosperous" year. From April 1 to July 1 of that year it carried almost a "record-breaking traffic in non-union coal." In fact, if the line suffered from any one factor it was that the expansion of the coal fields had been somewhat ahead of the railroad's expansion. Despite several strikes, the road's net operating income rose to $14,410,330, approximately $750,000 more than the previous year. By the time the Vans became seriously interested in the C. & O., the physical condition of the road bed, structures, and equipment was excellent and the morale of the line's employees high, reflecting the great ability of its president, W. J. Harahan.[3]

In 1869, Collis P. Huntington had added the C. & O. to an empire that already included the Central Pacific. After his death ownership of his 73,000 shares of C. & O. stock, representing only 12 percent of the total outstanding issue but still enough to elect the board of directors and thereby control the railroad, resided jointly with his nephew, Henry E. Huntington, and his nephew's wife (who, as Collis P. Huntington's wife—later widow— had also been his nephew's aunt!).

Terminal Tower Site (1925)

From a series of etchings of the Cleveland Union Terminal
and Tower, executed (1929-1930) by Louis Conrad Rosen-
berg.

Terminal Tower from the Federal Building (1928)

Terminal from West Third Street Bridge (1929)
(Including the Midland Bank Building, the Medical Arts
Building, and the Builders' Exchange-Terminal Garage
Building)

Terminal Tower from Public Square (1927)

Fortunately for the Vans, the Californian devoted more time to his library than to the C. & O. When, in 1919, the brothers learned that the Huntington interest in the C. & O. might be for sale, they first talked with representatives of J. P. Morgan & Company, "whom we regarded, as does the world, as wise counsellors in matters of finance," O.P. later recalled, adding that "they felt that it wasn't the time for us to make the expenditure." He continued, "We were going to have to have some money if we bought it—some that we didn't ourselves have. We took their advice and postponed our activities in that direction, keeping in touch with the Huntingtons, however." By October, 1922, following protracted negotiations that had begun in May of the preceding year, Huntington agreed to sell his holdings to the brothers. The Vans concluded the deal on January 29, 1923, when they paid the Huntingtons $7,300,000 for 73,000 shares of C. & O. stock.[4]

When the news of the purchase became public knowledge, many asked, "Why the C. & O.?" Initially, even *Railway Age* wondered "just how Chesapeake & Ohio would fit into the Van Sweringen system as it has thus far been assembled." But upon further study the journal concluded that "the point can well be made that operation of the Nickel Plate and the C. & O. in one system has come about at an opportune time," for "the Van Sweringens in acquiring control of the Chesapeake & Ohio have—because of the C. & O.'s financial strength generally—undoubtedly considerably strengthened their own financial position." *The Magazine of Wall Street* called the Vans' record in the railroad field "a good one" and advised C. & O. stockholders to "feel no uneasiness because of a change in control" that "may turn out to be a favorable development."[5]

Actually, purchase of the C. & O. by the brothers presented advantages to both the Nickel Plate *and* the C. & O. because of the intersection of the Nickel Plate with the C. & O.-controlled Hocking Valley at Fostoria, Ohio. While meeting John J. Bernet's request for fuel supplies adequate for all possible needs, as well as providing a route to the southern tidewater for produce and manufactures from Ohio, Indiana, and Illinois, the C. & O. would give the Nickel Plate a considerable share of the coal distribution business. This was an excellent type of traffic for the Nickel Plate; the line's low grades and curvature meant it could handle the longer and heavier trains the coal-carrying business demanded. One result would be a more balanced system, with trains travelling east with produce and west with coal. Such a desire for balance remained a keystone of Van Sweringen policy and became an important factor in their success as railroad operators. However, acquisition of the C. & O. by the Nickel Plate held out more advantages for the former than for the latter, specifically the benefits to be derived from an improved form of traffic interchange. The C. & O.'s greatest difficulty lay in disposing of the traffic it originated. Congestion in Cincinnati, created because the capacity of the C. & O. of Indiana did not equal that of the main line, meant delays and a loss of much business to other carriers. Also, the C. & O. could have supplied considerably more coal to the North and West but for the already overtaxed Hocking Valley route to Lake Erie. Now, however, the Nickel Plate could provide the necessary relief through its connection with the Hocking Valley at Fostoria, Ohio. This would offer the C. & O. a coal route to and through Chicago and east to Cleveland, thereby providing shippers more adequate and prompter service than they had been getting. Thus, any future expansion in the coal fields served by the railroad *required* such additional facilities as could be supplied by the Nickel Plate. Secondarily, the C. & O. would now gain access, via the Clover Leaf and Lake Erie & Western tracks of the Nickel Plate, to two additional gateways in the West, Peoria and St. Louis, for grain and livestock. Here might be the makings of a St. Louis-Tidewater route no more roundabout than that of the southern route of the Louisville & Nashville. All in all, the C. & O. looked like a good purchase.[6]

The next problem was paying for it. In financing their previous railroad purchases, the Vans had been able to convince the sellers of those roads to take long-term deferred payments; this the Huntingtons would not accept. The technique of creating a holding company, used so ably in their earlier purchases, would not work in this instance because they were already too deeply in debt—having not paid off the earlier consolidation debts—to come up with credit worth $7,300,000. Therefore, one of the existing companies had to be utilized. Since the

Nickel Plate Railroad was "well-to-do," it became the logical buyer. Six months earlier, in August, 1922, the ICC had authorized the Nickel Plate to issue $8,663,000 in second and improvement mortgage bonds for "additions and betterments to road and equipment"; the sale of these bonds in January, 1923, brought $7,274,000 into the Nickel Plate treasury. But another problem arose to complicate the situation. The Vans had agreed to pay $100 a share for 73,000 shares, or $7,300,000. Yet in January, 1923, C. & O. stock was selling at no higher than 75. To resolve this dilemma—and avoid criticism from Nickel Plate minority stockholders over paying $25 a share more than the C. & O. market price—the Nickel Plate bought 70,000 of the Huntington shares at $80 for $5,600,000 of the total while the Vans' Nickel Plate Securities Corporation bought the remaining 3,000 shares for $1,700,000, or $566.66 a share! Obviously the brothers were not overly concerned about complaints from stockholders of Nickel Plate Securities. That firm got *its* money from Vaness, which had just borrowed $3,000,000 from the Guaranty Trust Company of New York to repay a debt of $2,500,000 owed to Nickel Plate Securities.[7]

The controlling shares purchased, the Vans moved to take active control of the C. & O. When it was first announced that they had acquired a stock interest in the line, *Railway Age* commented: "Whether it is the intention of the Van Sweringens to merge the Chesapeake & Ohio and its controlled Hocking Valley into the present Nickel Plate system it is impossible to say." But, the journal added, "it is presumed that a union of the properties is included in the Van Sweringen contemplations." The first step toward that union occurred on January 23, 1923, before the actual purchase had been completed, when the Vans and several of their associates on the board of directors of the Nickel Plate—Otto Miller, John J. Bernet, J. R. Nutt, C. L. Bradley, and W. A. Colston—sought approval from the ICC to hold positions also as directors of the C. & O. and its subsidiaries. At that hearing in Washington, W. J. Harahan, the president and a director of the line, and Allan C. Rearick, another director of the C. & O., supported the proposal; no objections to granting the application were made. Within a week, and with only limited discussion, the commission voted its approval, observing that "all the evidence submitted tends to substantiate the applicants' contention that the proposed interlocking [directors] would facilitate and increase the movement of traffic between the C. & O. and the Nickel Plate and its connecting lines. . . ." It also noted that "neither public nor private interests will be adversely affected" by allowing the Vans and their associates seats on the C. & O. board. Commissioner Joseph B. Eastman dissented, finding as "not . . . in the public interest [or] . . . desirable as precedent for other cases that may arise" the proposal that "the Nickel Plate system, without any present direct financial interest in the Chesapeake & Ohio . . . shall have a large and probably dominating representation on the Chesapeake & Ohio directorate." Eastman still had his suspicions about the Vans.[8]

With ICC approval secured, the brothers now turned their attention to meeting another key element of Van Sweringen policy: the acquisition of more than a slight minority interest in a corporate investment. As O. P. later stated, "It is our aim to control by ownership a majority of the common stock of the corporations for the success of which we are responsible." That position made particular sense in the case of the C. & O., since no guarantee existed that the Vans could retain the management of the C. & O. with less than 15 percent of its stock. This basic philosophy, however, had to be squared with the Nickel Plate's "voluntary" offer made to the ICC during the Interlocking Directors hearing that "if the pending applications are granted, petitioner will not acquire in its own corporate name and right, directly or indirectly, more than 20 per cent of the outstanding stock of the Chesapeake & Ohio without an application to this Commission." The words "in its own corporate name and right, directly and indirectly" might have alerted the ICC to the planned solution, for the day after the Nickel Plate bought the Huntington shares, it spent another $1,399,780 for 18,700 shares of C. & O. By June, 1924, another 66,300 shares had been added to the Nickel Plate holdings, giving it a total of 155,000 shares, or 19.88 percent of the total. But while the Nickel Plate could not buy any more C. & O. stock, other Van Sweringen interests could—and did. From July to December, 1924, Vaness acquired 174,832 shares of C.

& O. common. Another 71,000 shares obtained early in 1925 gave the Vans the firm hold on the C. & O. they wanted. They now held over half of the common stock of that road in their own right. Two-thirds of the money for these purchases came in the form of loans from the brokerage houses of Paine, Webber and Hayden, Stone; the other third became part of a loan that now stood at $31,754,033.54 at J. P. Morgan & Company.[9]

Once upon a time a popular supposition had it that the Vans "were probably working in the interest of one of the trunk lines reaching the port of New York." W. A. Colston, the Nickel Plate vice-president, put this rumor to rest when he suggested that "it would be more likely for the Nickel Plate itself to acquire a New York-Buffalo connection rather than for one of the trunk lines to acquire the Nickel Plate." Such an eastern connection was both necessary and desirable for the Van Sweringen railroad system. The brothers' first choice for this outlet to the Atlantic seaboard was the Lehigh Valley Railroad (L.V.), and during 1922 several attempts were made to acquire the line. But the L.V.'s stock was too scattered and too expensive—and the line's owners were not interested in selling their financially strong and healthy property. However, the L.V.'s owners, a group that linked George F. Baker's First National Bank with the Morgan financial interests, were quite willing to dispose of a less profitable Buffalo-to-New York road— the weakest one, in fact: the Erie.[10]

Once the plaything of Daniel Drew, Jay Gould, and Jim Fisk, the Erie Railroad operated some 2,700 miles of track between a group of excellent terminals in Jersey City and equally good facilities in Chicago, reaching Buffalo, Rochester, Cleveland, Dayton, Cincinnati, and Indianapolis over branches or trackage rights, though touching no main centers by its main line. Primarily a freight-carrying railroad, the line ranked as an important carrier of anthracite coal, timber, minerals, agricultural products, milk, and meat, and it maintained an unexcelled reputation in the swift transport of fresh vegetables from the Far West and Southwest to the metropolitan New York area. Still, the Erie had financial problems. Although both track and equipment had been efficiently run and well maintained, low earnings prevented the payment of dividends on both the preferred and common stock—this the result of a perennial struggle to pay the fixed charges on a heavily funded debt incurred in an enormous improvement program. Other handicaps included having only one western terminus, Chicago, a 998-mile main stem that was the least direct route between that city and New York, a great deal of excess capacity, and the existence of very little on-line industrial activity west of Youngstown. As recently as 1920 the road had been on the brink of bankruptcy. In the six years from 1918 to 1923 the Lehigh Valley earned approximately $17,500,000; the Erie lost more than two and one-half times that amount in the same period of time.[11]

But the brothers needed an outlet to the Atlantic. As O. P. told Alfred H. Smith, "If we are to hold the business that has been developing on the lines we now control and continue in the expansion of that business, it is vital that we get from Buffalo to New York almost immediately." Therefore, with the Lehigh Valley unavailable, it had to be the Erie. It also had to be the Erie because the New York bankers to whom the brothers would no doubt turn for financing their next railroad purchase controlled both the Lehigh Valley and the Erie and were only interested in selling the latter. Actually, it made sense to join the Erie to the Nickel Plate, with which it connected at Buffalo, Dunkirk, Chicago, Cleveland, Lima, and, in Indiana, at Kingsland, Ohio City, and Rochester. *The Magazine of Wall Street* saw in the purchase "the probability of a more certain earning power and stronger financial position" for the Erie. *Railway Age* called the acquisition "a logical extension of the present Van Sweringen system" and suggested that "the feature that will prove of the greatest value to the new system is, of course, the fact that it gives the system an eastern connection and route of its own to New York." In fact, O. P.'s plans included construction south of Buffalo of a cut-off between the two roads, thereby creating the shortest line between New York and Chicago. In addition to administrative economies, O. P. forecast the line's gross business would increase by $25,000,000. This he attributed to an affiliation that would give the Erie entrance to the Lake ports at Erie, Conneaut, Ashtabula,

Lorain, and Toledo, to the automobile business in Detroit, to the western gateways of Peoria and St. Louis (avoiding Chicago's congestion), and, through its link with the Hocking Valley at Marion, Indiana, to Columbus and the coal business of the C. & O. and H.V.[12]

For most of 1923 the Vans dealt with Arthur M. Anderson of J. P. Morgan & Company, a director of the Erie, for control of the line. The brothers insisted that the Erie was overcapitalized and had to be "boiled down"; Anderson disagreed. As a result, little came of these discussions until November, 1923, when the Vans decided to go straight to George F. Baker, the principal and reigning person in the affairs of the Erie Railroad (and the First National Bank of New York). "That grand old gentleman," O. P. called him. "We talked with him as to our welcome as a participant in [the Erie's] ownership," O. P. later recalled. "He heartily concurred and said that if we decided to move into it, he would be glad to increase his own investment. . . ." Baker not only agreed to buy Erie shares with the Vans, but he also agreed to have First National Bank lend them the money for their part of the deal. By mid-1925 Vaness owned 386,989 shares common, 24,895 shares first preferred, and 52,605 second preferred—a total of 464,489 shares of 1,763,863 outstanding, acquired at a cost of $11,729,870.07. Combined with the 248,500 shares purchased by Baker, it was enough for working control of the road.[13]

The next railroad to which the Van Sweringens became attached, in this busy year of 1924, was the Pere Marquette (P.M.). Actually, the brothers first become interested in the line early in 1921, when Alfred H. Smith mentioned it to them, but they reached no agreement to buy the line at that time. Three-fourths of the system's 2,262 miles of track lay in Michigan, while another 583 miles stretched between Buffalo and Chicago by way of Detroit and southern Ontario, with branches south to Toledo and northwest to such Lake Michigan towns as Ludington, Manistee, and Charlevoix. At Ludington the railroad operated car ferries across the Lake to Milwaukee and the Northwest. The end result of a consolidation of several lumber-carrying roads in 1900, the Pere Marquette had gone through four successive managements since its founding as a unified road, as well as several receiverships brought about by deliberate mismanagement by its owners. But after 1917 a financial reorganization of the road combined with the automobile-based industrial development of southern Michigan to make the Pere Marquette a relatively healthy line. The ten-year period 1913–1923 saw the railroad's operating revenues climb 150 percent from $16,431,939 to $45,965,737, and this with negligible changes in the total mileage of the line. By 1923 the P.M.'s operating and financial effectiveness had so improved that its net income after fixed charges stood at $5,202,810—a definite improvement over the deficit of $7,152,895 experienced in 1913. Obviously the bright prospects for the automobile encouraged even brighter prospects for the railroad.[14]

Remembering Smith's advice of several years earlier, the Vans saw what the future held for the Pere Marquette and what acquisition of the line could mean for their own system, with which it connected at Toledo and Chicago. As O. P. later noted, "We decided the Chesapeake & Ohio should have additional outlets for its coal shippers. Industrial Michigan seemed to fill the bill, and so we bought into the Pere Marquette." The line also offered a less congested route, one that avoided Chicago, for moving coal into the Northwest. For balance, the rest of the Van Sweringen system offered the Pere Marquette a large market for the glossy automobile. *Railway Age* found it "not difficult to see the value of the Pere Marquette to the Van Sweringen system." Therefore, beginning in April, 1924, the brothers and their newly found ally George F. Baker "quite vigorously" acquired 200,000 shares, or approximately 30 percent, of the Pere Marquette stock at a cost of over $10,300,000. Of the 200,000 shares, 120,000 were assigned to the Nickel Plate Railroad, 30,000 to Vaness, and 50,000 to Baker and two associates. To pay for the first bloc of shares the Vans secured a $1,000,000 loan from Cleveland's Union Trust Company. The loan was needed for only a short time, since in early June, 1924, the ICC authorized the sale of nearly $24,000,000 worth of refunding mortgage bonds which, when sold to the public, provided the Nickel Plate with enough money to repay Union Trust its $1,000,000 and to buy the rest of the Pere Marquette stock. The good offices of J. P. Morgan & Company assisted throughout the entire purchase. The brothers formally took over the direction of the Pere Marquette in 1929, but from the summer of 1924 the railroad cooperated with the Vans.[15]

Van Sweringen policy dictated continuing efforts at improving the physical plant of their railroads. Not yet in the position to work on the Pere Marquette, which needed the least number of improvements anyway, the Vans began development of the C. & O. and the Erie. During the ICC hearings in 1923 on the brothers' request to become directors of the C. & O., O. P. had promised financial aid for expanding and improving that line. With that financial backing, the talented W. J. Harahan led the C. & O. on a comprehensive program affecting equipment, additions, and improvements that made the line one of the strongest railroads—physically as well as financially—in the United States. In each of the states through which it passed, including Virginia, West Virginia, Kentucky, and Indiana, betterments were made: new warehouses, storage yards, and coal bins were constructed; new bridges and tunnels were built and old ones strengthened; heavier locomotives and all-steel freight and passenger cars were obtained. One of the most important improvements was completed in 1926 when the C. & O. built its own connection to the Hocking Valley, thus eliminating the necessity of using the already congested tracks of the Norfolk & Western. By the end of Harahan's first tenure as president of the C. & O. in 1929, more than $234,820,000 had been invested in road and equipment—an amount adequate to sustain the road during the depression years of the 1930s. A similar story can be told of the Erie under presidents Frederick D. Underwood and John J. Bernet. Operating reforms, new track, and replacement of obsolete rolling stock marked the Erie under Van Sweringen control. Physically, it was a better railroad than ever before.[16]

Purchase, financing, physical improvements, and consolidation—that was the Van Sweringen formula. Rumors of another Van Sweringen merger circulated freely following their purchase of the Erie, the *New York Times* noting that "the contemplated Van Sweringen system promises to become one of the outstanding railroad systems of the country." In fact, the next logical and obvious step for the brothers was to unify their properties into a single system, a project to which they now devoted their energies. They took the first step towards meeting this goal by initiating a series of conferences with representatives of the other major eastern trunk lines, the New York Central, the Pennsylvania, and the Baltimore and Ohio. These meetings brought the brothers the results they had hoped for, namely, the support of these roads for a unification of the Nickel Plate with the C. & O., the Pere Marquette, the Hocking Valley, and the Erie.[17]

By August, 1924, the Vans presented to the stockholders of these five railroads a proposal calling for the organization of a "New Company" designed to "acquire control of the railroads and properties of your companies . . . by lease . . . for 999 years . . . and/or by acquisition of at least a majority of all their outstanding capital stock." With $1,400,000,000 in assets, the New York, Chicago, & St. Louis Railway Company—as the "New Company" would be known—would operate over 9,100 miles of track from the ports of New York and Newport News to "the principal western, northwestern and southwestern roads at the gateways Chicago, Peoria and St. Louis; also to the gateways of Louisville, Cincinnati and Indianapolis" as well as "such important cities as Rochester, Buffalo, Erie, Cleveland, Sandusky, Toledo, Columbus and Ft. Wayne." The consolidated lines could be expected to haul automobiles from Michigan, steel from the Mahoning Valley, rubber from Akron, bituminous and anthracite coal from northern Pennsylvania, and bituminous coal from West Virginia, Ohio, and Kentucky. Though smaller than such eastern trunk lines as the Pennsylvania and the New York Central, this "greater Nickel Plate" would be much larger than the Baltimore & Ohio and would compare favorably in terms of earning power with these other lines. The initial issue of capital stock in the company would consist of two classes of shares worth a total of $329,102,920.28: 6 percent cumulative preferred stock, Series A, par value $100 each, non-voting (except under certain special circumstances), and common stock with voting power.[18]

This unification plan did not provide for the outright consolidation of the lines involved because several of them (notably the Nickel

Plate, Erie, and Pere Marquette) paralleled and more or less competed with one another. The ICC had approved the consolidation of 1923 when it involved three relatively small non-competing roads totaling some 1,700 miles, a union actually proposed by the ICC itself in its tentative consolidation plan. But would the commission now assent to a full-scale merger, involving 9,000 miles of track, that conceivably violated the Clayton Anti-Trust Act? It seemed unlikely. Thus, when it came time to present the proposal to the ICC, the Vans did so not under Section 5, Paragraph 6 of the Transportation Act of 1920, which gave the ICC authorization to approve a merger, but under Section 5, Paragraph 2, which gave the commission authority to approve the control and acquisition of the property of one road by another when obtained by lease or stock control if such control would be in the public interest. The proposed leases did leave open the possibility of an outright merger when authorized by the ICC or other proper governmental agency.[19]

While the actual form of the plan of 1924 differed from the earlier one, the financial motives and techniques were similar. The Vans' acquisition of their shares of the Erie, Pere Marquette, and C. & O. had increased their debts by over $30,000,000. The consolidation by lease would supply the brothers with the non-voting preferred stock that could be sold to pay off these debts—exactly the way it was done a year earlier. Also, following their standard practice of trying to obtain majority control of any railroad in which they were involved, the Vans planned to use a ratio in exchanging securities between the old and new companies that would get them a larger equity in the new company and increase their control over the combined properties. They proposed an exchange on the following basis:

For 100 Shares of:	New Preferred	New Common
C. & O. preferred	115	
C. & O. common	55	55
Hocking Valley common	50	50
Erie first and second preferred	50	
Erie common		40
Pere Marquette prior preference	100	
Pere Marquette preferred	90	
Pere Marquette common		85

The *stockholders* of the Nickel Plate would not receive shares in the "New Company" but the Nickel Plate *railroad*, as a corporate structure itself, would "receive . . . shares of the preferred and common stock of the 'New Company' equal in number to the shares of the preferred and common stock respectively" of the Nickel Plate actually outstanding. This would give the brothers, as managers of the Nickel Plate, control of 304,000 shares of common stock in the "New Company" as opposed to the 153,000 shares they would receive as Nickel Plate stockholders. By converting voting common to a higher dividend, non-voting preferred, approximately one-third of the stock in the lessor companies would be disenfranchised and, without any additional expense, give the Van Sweringens slightly more than a majority of the "New Company's" common stock, 50.93 percent.[20]

With such terms, the Vans tempted the stockholders of the five railroads involved to vote for the proposed unification. By the end of August, 1924, the boards of directors of each line had given their approval to the proposal. Stockholders of the Pere Marquette, Erie, Hocking Valley, Chesapeake & Ohio, and Nickel Plate met in March and April and also approved the terms of the proposed lease. On January 20, 1925, the Articles of Incorporation of the "New Company" were drawn up, thus forming the New York, Chicago & St. Louis Railway Company under State of Ohio laws. Actually, by January 29, 1925, enough stock in favor of the "Greater Nickel Plate" plan had been deposited with several banks and stock brokerages in New York, Chicago, Cleveland, Boston, and London to declare the plan operative as to all five companies. The next step towards consolidation meant many train rides to Washington.[21]

Interstate Commerce Commission hearings on the *Nickel Plate Unification Case* began on April 15, 1925, and lasted ten months. Testimony ran to 10,000 pages, focused the public's attention on the Vans and on their planned consolidation, and occasioned much comment, rhetoric, and opinion, in and out of the hearing room, on the proposal. On the opening day, according to the *Plain Dealer*, "There was a large attendance, including not only executives and experts of the roads involved in the proposed merger but also counsel and officers of other roads directly and indirectly interested and other persons especially interested in the whole consolidation question." W. A. Colston, counsel of the Nickel Plate, and Newton D. Baker, personal counsel to the Van Sweringens, brought forth witness after impressive witness to testify in behalf of the unification. John J. Bernet, president of the Nickel Plate and a proven leader in the field of railroad operation, pointed to numerous operational economies, smaller capital expenditures, fewer delays, and less traffic congestion as reasons for insisting that "the proposed unification, in addition to being a logical railroad development, presents opportunity for economical and efficient operation and for serving the interest of the public to better advantage than is possible under separate operation." Noted academic experts added their support. Emory R. Johnson, Professor of Transportation and Commerce and Dean of the Wharton School of Finance and Commerce at the University of Pennsylvania, justified the proposed unification on the grounds that ". . . a large financially stable railroad system—such a one as was contemplated by the Act of 1920—will have been created. . . ." Professor William J. Cunningham of the Harvard University Graduate School of Business Administration found the plan "sound in public interest" and praised the Van Sweringens for having taken "the first, definite constructive step to bring about the objects sought by the consolidation section of the Transportation Act." An important voice of the business world, Richard F. Grant, president of the United States Chamber of Commerce, testified that in his opinion "the plan is in the public interest from the standpoint of improved service and reduced cost of operation and that it ought to be encouraged as blazing the way toward further progress in the same direction." John E. Oldham, of the Boston firm of Merrill, Oldham & Company, himself the author of a plan for the consolidation of American railroads, found the Nickel Plate plan to be "generally fair, generally sound and essentially fair to the security holders, as well as in the public interest as a first important step toward such consolidations as are contemplated by the transportation act." In addition to testimony presented in person to the ICC, hundreds of letters and resolutions from individuals, businesses, and civic organizations favoring the proposed unification poured into the ICC offices. Dozens of Chambers of Commerce in New York, New Jersey, Pennsylvania, Virginia, West Virginia, Indiana, Illinois, Kentucky, Missouri, and Ohio, and industries including George A. Hormel & Company (packers), Union Carbide Company, Youngstown Sheet and Tube Company, and the Pierce-Arrow Motor Car Company expressed support for a "Greater Nickel Plate."[22]

What the opponents of the plan lacked in national reputation and in numbers, they made up in vocal activity. The well-financed opposition centered around a group of C. & O. minority stockholders headed by George Cole Scott, a wealthy businessman from Richmond, Virginia. The basic thrust of their attack revolved around the belief that the stock-exchange ratio did not give a fair value to the C. & O. shares. They also took numerous "swipes" at the brothers' careers, their real-estate and terminal interests, and their previous railroad con-solidations. These critics attempted to demonstrate that all of those transactions, as well as the proposed unification, had been designed to serve the brothers' personal interests and those of their associates. Col. Henry W. Anderson, a former special assistant attorney general in the Wilson administration now serving as counsel for the minority stockholders, insisted that the Vans were the "little brothers" of the New York Central and were controlled by New York banking interests. He attacked the plan as being "conceived by promoters and bankers in the interest of promoters and bankers for the purpose, through the manipulation and exchange of securities and taking from stockholders their voting rights, to vest in themselves complete control of five great transportation systems and to enable these promoters and bankers to realize for themselves immediate profits running into many millions of dollars at the expense of the transportation services of the country." Particularly criticized was that voting-trust agreement relating to the control of the Vaness Company through which "they may divest themselves of all beneficial interest in Vaness Company stock and still retain voting control of the New Company, without direct or indirect ownership of a share of stock therein." Anderson concluded that "this was not the intent or purpose of the transportation act; it is not just to the stockholders of these companies; it is not in the interest of the public;

it cannot fail, if approved, to react to the serious prejudice of the railroads of the country and to discredit the whole policy of railroad consolidation."[23]

Letterwriters objected along similar lines, claiming the entire proposition related more to banks than to railroads. One letter to the ICC, signed HONESTY, stated:

> People in this section generally feel that but one barrier remains between the consummation of the first big steal of the gigantic railroad mergers that are contemplated. The barrier is the Interstate Commerce Commission and the merger referred to is the socalled Van Sweringen group, tho of course they have as much to do with it as the King of Dahomey.
>
> How, in God's name, the Commission is going to find its instructions from Congress elastic enough to permit of this MONEY affair being "pulled off " is beyond comprehension. . . . The BIG BOYS should have all the gravy, and should be in a position to suppress ruthlessly any attempt at an uprising to clean such things out. . . .
>
> Should you obey your consciences, you would demand (the parties to be under oath) information as to just who are behind the Van Sweringens, because they are still nothing more than newsboys, as you know.

Another letter, signed by "Many Citizens of Virginia," suggested that :

> the fetters that [the new system] will put on the section through [which] it passes will make the days of the Reconstruction pale into insignificance. . . . The Van Sweringens may sware [sic] until they are black and blue but they very well know as well as any intelligent person, that it is a scheme of them to eventually dump the C & O R R into the control of the New York Central RR. That is the intention pure and simple and the next prime move will be the Penna R R taking over the Norfolk & Western Ry. In other words the Penna R R and the New York Central R R are fixing to get absolute control of the Trunk Lines in the Eastern part of the United States and God help us all when that comes to pass.

Finally, John B. Thomas of Murfreesboro, Tennessee, expressed his concerns to President Calvin Coolidge in strong but illiterate language:

> I am writing to you and asking of you to knot let the Van Sweringen

Bro Consolodate the N Y C & St L Railroad the Knickell Plate Rout with those other Roads that they are trying to do for I own the controling inerest in that Railroad and they are trying to beat me out of the Road and I dont want them to have anything to do with nothing that belongs to me. and I have writen to Dillon & Read of the Dillon & Read Banking co of New York to look after my inerest in the Road for me. Hopping you wont let them consolidate.

More serious, however, were Senator Burton K. Wheeler's references to the proposal as "one designed primarily for the purpose of making profits for promoters and bankers." His resolution introduced on February 16, 1926, called on the ICC to withhold a decision on the Vans' application "until Congress has prescribed the conditions and means by which such consolidations may be effective."[24]

But the highlight of the hearings was the appearance of O. P. Van Sweringen himself. According to the *Plain Dealer*, "a hush fell over the room as his name was called and then there was a buzz of expectancy in the audience as he came forward. . . ." Few knew what to expect from this man with a well-known aversion to publicity. James L. Wright, the Washington correspondent for the *Plain Dealer*, writing in *Nation's Business*, described it:

> With minute exactness and without reference to a book or a note, Mr. Van Sweringen testified and was cross-examined for days and weeks about the interwoven relationships of a score of his corporations, involving hundreds of millions of dollars, and a variety of interests, ranging from the ratios of exchange of stock in one company for stock in a new company, congested gateways, air rights over terminals, through a myriad of other things.
> Financial transactions that were bewilderingly complicated to those who heard him give their details out of mind, and left mystified even those who spent hours in an endeavor to unravel their multitudinous activities, were as simple as a two-plus-two problem for Mr. Van Sweringen, but when he was asked what salary he receives, a question that most men can answer without a moment's hesitation, and to the penny, he had to admit that he was stumped.[25]

Throughout a prepared statement which traced the development of the Van Sweringen railroad system from 1916 to 1925, and while responding in "a vigorous cross-examination" to numerous questions from Col. Anderson, this "low-voiced, mild-mannered railroad builder of modern times, so unlike the gruff 'Jim' Hill of other days" insisted that he and his brother were "engaged in a constructive undertaking which will promote the public interest." Calmly, quietly, almost matter-of-factly, he answered dozens of questions. To objections to their methods of obtaining majority control of a railroad by eliminating the voting preferred stock, O. P. countered:

> We had a feeling, and still have, that one of the most unfortunate conditions in the railroad world is the absence of parental interest, guidance and encouragement—someone to be responsible for the policies and pursuits of the company through having the major stock interest. If we could not control the properties to the extent necessary to assure continuity of policy, we did not want to be interested in them. We have had a natural pride in feeling that we were constructive. We have tried to look into the future and be progressive, and we wanted a free hand in doing so. . . .
>
> As we have heretofore stated, it is our aim to control by ownership a majority of the common stock of the corporations for the success of which we are responsible. These railroad operations have become our principal occupation.
>
> We make no apologies for wanting to control the policies of the properties for whose management we are responsible, and in which we have a larger investment than any other stockholder in the shares which are first to suffer by reason of a mistake in policy, an error in judgment or mismanagement of the company. All other classes of shareholders and investors have their investment and their income protected ahead of our position.

To those who claimed that the entire proposal represented a get-rich-quick speculator's, not a railroader's, proposition, O. P. retorted:

> All sources of gain to us were by reason of the improvement of the shares purchased and not one dollar by promotion fees or charges, stock manipulation or watering processes—the same as the ratio of gain to all stockholders, and no more. What is more, if this plan is approved by this commission, we will have reduced the aggregate outstanding capital stock by reason of this unification and the former Nickel Plate consolidation about $125,000,000. . . .
>
> Dollars don't have the attraction for me they have for some

people. I am not sure whether to be rich is to be poor or to be poor is to be rich. I am inclined to believe the latter.

To charges that the stockholders had been treated unfairly in terms of the ratio of exchange between old and new securities, O. P. argued:

> Our intent was to provide a fair basis of settlement for those who wished to drop out of the enterprise, a fair method of rental payments to the present corporations for the benefit of those who wished to retain their ownership in their present companies, and to accord a full partnership in the new enterprise to those who wish to participate therein.

But would such arguments convince the commissioners? The hearings dragged on for several months until final briefs were delivered in the waning days of December. Two months later the Vans received a shock.[26]

On March 2, 1926, the ICC issued its decision: by a vote of 7 to 1 the Vans' application was denied. In the majority opinion written by Balthasar H. Meyer, the commission admitted that "viewing the grouping presented in this application strictly from a transportation standpoint, we find that the proposed acquisitions of control are in the public interest" and "a step in the right lines in carrying out the policy of Congress . . . of encouraging the formation of a limited number of systems." But the commission also found the financial considerations of the proposal "not just and reasonable" and therefore not in the public interest. Basically, the ICC objected to the brothers' attempt to increase their percentage of stock control in the companies from 32.85 to 50.93 percent "without purchasing a single additional share" but by issuing new non-voting preferred and by disenfranchising the preferred stockholders of the lessor companies. Noting that the Nickel Plate was "the only railroad of importance in the country in which preferred stockholders do not have the vote," the commissioners suggested that the Vans' plan was designed to keep "control in the hands of its proponents even though their interest is a minority one in fact" and called such an arrangement "not in accord with sound railroad practice." "Hovering in the background of this entire question of control in this case," wrote Commissioner Meyer, was the Vaness Company and the trust agreement between the Vans, C. L. Bradley, and J. R. Nutt, which provided, as the ICC saw it, that "the Van Sweringens may divest themselves of all beneficial interest in the Vaness Company stock and still retain voting control of the New Company without direct or indirect ownership of a share of stock therein."[27]

In addition, the ICC strongly criticized the treatment of minority stockholders, referring to the use made by the Vans and their associates of "every weapon at their command to crush all opposition to their predetermined course of action" and citing the "utter lack of independent and impartial representation of all of the stockholders of the Chesapeake and Hocking when consideration was being given by their directors to approval of the plan and the terms of the proposed leases." In a related matter—the question of the fairness or unfairness of the ratios of stock exchanges—the commission held that the brothers had "not sustained the burden of showing that the ratios are just and reasonable as between the stockholders of the respective lessor companies." And to the Vans' oft-repeated request for guidance in determining "just and reasonable" ratios of exchange, the ICC, fearing an onslaught of similar applications from other railroads, insisted that "the burden of ascertaining or determining proper ratios of exchange should not be cast upon us." The commissioners concluded, "We therefore find that the considerations, terms and conditions of the proposed acquisitions of control are not just and reasonable. Aside from the transportation aspect the proposed acquisitions of control upon the considerations, terms and conditions proposed have not been shown to be in the public interest. The application must be denied."[28]

Reaction to the ICC's decision was both negative and positive. On March 3 an already jittery Wall Street registered the biggest day's trading in its history, with over 3,785,700 shares exchanged. Nickel Plate common plummeted 33 points to 130 with the overall average declining to 121.46, down 17½ points from the year's high, which had been reached on February 13. One newspaper doubted "if there ever has before in Wall Street's history been such a drastic shake-out in such a short time." Several newspapers feared the effects of the decision on future consolidations: the *Philadelphia Public Ledger* declared that "consolidation as a national rail policy has received a savage setback." while the *New York Times* remarked that "the fulfillment of the purposes of the transportation act would have been promoted by a Nickel Plate merger which had won the commission's approval, and will be impeded by what has actually happened."[29]

But, as Commissioner Joseph B. Eastman wrote to a friend in Chicago, the decision "met with rather widespread approval throughout the country." Many segments of the corporate sector reacted quite favorably. The *Financial World* called the decision "highly constructive"; *United States Investor* praised the commission for handing down "a decision of undeniable value to railroad managements, railroad financiers, individual stockholders, and the public at large." *The Wall Street Journal* applauded the commission for telling the Van Sweringens "how not to Nickel Plate." In the *Journal's* opinion, the proposed combination "would have been a satisfactory vehicle for public transportation service, but should have been designed with fewer nickle-plated trimmings. It was to be fashioned with too much consideration for the driver and his personally selected crew and too little for those who were expected to supply the parts." The financial commentator, F. J. Lisman, writing in *Railway Age*, called the decision "a disappointment to the speculator and a solace to the far-sighted investor." Analyst Benjamin Graham, commenting in *The Magazine of Wall Street*, praised it as "a victory for the real Wall Street—the intelligent, conservative security owners of the country."[30]

Letters to the ICC echoed these same sentiments. M. H. Hutchinson of the New York brokerage house of Edward B. Smith & Company congratulated the commission on its decision, saying that "I think the public, and also all holders of railroad securities, may feel assured that their interests are in sound hands." M. F. Connors, the railroad expert at L. F. Rothschild & Company, expressed "the views of a conservative investment house with no ax to grind in this consolidation" when he wrote that "the denial of the Nickel Plate application has been one of the most constructive occurrences in recent railroad history and will perhaps do more to firmly establish confidence in railroad securities than any recent legislation or acts by the Commission."

Davis R. Dewey, a well-known professor of economics at M. I. T., thought the decision would be "a landmark, and have a most healthy influence"; the railroad expert William Z. Ripley telegraphed his sentiments: "THANK GOD FOR A REAL COMMISSION. NO HIGHER PRAISE THAN THAT I MIGHT HAVE WRITTEN IT MYSELF." Newspapers across the country—the *New York World*, the *Chicago Tribune*, the *Baltimore Sun*, the *Kansas City Star* and the *St. Louis Globe-Democrat*—gave editorial support to the ICC's decision. The *Globe-Democrat* best expressed the feelings of many papers when it applauded a decision which affirmed "the economic and transportational advantages of unification" but insisted "that the fiscal arrangements shall be fair to all concerned."[31]

The Van Sweringens themselves did not make their views on the ICC decision known to the public. W. A. Colston issued a statement which they no doubt supported:

> The paramount purpose of the transportation act is the establishment and maintenance of an adequate national transportation system. The commission, in the first nineteen and one-half pages of its mimeographed report, finds that the proposed acquisitions of control are in the public interest as accomplishing this purpose, but denies the application under consideration of purely private arrangements between stockholders, of which the commission's jurisdiction is at least doubtful and as to which the commission indicates definite exception. . . .
>
> The commission does not even say what changes in the private arrangements between stockholders would be acceptable to it and apparently strikes down without suggested remedy the congressional policy of consolidations in a meritorious case which, according to the commission's own ruling, was estimated to result in a saving to the transportation system of the nation of more than $6,000,000 per year.[32]

What would the brothers do? Aside from the operational and economic benefits that would have resulted from consolidation, the Vans had also expected to be able to free themselves—meaning Vaness—from the onerous weight of the $35,000,000 in debts to brokers and banks incurred in securing their blocs of stock in the five railroads. Several options were open to them. First, they could alter the plan by removing the objectionable feature of non-voting preferred stock. Second, they could continue to operate the five roads as separate entities. Third, the commission could be asked to rehear the case and give the Vans a possible duplicate of their ultimate success in the Terminal Tower case. Such alternatives would be carefully and deliberately examined during the succeeding months. But no matter the option chosen, the Vans had suffered their first major defeat. Shaker Heights, Terminal Tower, Nickel Plate, C. & O., Erie, Baker, Morgan— the seemingly endless series of successes had been broken. The sense of disappointment could not have lasted long, however. On April 20, 1926, one month after the ICC's decision, the Cleveland Chamber of Commerce awarded its Cleveland Medal for Public Service to O. P. and M. J. Van Sweringen, "masters of business, builders of great enterprises, eager participants in every movement for a better Cleveland." Even without this distinguished award, the brothers' chagrin would have lasted only a brief time, for they soon set off on another course to meet their goals.[33]

VI

The C. & O. Unification Case

THE INTERSTATE COMMERCE COMMISSION'S DECISION of 1926 in the *Nickel Plate Unification Case* meant, among other things, that the Van Sweringens still owed almost $35,000,000 to the banks and brokerage houses whose support had enabled them to purchase the stock in the railroads they had tried to consolidate.[1] Further plans for the unification of their railroads would have to wait until their debts had been paid. The wait would not be a long one. Two weeks after the ICC handed down its decision, the brothers secured for Vaness a six-month, 6 percent loan of $31,754,033.54 from J. P. Morgan & Company. Their creditors received their due immediately thereafter. Obviously these debts had not been "paid," but merely consolidated and refunded. Yet this arrangement proved of considerable importance, for it carried the brothers through a potentially serious financial crisis, while simplifying the "corporate tangle of purchases, loans, and companies." Furthermore, it set the stage for future multi-million-dollar Morgan loans to the Vans.[2]

89

Their financial obligations resolved, the Vans returned to the task of perfecting a workable and acceptable plan for unifying their railroads. The criticisms expressed by the C. & O. minority during the hearings of 1925 and 1926, and by the ICC in its decision, had to be recognized and accommodated in any new proposal—and in fact, by the time the Vans presented a new proposal to the ICC, nearly all of these objections had been met.

When the ICC turned down the planned consolidation of the Nickel Plate, C. & O., Hocking Valley, Erie, and Pere Marquette, the commissioners revealed their concern over the brothers' attempt to "control . . . this large transportation system without the necessity of owning an actual majority of even the voting stock, much less all of the stock." To eliminate this objection, the Vans devoted most of the remaining months of 1926 and the first months of 1927 to a stock-purchasing campaign designed to give them greater control of the companies in which they were involved. Further additions of Nickel Plate stock were unnecessary since they were already majority stockholders in that railroad. However, the brothers did obtain considerable quantities of Erie, Pere Marquette, and Chesapeake & Ohio. And they adopted an ingenious method for doing it.[3]

The Vans knew that ICC approval would be required for one of their railroads to acquire stock control of another and to issue more stock or bonds to pay for the purchase of the controlling stock. Therefore, in order to avoid going to the ICC, they had their railroads incorporate subsidiaries, contending that these wholly owned holding companies did not need permission from the ICC to obtain the stock of another railroad.[4]

Vaness increased its investment in C. & O. stock by 93,344 shares, while the Nickel Plate, through its newly born (April 12, 1926) subsidiary, the Special Investment Corporation, bought 190,000 shares of the same road. For $38,423,000 the Vans had secured the majority control of the C. & O. which came with ownership of 598,344 of the 780,000 shares outstanding. By spending $7,100,000 Vaness also extended its holdings of Erie to 391,239 shares. The C. & O. purchased 475,000 shares of Erie for $19,535,084.92 but, to avoid any new problems with the ICC, quickly turned the shares over to its new subsidiary (October 13, 1926), the Virginia Transportation Corporation. That company then plunged into the market for another 70,200 shares costing $3,002,391.68. As a result, the brothers' investment in Erie consisted of 936,439 shares of 1,763,863 outstanding, worth $34,744,-224.44. Finally, a year's purchases of Pere Marquette doubled the Vans' investment in that company. The Special Investment Corporation, to which the Nickel Plate had already turned over its previously acquired 120,000 shares of Pere Marquette, obtained another 64,900 shares for $6,637,607.08; Vaness raised its ownership of Pere Marquette from 25,900 to 36,500 shares with an expenditure of $1,092,900; and, lastly, the C. & O.'s Virginia Transportation Corporation bought 16,000 shares for $1,556,430.13. The brothers now controlled 238,000 shares of Pere Marquette worth $16,547,538.51, representing 35 percent of the road's stock.[5]

Other problems were solved. Six weeks after the defeat of the unification plan, the Vans responded positively to the ICC's complaint of "an utter lack of independent and impartial representation of all of the stockholders" in the consideration of their previous proposal. On April 20, 1926, they secured the election to the C. & O. board of directors, "with full freedom to act as their judgment may direct," of George Cole Scott, chairman and organizer of the C. & O. minority stockholders' committee, and John Stewart Bryan, a member of the committee. A year later the Vans eliminated another sore spot. In early 1927 F. H. Ginn and Herbert Fitzgerald, whose legal advice the brothers respected, suggested the much criticized Vaness voting-trust agreement with J. R. Nutt and Charles Bradley be dissolved. The two lawyers argued that it would be "an aggravating circumstance requiring much explanation and provoking unfavorable comments and criticism and possibly with finally harmful results." The Vans agreed, and by May, 1927, the trust agreement had been dropped.[6]

The ICC had not considered the stock-exchange ratios "as between the stockholders of the respective lessor companies" to be "just and reasonable." Thus, throughout June and July of 1926, a special committee of five C. & O. directors—George C. Scott, John S. Bryan, F.

H. Ginn, W. J. Harahan, and Otto Miller—discussed a modification of the terms of the merger plan with representatives of the five roads involved so as to make them "just and reasonable."[7] The special committee agreed on the wisdom of unification and supported the basic premise of the previous plan—the leasing of the five roads by a "new Nickel Plate" in exchange for stock in the new company. The modifications proposed by the committee would change the stock-exchange ratios and give voting rights to all classes of stock in the new company. No one objected to conferring voting privileges on all stockholders—a practice the ICC had in fact urged. But the railroads' representatives could not reach a consensus as to the relative value of the contributions of their carriers, a necessary prerequisite for determining the ratio upon which the several stocks would be exchanged. The Pere Marquette directors supported the suggested modifications since they would have meant better terms for Pere Marquette common and preferred shares than the previous plan. But with the Erie unsteady in its support and the C. & O. still facing an unsatisfied and ever louder minority which saw "manifest inequity to the Chesapeake & Ohio stockholders" in the proposal, it became apparent that any plan involving an exchange of stock would never work. A new approach was needed—and it had to avoid the difficult matter of fixing the trading ratios for the shares of the C. & O., Erie, Pere Marquette, and Nickel Plate.[8]

In September, 1926, after five months of fruitless negotiations, Otto Miller presented to the C. & O. committee the seed of an idea that flowered into the plan ultimately presented to the ICC. Its underlying premise derived from two observations the ICC had made in its decision of February, 1926. First, the commissioners had written, "the traffic of the Chesapeake [& Ohio] and Hocking [Valley] has increased greatly year by year, and together these two roads now constitute one of the most efficient coal transportation machines in the country and *undoubtedly would constitute the backbone of the proposed system*" [italics added]. Second, they continued, "many, if not all of the savings are not dependent upon unification in the exact manner proposed here but *could be brought about if control were only by stock ownership* [italics added], or in many cases by intercompany contracts provided for the use of such joint facilities. . . ."[9]

On February 11, 1927, the Chesapeake & Ohio asked the ICC for permission to acquire stock control of the Erie and Pere Marquette. Where would the C. & O. obtain the stock it wanted? The Virginia Transportation Corporation was holding 545,200 shares of Erie for it and Vaness had optioned 391,239 shares to it. Thus, "the aggregate of all Erie shares, purchased, contracted for, or optioned in behalf of the C. & O." stood at 936,439 shares of the 1,763,863 shares of Erie outstanding. Furthermore, the C. & O. board had authorized the acquisition in the open market of another 134,900 shares of Erie. Virginia Transportation Corporation was also holding 16,600 shares of Pere Marquette for its parent, Vaness had optioned 36,500 shares of Pere Marquette to the C. & O., the Nickel Plate's Special Investment Corporation had another 174,900 shares available to the C. & O., and the C. & O. board had authorized further purchases up to 50,000 shares. These options and holdings—through Virginia Transportation Corporation—gave the C. & O. 228,000 of the 686,750 shares of Pere Marquette outstanding. Even without going into the marketplace for more shares—and the C. & O. board had authorized further purchases up to a numerical majority of the Pere Marquette stock—the C. & O. would have to spend $37,144,005.33 for its Erie shares and $24,817,-297.69 (plus carrying charges) for the Pere Marquette shares.[10]

All of these purchases gave the Van Sweringens tighter control over the C. & O., Erie, and Pere Marquette; they also increased the brothers' debts to several banks and brokerage houses to $85,500,000. Vaness owed the Morgan syndicate $35,000,000 and Paine, Webber approximately $11,500,000. The Nickel Plate's Special Investment Corporation was in debt to the Cleveland Trust Company for $16,000,000, to the Guaranty Trust Company for $11,000,000, and to Paine, Webber for $7,500,000. The wealthy C. &. O. had paid for most purchases out of its own treasury; still, a debt of almost $4,500,000 remained outstanding to several banks and brokerage houses. The necessity of paying these bills led the Vans to create another holding company, the Chesapeake Corporation.[11]

Nearly half of the outstanding debts—$40,500,000—resulted from purchases of C. & O. stock. The creation of the Chesapeake Corporation in May, 1927, enabled the Vans to shift the burden of paying off those debts onto the shoulders of a hungry, stock-investing public while still maintaining control of the railroad. The new company had authority "to hold and dispose of securities of any corporation or association, and to engage in every kind of business except banking." During the very busy month of its creation, the Chesapeake Corporation secured 600,000 shares of C. & O. stock from the Nickel Plate and Vaness. This involved several intricate operations. First, the Nickel Plate created a wholly owned subsidiary called the Pere Marquette Corporation and transferred to it all of the assets, except for 345,000 shares of C. & O., of its other subsidiary, the Special Investment Corporation. Then the Special Investment Corporation transferred those 345,000 shares of C. & O. to the Chesapeake Corporation, which turned over 589 shares of its own stock to the Nickel Plate and 516,911 shares to the Nickel Plate's stockholders, and assumed the $23,875,000 liability on the 345,000 shares. Chesapeake Corporation secured Vaness' C. & O. shares in a slightly less complicated manner. Vaness created another holding company, the General Securities Corporation, to which it transferred its 255,000 shares of C. & O., and the $17,212,500 liability on those shares, in return for the entire issue of General Securities stock. On June 6 the Chesapeake Corporation exchanged 382,500 shares of its own stock for the C. & O. stock—and liability—held by General Securities Corporation. Thus, by early June, 1927, this non-operating holding company, the Chesapeake Corporation—ownership of which was vested in the Nickel Plate—had 600,000 shares of C. & O. plus a debt fixed at $40,500,000. And now the Vans gave the only too willing public the opportunity to pay off fully half of these financial obligations.[12]

The first public announcement of the creation of the Chesapeake Corporation came on May 10 with the advertisement of the successful sale of $48,000,000 worth of twenty-year 5 percent convertible collateral trust bonds to a group of New York banks and brokerage houses, including J. P. Morgan & Company. O. P. Van Sweringen described these bonds as being necessary for paying indebtedness and providing working capital. This issue was "impressively over-subscribed" by some $213,678,000, and its sale (plus interest) brought the Vans $43,549,808.22. With half of their debts erased, they now returned to the ICC with another consolidation plan that would, they hoped, ultimately eliminate the rest.[13]

The application was proposed to the ICC on February 11, 1927, as "an intermediate step toward unification, to exercise that character and degree of administrative control by stock ownership for the benefit of all the carriers within the group proposal, and at the same time consistent with separate operation of, and accounting by, each carrier within the group." The plan omitted any mention of the Nickel Plate, the backbone of the system suggested in 1925, for this new railroad system of some 7,890 miles would center around the Chesapeake & Ohio—just as the ICC had suggested a year earlier. An accompanying petition asked for authority to issue $59,502,400 of additional C. & O. common stock, which would provide the cash needed to finance the purchase of the stock to be acquired.[14]

The hearings conducted by the ICC's Director of the Bureau of Finance, C. D. Mahaffie, began on May 10, 1927—the same day the public announcement of the creation of the Chesapeake Corporation was made—and concluded a little over a month later on June 22. The proponents and opponents of the proposal argued their points in briefs, oral statements, and published materials before the ICC. The C. & O. emphasized the necessity of acquiring the Erie as the best way to solve an increasingly difficult problem, that of transporting bituminous coal from southern West Virginia and eastern Kentucky to Chicago. With its Columbus-Toledo route taxed to the limit and the single-track Cincinnati-to-Chicago line ill-designed for the economical transporta-tion of heavy coal, the C. & O. contended that only two possible solutions for its problem existed. It could either improve the Cincinnati-Chicago line for almost $34,000,000; or, for $36,500,000, it could obtain the low-grade, high-capacity Erie. What attracted the C. & O. to the Erie was its section of track joining Marion, Ohio, where the Erie connected with the C. & O., and Chicago. This link could provide the C. & O. with a ready-built direct route from the coal fields to Chicago. The applicant also noted that the Erie would provide it with an entrance into the industrial regions of eastern Ohio and western Pennsylvania—and all of this for only $2,500,000 more than the cost of improving the Cincinnati-Chicago route. Similarly, the Pere Marquette would provide the C. & O. with a way into Detroit, industrial Michigan, Wisconsin, and the Northwest. Other more general advantages were expected to accrue to the C. & O. and the public: greater operating savings and earnings; more direct and efficient service with fewer delays; increased traffic; and a move towards a realization of the Transportation Act of 1920 by effectuating "the formation of a system geographically co-extensive with, and in financial stability and transportation ability comparable to, the three powerful existing systems, to wit: The New York Central, Pennsylvania and Baltimore & Ohio, serving the territory between Chicago and the Mississippi River on the west and the Atlantic seaboard."[15]

The C. & O. minority "Stockholders Protective Committee" disagreed, calling the plan "not in the public interest" and its terms and conditions "not just and reasonable." The minority detailed its objections. First, the proposal only revived "in substance, though not in form" the Van Sweringen plan which the ICC a year earlier had called "not just and reasonable." To the members of the minority committee, little difference existed between a "lease" and "acquisition by stock control"—both were "equally objectionable means." Furthermore, they could not see "either operating reason or financial necessity" for allying the C. & O. with the Erie and Pere Marquette. The "position of independence" of this "greatest of all the bituminous coal carrying roads" should be retained, free from "stock controlling alliances with connecting carriers." The committee called the prices to be paid for the Erie and Pere Marquette stocks "artificial," "greatly in excess" of the stocks' value, and reflective of the "effect of the present and con-templated purchases" by the C. & O. This group also worried about expending $36,000,000 to put the C. & O. into the anthracite coal business in Pennsylvania, "the successful conduct of which is constantly affected by disturbed labor conditions, strikes, etc., incident

to 'union' mine operations, for which no remedy has ever been found."
Finally, the Stockholders Protective Committee asserted,

> the proposal, though in the name of the Chesapeake & Ohio, is
> in effect an effort on the part of O. P. and M. J. Van Sweringen and
> their financial associates in control of the Chesapeake to consum-
> mate, with the commission's approval, and at large personal profit
> to themselves, a plan to create a new and fourth transportation
> system in [the] eastern trunk line territory, which is economically
> unsound, unjustifiable in cost to the Chesapeake, and, if approved,
> cannot fail but prejudice the ultimate plan of railroad con-
> solidation.[16]

Following the open hearings, the submission of written briefs,
and the final oral arguments before the ICC, the commission made its
decision public on May 18, 1928. The majority opinion detailed the
history of the case, catalogued the arguments in support of and in
opposition to the C. & O.'s application, and then approved it—in part.
"No specific objection from a transportation standpoint has been
presented to us with respect to the applicant's proposed control of the
Pere Marquette," wrote the majority. The commissioners saw the
transportation functions of the C. & O. and Pere Marquette as
"supplemental," and they disagreed with the minority stockholders
who argued that the C. & O. should be kept separate for independent
operation. They said that "no restriction on [the C. & O.'s] coal
distribution would result from the applicant's control of the Pere
Marquette"; rather, "the applicant would be in a position to transport its
coal more directly and efficiently to a territory where much of its coal is
now marketed, and to connections which it does not at present reach by
its own lines." "We are convinced," the majority reported, "that as
regards the Pere Marquette, the proposal is sound from a transportation
standpoint."[17]

The ICC did not, however, feel as sympathetic towards the idea
of linking the C. & O. and the Erie. The commissioners saw such an
association as neither "complementary [nor] supplementary." The
Erie's east-west connection bore little relationship to the northerly
extension provided the C. & O. by the Pere Marquette. The C. & O. had

demonstrated neither "a necessity for control of the Erie because of lack of outlet for its coal traffic," nor the "extent of demand for its coal at points on the Erie not reached by its own lines," nor "the merits of the proposal to utilize the Erie's route between Marion and Chicago for a portion of its westbound business, except to the extent that the Hocking Valley and Erie would benefit thereby." As far as the commission was concerned, the C. & O. and Erie could have made a joint-trackage agreement to provide for the operation proposed, just as the C. & O. had used the Norfolk & Western's tracks between Gregg and Valley Crossing before it built its own road between those two points. Finally, the issue of the unification of the country's railroads—still unresolved since 1920, when Congress had given the ICC its mandate to devise a plan for consolidation—reared its head. The proposed acquisition, the commissioners held, "would constitute practically an allocation of an important New York-Chicago trunk line in advance of the adoption of any general plan for the formation of competitive systems in the eastern territory."[18]

The commission considered the minority stockholders' charge that the proposal "is a great speculative enterprise rather than a transportation development," but concluded that "the evidence showing personal and corporation profits, use of company credit and control, and factors of similar character has received attention in the degree which these matters have a bearing upon the public interest in the plan immediately before us." The majority did express "grave doubts" as to the legality of the operations of the Special Investment Corporation and the Virginia Transportation Corporation, the subsidiary companies established by the Nickel Plate and the Chesapeake & Ohio, but they took no action beyond issuing the following *caveat*:

> Financial manipulation of great railroad properties as an accompaniment of acquisition or consolidation under the law should not be tolerated. Unification of existing lines should have its inception primarily in the traffic and transportation conditions of the territory served. If the regulation of railroads, with especial reference to their unification and capitalization, can be effectively and justly administered under the acts passed by Congress for that

purpose, these projects should be so controlled and governed as to be made productive of large benefits in transportation.[19]

The C. & O. had also asked for ICC approval to issue 595,024 additional shares ($59,502,400 par value) of common stock to be used to pay for the Erie and Pere Marquette stocks already and about to be acquired. But having pulled in the reins on the Van Sweringens on the Erie, the ICC also curbed them by not approving the C. & O.'s issue of as many shares as requested, and by setting a price on the shares which it did authorize. The commission agreed to a new issue of C. & O. stock "not to exceed 200,000 shares of its common stocks," to be offered to present stockholders for $150 per share for the purpose of acquiring the 16,600 shares of Pere Marquette held by Virginia Transportation Corporation, the 36,500 shares of Pere Marquette in Vaness' control, and "such other shares of Pere Marquette common stock as may be obtainable at a price not to exceed $110 per share, or such prior preference or preferred stock as may be obtainable at a price not to exceed $100 per share." The ICC acknowledged that these expenditures might not be enough to obtain majority control of the Pere Marquette, and it stipulated that "the applicant may, if found necessary, submit a supplemental application for authority to issue additional stock for that purpose."[20]

As in the Nickel Plate decision of two years earlier, the commission's opinion had not been unanimous: seven supported the majority views while four dissented. Of the four dissenting opinions, the two most interesting represented opposite points of view. Commissioner Joseph B. Eastman continued his now eight-year-old war against the Vans by first blasting his fellow commissioners for approving as much of the C. & O.'s request as they did. Acquisitions must be "in the public interest" and based on "just and reasonable" terms, Eastman noted. But, he claimed, "the majority do not state with any clarity and strength the advantages which they believe will flow from acquisition of the Pere Marquette. The impression is left that they approve the acquisition largely because they see in it no clear public disadvantage." Furthermore, he wrote, "so far as economy and efficiency are concerned it has not, I think, been shown that the public interest has anything to gain from the Pere Marquette acquisition here proposed." But something else troubled Eastman, something that always bothered him when dealing with the Vans—the way they operated. "The policies and practices of these interests in many important respects have not been such as to inspire public confidence . . . , " he complained. He specifically objected to the methods the brothers used to promote and finance their various railroad projects. In his judgment, "these projects have been characterized by the creation and use of a maze of dummy corporations [which] are legal perversions, commonly used for purposes of conceal- ment and evasion." The Vans adopt them, he said, "to facilitate shoe- string financial operations on a very large scale" and "to escape supervision by this commission." At the bottom of all Van Sweringen schemes—past, present, and future—Joe Eastman saw "speculation and private profit." He would never be a supporter of theirs.[21]

But the recently appointed Commissioner Claude R. Porter felt quite differently, arguing that the C. & O. should have been permitted to obtain both the Pere Marquette *and* the Erie. Porter wanted the commission to move on the long-stalled plan for the consolidation of American railroads: "I am convinced that it is our duty, irrespective of individual opinions and beliefs, with all of the ability at our command, earnestly to strive in sincerity and truth to carry out this declared program of Congress placed in our hands as its servants for its execution." As far as he was concerned, a union between the C. & O., Erie, and Pere Marquette would be "in thorough obedience to the plain mandate of Congress for us to assist in the building up of as nearly competitive systems as we can." Porter accepted the arguments advanced by the C. & O. He agreed that the Erie would not only supplement the C. & O. and Pere Marquette but would complement the C. & O. by providing the desired second route to Chicago as well as new markets for C. & O. coal along the Erie's territory in the East. In all of this the commissioner saw "increased traffic with increased revenues and increased facilities of transportation [which] ought ultimately to result in increased economies with the resulting benefits in the way of reduction of freight rates." Claude Porter cast only one of eleven votes.

Still, the Cleveland *Plain Dealer* called the majority's report "the most encouraging gesture yet made toward the Van Sweringen consolidation program, even though the Erie was denied a place in the system."[22]

The Vans reacted in silence but two and one half months later they accepted the commission's invitation and proposed two modifications of the decision. The first requested authorization to purchase the shares of Pere Marquette common held by the Nickel Plate at a price of $133.33 per share; this required a reconsideration of the order stipulating that the purchase price of those shares be no more than $110 per share. The second petition asked for permission to issue 300,000 shares of C. & O. common at par ($100) instead of the 200,000 shares of C. & O. common at $150 per share the commission had specified in its earlier decision.[23]

The reason for the first petition lay in the Nickel Plate's refusal to extend past the deadline of June, 1927, the $110-per-share option on its Pere Marquette stock it had granted the C. & O. Now, a year later, the stock's market price had risen to $140 and the Nickel Plate management would not accept the $110 per share specified by the commission when the prevailing market price stood almost 30 percent higher. Despite the closeness of the relationship between these two Van Sweringen companies—C. & O. and Nickel Plate—the Nickel Plate directors would have faced serious criticism from the stockholders if they had sold the road's Pere Marquette stock to the C. & O. at a price so far below the current market level. Following discussions between representatives of both the Nickel Plate and the Chesapeake & Ohio, an agreement was reached in which the Nickel Plate offered its Pere Marquette stock to the C. & O. for $133.33 per share, subject to ICC approval by June 12, 1929.

In the second petition, the C. & O. called for ICC approval of an issue of 300,000 shares of its common at par. The railroad argued that the previously mandated limit of a stock issue of 200,000 shares at the "premium" price of $150 per share constituted "an inexpedient and unwise policy [which] would unreasonably invade the private affairs of the company, would amount to usurpation of the legitimate functions of the board of directors and stockholders, and would unconstitutionally deprive the company of its right to manage its property." Moreover, the C. & O. noted, "the wider distribution of stock by reason of the issuance of 300,000 new shares at par instead of 200,000 new shares at $150 would tend to increase the demand for the shares because the assets would be distributed over a larger number of shares, leaving each share somewhat more in reach of the pocketbook of the average investor."[24]

On April 6, 1929, the commission made what a later investigator would call "its most important concession to the Van Sweringens' ambitions and necessities." It announced its decision to grant both applications. The arguments advanced regarding the increased value of the Pere Marquette stock convinced a majority of the commissioners. "There appears to be no reason," they wrote, "to deny the applicants petition as it relates to the payment of $133.33 per share for the block of Pere Marquette common stock described. . . . The proposed price is not an unreasonable one, and we are not disposed to question the judgment of those who fixed it." The majority also agreed that the $30,000,000 worth of par value stock could be issued on a "sound financial basis," and that "the proportional interests of the stockholders in the property, its assets, and earnings [would be] . . . unchanged whether 200,000 or 300,000 new shares are distributed." In both cases, the assets in the company's treasury would go up by $30,000,000. To these commissioners, it was "clear that the proposed issue at par may, within a reasonable probability, yield to present stockholders who sell their rights a money benefit of more than double the amount which would follow from an issue at $150 per share." This led them to conclude that "the desire for the larger probable 'compensation' to the shareholders is a factor in the applicant's present request." For all of these reasons, the ICC approved the Vans' request.[25]

As before, this was not a unanimous decision. Again Commissioner Eastman dissented and continued his attack on the Vans' aims and methods:

> It is plain that the transfer of a large block of stock from the Nickel Plate to the Chesapeake & Ohio will not change the real situation so far as control of the Pere Marquette is concerned. The Van Sweringens can as easily vote the stock in one place as in the other.

All that will be accomplished by this shifting of the stock from one pocket to another is that the Nickel Plate will be able to realize a cash profit of more than 100 percent at the expense of the Chesapeake & Ohio. Just what public interest will be served by this transaction I am unable to see. . . . We pass upon various applications for authority to acquire control which are brought to us by the Nickel Plate or the Chesapeake & Ohio, but apart from causing some passing comfort or discomfort to the Van Sweringens I can not see that our decisions affect the ultimate situation very materially. The process of acquiring control goes steadily on regardless and the same may be said of the process of keeping control.[26]

Surprisingly, the C. & O. minority stockholders were quiet. Late in the summer of 1928, when the Vans had submitted their request to the ICC, the Stockholders' Protective Committee of the C. & O. filed a brief opposing the petition on the grounds that "the price of $133.33 per share for Pere Marquette common stock is largely in excess of its value to the Chesapeake" and that "it would involve large additional profits to the Van Sweringen interests." Earlier that year this same group of protestors had presented a resolution at the annual C. & O. stockholders meeting in April calling upon the directors of the road to account for profits they made in the purchase of the Erie stock. Furthermore, they had introduced this resolution with a preface that led the Vans to consider a libel suit against them. However, by December, 1928, a peace treaty between the two factions was negotiated. Vaness paid $350,000 worth of legal expenses incurred by the minority committee in its various battles against the brothers. In exchange, the committee sponsored a motion at the C. & O. meeting in April, 1929, expunging from the minutes of the previous year's stockholders' meeting the resolution that called for an accounting of the directors of the company. The minority ended their attacks on the Vans' case before the ICC and opposed neither the issue on July 1 of 296,222 shares of common stock worth $29,622,200 nor the payment of almost $28,000,000 that same day for 230,400 shares of Pere Marquette held, variously, by the Pere Marquette Corporation, the Virginia Transportation Corporation, and Vaness. This successfully marketed stock issue gave these Van Sweringen companies sufficient funds to pay off the loans they had incurred while purchasing their several Pere Marquette holdings. All of this became possible on May 25, 1929, when the ICC granted the applications filed with it three days earlier on behalf of the officers and directors of the C. & O. for authority to hold similar positions with the Pere Marquette. John J. Bernet, the Vans' chief operating officer and president of the Erie, became president of the C. & O., Hocking Valley, and Pere Marquette. The Vans finally had their merger—if not with the Erie, at least with the Pere Marquette.[27]

VII

The Consolidation Problem, 1924-1932

ON MAY 17 AND 18, 1928, the same two days on which it gave partial approval to the C. & O. merger proposal, the ICC announced two additional decisions that affected other Van Sweringen consolidation plans. These involved still another railroad, the Wheeling & Lake Erie. Consisting of over 512 miles of track, all located within Ohio, this important road carried bituminous coal, iron ore, steel, and various manufactures into many of the state's industrial centers. But to the Vans and several others in railroading, the Wheeling represented much more than a mere carrier of natural resources and industrial products. It meant the difference between four trunk lines or five in the eastern region of the United States.[1]

The question of the number of trunk lines in that region had been the subject of much debate since 1921, when the ICC issued its tentative consolidation plan that called for five trunk lines. When the commission proved unable to resolve this and other difficulties and formulate a final consolidation plan, the Vans took the initiative in arranging a series of four-party conferences with the Pennsylvania, the New York Central, and the Baltimore & Ohio "with the aim of obtaining . . . an allocation of eastern carriers among the four parties which could be presented to the Commission as an alternative to that part of the tentative plan which dealt with trunk line territory." From these meetings, begun in April, 1924, and welcomed by the commission, there emerged a general plan supported by the "triple alliance"—the B. & O., the Central, and the Vans—and opposed by the Pennsylvania. As finally presented by the alliance to the ICC in January, 1925, the plan proposed the following distribution:

1. *To the New York Central*: Lehigh Valley; New York, Ontario & Western; most of the Buffalo, Rochester & Pittsburgh

2. *To the Pennsylvania*: Norfolk & Western; Alton; Grand Trunk Western

3. *To the Baltimore & Ohio*: Reading; Western Maryland; Monon (Chicago, Indianapolis & Louisville); Ann Arbor; Buffalo & Susquehanna; Detroit, Toledo & Ironton; Cincinnati, Indianapolis & Western; Wabash lines east of the Mississippi

4. *To the Nickel Plate*: Virginian; Lackawanna; Bessemer & Lake Erie

5. *Joint control of*: Chicago & Eastern Illinois; Wheeling & Lake Erie; Delaware & Hudson; Lehigh & Hudson River; Lehigh & New England.

But with the Pennsylvania unwilling to support the plan, the ICC refused to accept it. Still, the alliance continued to defend and protect the concept of four eastern trunk lines—whatever their composition. The most serious threat to that idea came three months after the plan had been given to the ICC, and it came in the person of Leonor F. Loree.[2]

Known as the "schoolmaster of American railroads,"[3] Loree

made a major attempt to upset the alliance's applecart when he submitted a five-system proposal to the ICC in April, 1925. Accepting the Pennsylvania, B. & O., New York Central, and Van Sweringen systems as they existed, Loree proposed the creation of a fifth system which would include all the remaining carriers of any importance in the eastern region: the Lackawanna, Lehigh Valley, Wabash, Western Maryland, Wheeling & Lake Erie, Bessemer & Lake Erie, Pittsburgh & West Virginia, and Buffalo, Rochester & Pittsburgh. Such a system would give Loree's Wabash, which ran from Toledo to St. Louis, the Mississippi, and beyond, routes to the Chesapeake Bay tidewater and New York City. To stop Loree, who acted with Pennsylvania support, the alliance sought control of the Wheeling and Lake Erie.[4]

Why was this road of such strategic importance? A lesson in railroad geography can explain. The Wheeling's lines ran from the Lake Erie ports of Toledo, Lorain, and Cleveland southeasterly to Wheeling and the Pittsburgh vicinity. The Western Maryland travelled westward from Baltimore to Connellsville, Pennsylvania, a little town approximately forty miles south of Pittsburgh. The Pittsburgh and West Virginia bridged the Wheeling & Lake Erie and the Western Maryland. Anyone controlling one of these roads could decide whether there would be four or five eastern systems; conversely, anyone controlling all three had a seaboard-Lake Erie route and the nucleus of a fifth eastern system. This was what Leonor Loree tried to accomplish, since his Wabash joined the Wheeling at Toledo. It was also what the Van Sweringens, both as a part of the triple alliance and by themselves, spent two and one-half years trying to prevent.[5]

The Wheeling & Lake Erie story of 1926-1929 reminded many observers of the great railroad battles of the nineteenth century. Control of the road rested with John D. Rockefeller. As early as January, 1925, the triple alliance had indicated its interest in the Wheeling, but serious negotiations advanced little until late December, 1926. By then, the alliance's fears about Loree's establishment of a fifth system had grown considerably. Another pair of railroading brothers from Cleveland complicated the situation even further. Frank E. and Charles F. Taplin, owners of the Pittsburgh & West Virginia, had also begun purchasing

Wheeling stock. Their unannounced intention was to either form their own fifth system or, more likely, sell the stock to Loree.[6]

Operating under these suspicions, fears, and pressures, the alliance offered Rockefeller $18,000,000 for his holdings in the Wheeling. John D. Rockefeller, Jr., who conducted the negotiations for his father, declined to accept. He noted that they "had held [the stock] for a long period and felt that the Wheeling and Lake Erie had now reached a point where they could look not only for a return on their investment but to the repayment of the back dividends." The Rockefellers obviously knew they had the alliance where they wanted it. By dropping hints that "others who were negotiating for the property seemed to be prepared to pay" much more than the alliance had offered, Rockefeller only increased that group's anxieties. On January 18, 1927, when he made a counter offer of $21,300,000—"a definite price . . . that . . . would not be changed"—resistance crumbled; the alliance accepted the terms of the offer two days later and signed the final agreement on February 3. Since the members of the alliance could not agree on which one of them should control the Wheeling, they divided control equally among all three. Within a week of signing the agreement, each member of the alliance announced publicly the acquisition of 95,000 shares of stock, representing slightly more than a one-sixth interest in the road, for $7,100,000 in cash.[7]

But that was not all the Wheeling stock the alliance obtained. Beginning in early January the Vans, acting for the alliance, had started buying Wheeling stock in the New York market. Combined with the Rockefeller shares, these and other purchases gave the three roads a total of 296,993 shares. Working control of the Wheeling required 279,344 shares; by expending $9,749,000 each, the railroads, acting together, had secured it.[8]

The *Plain Dealer* called "imaginative" this plan which provided for the Wheeling's "exchanging freight with all three [members of the alliance] on even terms. . . ." But the chief benefit, as *Railway Age* astutely noted, would be "to protect a strategic position in future consolidation proceedings in [the eastern] territory." And, indeed, by early February, 1927, the alliance succeeded in preserving its four-party plan by scuttling Loree's attempts to create a fifth independent trunk line from the Great Lakes to the eastern seaboard. The Taplins were also blocked. At worst, the alliance hoped, they would be only a troublesome minority—a false hope, as the next year and one-half demonstrated, for the Taplins joined with Loree to give the alliance many headaches.[9]

In April, 1927, representatives of the New York Central, Baltimore & Ohio, and Nickel Plate railroads submitted applications to the ICC requesting "authority to act as directors or officers of the Wheeling & Lake Erie Railway Company while continuing to hold positions as directors or officers of certain other railroad companies."[10] Hearings on this "interlocking directorates" case were held from June 20 to June 25. The Pittsburgh & West Virginia (the Taplins) and the Wabash (Loree) intervened in opposition. The Taplins explained that their road had a large interchange of goods with the Wheeling, which served as its principal outlet to the West; therefore, they feared that control of the Wheeling by the alliance could "depress the value of its stock and destroy or injure its trade relations with the Wheeling." Similarly, the Wabash had made extensive use of the Wheeling as an outlet to the East for more than twenty years. Because nearly all of its traffic competed with the B. & O., Central, and Nickel Plate, the Wabash expressed concern that control of the Wheeling by its competitors would mean the loss of its eastern outlet and the enforced use of one of the three trunk lines for that purpose. The proponents of the application insisted that "absolutely no agreements or understandings" existed between the three companies to eliminate competitive through routes. Nothing prevented any one of the roads from selling its stock at any time. Rather, they explained, the three trunk lines had acquired the Wheeling stock "to perpetuate its independence in accordance with the four-system plan recommended to the commission in 1924." They argued that "this proceeding does not present for the decision of the commission the propriety of the four-system plan, nor . . . is [it] necessary in this proceeding that such issue be presented. . . ."[11]

The commission remained unconvinced and by a narrow 6-5 vote denied the application. The entire arrangement bothered the six concurring commissioners, who questioned "the wisdom of providing joint control instead of single control of important lines." Also, these commissioners could not understand why the applicants had not come before the ICC to ask approval for the acquisition of control *prior* to making a request for representation on the board of directors. But the commissioners also had a far greater concern: "Notwithstanding the form of this proceeding, the issue of the most advantageous disposition of the Wheeling in a general consolidation is presented. . . . Obviously, we are not in a position . . . to render a decision upon the important questions involved, or to take any unnecessary step which might be construed as an approval of this plan or any other." In other words, the commissioners feared that allowing the alliance to seat directors on the Wheeling would signal approval of the four-system plan. The five dissenters did not consider that representation of the alliance on the Wheeling board would "be construed as an indication of a position either favorable or unfavorable toward the four-party plan or any other plan," especially since the applicants had "stated their willingness to accept a provision for termination of their directorships by our further order."[12]

  The interveners in their petitions claimed that the purchase of the Wheeling stock by the members of the triple alliance violated the Sherman and Clayton Acts as it allegedly lessened competition. The commission acknowledged this complaint but noted: "That question is not properly an issue in this proceeding." The matter did not end there, however. On the next day, May 18, the ICC formally issued complaints against the New York Central, the Baltimore & Ohio, and the Nickel Plate charging them with violating the Clayton Anti-Trust Act in their acquisition of the stock of the Wheeling & Lake Erie on the ground that the effect of the acquisition might be to lessen substantially competition between it and the roads. Each road was given until June 25 "to show cause why an order should not be entered requiring it to divest itself of its interest in the capital stock so acquired."[13]

  The ICC hearings on the alliance's attempted acquisition of the Wheeling & Lake Erie did not interfere with the Van Sweringens' involvement in another railroad purchase, that of the small but profitable coal-carrying Buffalo, Rochester & Pittsburgh (B.R.&P.). This railroad's tracks ran from the Great Lakes cities of Buffalo and Rochester to Butler, Pennsylvania; a trackage agreement with the B. & O. brought the line from Butler into Pittsburgh. A variety of interests coveted this strategically important line. The Central and the B. & O. saw the road as forming part of a projected shorter freight route between Chicago and New York. The Van Sweringen-controlled Erie could utilize it between Salamanca and Buffalo. Leonor Loree wanted it for his fifth system, but in December, 1927, the ICC refused to approve a lease of the road to his own Delaware & Hudson. This decision by the ICC set the Vans off on their own way to acquire the road.[14]

John J. Bernet, acting for the Vans, opened discussions with the owners for purchase of the controlling interest in the Buffalo, Rochester & Pittsburgh. On October 9, 1928, following six months of negotiations, the Vans announced that they personally had obtained approximately 67 percent of the total outstanding stock of the road for $14,251,035. In a formal statement they gave the basic reason for this acquisition: "We have in mind that this step may facilitate the Eastern grouping in an effort to reach an agreement which will be fair to all the roads concerned, and in the general public interest." Since they bought the road as individuals, the Vans did not have to be concerned with the Clayton Act or the ICC. They did, however, inform the chairman of the commission of the purchase and expressed their willingness "to discuss with you or other members of the Commission the purpose of this transaction which we think is a helpful and constructive move." While they could ignore the ICC on this matter, they did have problems coming from another corner.[15]

This entire maneuver had been accomplished without the knowledge of the other members of the alliance. Only three days before the announcement did O. P. Van Sweringen advise them of the impending purchase. B. & O. vice-president George M. Shriver expressed surprise and concern over the forthcoming purchase and the secrecy surrounding it; O. P. replied that his own fear that Frank E. Taplin might obtain the road, thereby complicating an already complex consolidation, had prompted him to act. He added that the shares were being purchased "with the idea that if the four-system plan became possible of accomplishment the B.R. & P. property would be available in that connection." O. P. reiterated these comments several weeks later to the president of the B. & O., Daniel Willard: "He had become convinced [Willard recorded] that Mr. Taplin was either negotiating for the B.R. & P. property or was to do so and he was afraid that if the matter remained as it was, that it would be found that Taplin was in possession of the property, which would mean another obstacle in the way of working out the Four-Party program as originally agreed upon." The B. & O. doubted all of this, and relations between these members of the alliance were strained for several months.[16]

The ICC based its investigation of the alliance's purchase of the Wheeling & Lake Erie stock on Section 7 of the Clayton Act. This section states "that no corporation engaged in commerce shall acquire, directly or indirectly, the whole or any part of the stock or other share capital of another corporation engaged also in commerce, where the effect of such acquisition may be to substantially lessen competition between the corporation whose stock is so acquired and the corporation making the acquisition. . . ." In other words, did the stock acquisition of the Wheeling & Lake Erie by the alliance result in "substantially lessened competition?"[17]

In an earlier case, the commission had expressed the view— repeated here—that "competition between carriers . . . exists wherever there is such possibility of election of routes as may have influence upon service or rates." Following this as precedent, the ICC saw competition in this case as the number of "carloads hauled by the Wheeling but which could have been moved over other *one-line* routes." Using that definition, and citing fourteen points common to the Wheeling and the Central, twelve common to the Wheeling and the B. & O., and five common to the Wheeling and the Nickel Plate, the commissioners concluded that "48.6 per cent of the carloads were found . . . to have been competitive with the Baltimore & Ohio, 29.4 per cent with the Central, and 13 per cent with the Nickel Plate."

Therefore, the commission stated, "That there is competition suscepti-ble of substantial lessening is amply shown."[18]

The three railroads disagreed with this interpretation, conten-ding the Clayton Act did not apply to a simple purchase of stock in a competing road unless something *had* been done or was likely *to be* done to lessen competition. The B. & O. took the position that the statute had not been designed "to correct a supposed violation" or forbid "the mere acquisition of the shares of stock in the absence of any showing that competition has been lessened." Neither a lessening of competition nor an intent to lessen competition had been shown by the ICC, the B. & O. maintained. In fact, the road noted, "competition between the Wheeling & Lake Erie and the Baltimore & Ohio has increased since the purchase of the shares of the capital stock of the former by the latter." The New York Central submitted that "the competitive relationships existing between the Wheeling, the New York Central, the Nickel Plate, the Baltimore & Ohio, the Pennsylvania and the Erie are such as to make it manifestly absurd and preposterous to assume that the New York Central System can conceive it to be to the financial interest of that system to undertake a policy of suppression of Wheeling competition, even assuming, another manifest absurdity, that it could secure the cooperation in such a policy of the other carriers involved." The Nickel Plate echoed these sentiments on the supposed lessening of competition and denied the existence of "any agreement or understanding between the trunk lines to control the Wheeling, to dictate or interfere with its policy or vote in any particular manner for any purpose any Wheeling stock." Furthermore, "had the plan been fully carried out, the Wheeling would be held intact, be operated independently and continue to serve, as it has in the past, the interests of all its connections."[19]

The ICC did not accept these arguments but rather insisted that "the value of the Wheeling as a competitive factor in the territory it serves, and in the territories which it aids other carriers in serving, would be greatly impaired" if the arrangement were not dissolved. In fact, the ICC suggested, "it is not improbable that the presence of the Wheeling in this field, offering its facilities and diligently seeking traffic in competition with the respondents, is a factor of greater value to the shipping public than the transportation service it performs." The commission also returned to the larger question of consolidation. To the ICC, the Wheeling purchase appeared to be actuated "by a desire . . . to prevent the consummation of the plans for a competing through system, to which the geographical position of the Wheeling lends itself." Any such change in the railroad *status quo* bothered the ICC for fear that it would affect any general consolidation plan the commission might propose in the future.[20]

Thus, the majority report of March 11, 1929, found the acquisition of Wheeling & Lake Erie stock by the B. & O., New York Central, and Nickel Plate railroads "may . . . substantially lessen competition" between the Wheeling and those roads. The commission therefore ordered the three roads "to divest themselves of the stock so acquired." Four commissioners dissented and concluded, with the railroads, that the stock had been obtained as an "investment" in furtherance of their four-party consolidation plan. As Commissioner Woodlock noted, "The record shows that they have, since their acquisition of Wheeling stock, pursued a policy of inertia about as complete as could practically have been followed . . . so far as interference with, influence over or control of the Wheeling's actions are concerned." The three railroads had been operating, he said, within another clause of Section 7 of the Clayton Act which states that "this section shall not apply to corporations purchasing such stock solely for investment and not using the same by voting or otherwise to bring about, or in attempting to bring about, the substantial lessening of competition." Commissioner Porter agreed with Woodlock but added that the alliance had acted with some justification in acquiring the Wheeling stock because the commission itself had encouraged the conferences which resulted in the four-system plan. Porter also recalled that annually, from 1924 to 1928, the commission had actually asked Congress to be relieved of the responsibility of formulating a final plan for consolidating all of the country's railroads into a limited number of systems. "It is undisputed in this record," he stated, "that in an honest attempt to assist the commission in working out a solution of this important problem several purchases of various lines of railroads have been made, among them the one before us." Porter could not see contemplated conspiracies or combinations in restraint of trade or competition, nor could he see actual lessening of competition between any one of the alliance members and the Wheeling & Lake Erie. In fact, to him, the majority's arguments seemed "little less than absurd."[21]

But what the minority had to say mattered little, since the majority of the commission had demanded that the three railroads dispose of their Wheeling stock. Other events, however, made the commission's decision less significant—events it recognized in its majority opinion: "Informal representations have recently been made to our chairman, to the effect that the Baltimore & Ohio and Central have disposed of, or are in the process of disposing of, the Wheeling stock owned by them. Of course, such representations can have no weight in this proceeding which is necessarily determined on the record formally before us."[22]

What had happened to make the ICC's decision a moot point? On January 26, 1929, the Alleghany Corporation[23] made what *Fortune* would later call its "ponderous entrance." This company had the power "to enter into, assist, promote, conduct, perform, or participate in, every kind of commercial, mercantile, mining or industrial enterprise, business or work, contract, undertaking, venture, or operation in the United States or in any foreign country." Actually, as O. P. Van Sweringen later explained, Alleghany had a much more concrete *raison d'être*:

> It was not [sic?—probably should be "now"] clear that there was a definite need for a vehicle in which to carry . . . and to mobilize in the financial sense, our activities looking toward the ultimate goal of final upbuilding of the Chesapeake & Ohio, or so-called fourth system for the eastern region. . . .
>
> All of these efforts and activities could more readily be treated with by a proprietary interest than otherwise, and to that end also we had been accumulating and developing the separate parts of that ultimate whole, as we saw that fourth system to be.
>
> To meet the need to which we have just referred, early in 1929 we brought Alleghany Corporation into being, to take over shares held by us and to furnish a corporate instrumentality to provide funds for carrying on.[24]

To ensure the success of this venture, the Vans turned to their financial counselors, J. P. Morgan & Company, for assistance. The Morgan bank helped the brothers determine the assets Alleghany would obtain and develop a procedure for providing the money the new holding company needed to acquire those assets. By the time Alleghany was officially incorporated, with authority to issue up to 7,500,000 shares of common and 1,000,000 shares of preferred, the Morgan had already agreed to buy and market the first $85,000,000 worth of securities issued.[25]

The sale of Alleghany securities in mid-February, which J. P. Morgan & Company accomplished with ease, brought into the company's treasury almost $83,000,000.[26] With that money Alleghany could take its first steps and acquire its assets, held either by O.P. and M. J. Van Sweringen personally, or by their General Securities Corporation, or by Vaness. Within a few days the total listing of assets agreed upon by the Morgan and the brothers had been secured:

    100,000 shares of Nickel Plate common
    492,000 shares of Chesapeake Corporation common
    215,000 shares of Erie common
     26,100 shares of C. & O. common
     96,000 shares of B. R. & P. common
     43,000 shares of B. R. & P. preferred.[27]

This series of transactions had several results. First, by the end of February, 1929, Alleghany Corporation had been established and had secured the various holdings in Van Sweringen railroads and holding companies it had been set up to obtain. Second, $36,000,000 of the cash received from the sale of securities, when channeled to the brothers and Vaness, provided the funds needed to pay off some pressing debts, notably $10,000,000 incurred in the acquisition of the Buffalo, Rochester & Pittsburgh several months earlier, $13,500,000 to their brokers Paine, Webber & Company, and $12,000,000 to the Morgan for a loan payment. Third, since many of Alleghany's assets had been acquired simply by an exchange of stock and not by an expenditure of cash, there remained some $46,000,000 in Alleghany's treasury for other ventures. And it was one such "other venture" that made the ICC's decision in the Wheeling case meaningless. Just prior to the ICC's issuance of that decision in March, 1929, Alleghany paid $10,680,000 for the New York Central's Wheeling shares and exchanged its controlling interest in the Buffalo, Rochester & Pittsburgh for the B. & O.'s Wheeling shares. This eased the strain with the other members of the alliance that had been created when the Vans first purchased the road. As a result, O. P. and M. J. Van Sweringen, through the Nickel Plate and Alleghany, now controlled the Wheeling and, as *Railway Age* commented, "a new chapter in the rather involved history of the contests for control of the Wheeling & Lake Erie" had begun. On April 15, 1929, the Nickel Plate asked the ICC to vacate its order of a month earlier requiring it to divest itself of its 17 percent of the Wheeling stock, and to approve an application for authority to obtain control of the Wheeling by acquiring from Alleghany the stock that would give the Nickel Plate a total of 53 percent of the outstanding Wheeling stock.[28]

In stating its reasons for desiring control of the Wheeling, and explaining why it thought this acquisition would be in the public interest, the Nickel Plate pointed out that, "unlike its principal competitors, it has no access to the Pittsburgh district nor to any important soft coal deposits." The railroad also recalled Professor Ripley's and the ICC's tentative consolidation plans of 1921, both of which had included the lines of the Nickel Plate and Wheeling in the same system, and noted that "there are and have been for a number of years important and well-established routes and channels of trade and commerce involving the use of the Nickel Plate and the Wheeling." Adopting arguments its own opponents had used in the two earlier cases, the Nickel Plate stated that "unless the two lines are operated and managed so as to afford through and co-operative service (and especially if the Wheeling should be under control adverse to applicant), [the] applicant would be at the mercy of its competitors in respect of the important traffic which has been referred to." Finally, the Nickel Plate referred to another portion of the Clayton Act, which "provides explicitly that nothing in the statute under consideration shall be construed . . . to prevent this respondent from extending any of its lines through the medium of the *acquisition of stock or otherwise* of any other such common carrier where there is no substantial competition between this respondent and the company whose stock, property, or an interest therein is so acquired." Along these lines, the railroad quoted the ICC's own words from the previous year's "interlocking directorates" decision: "The Wheeling and the Nickel Plate are complementary and supplementary to a greater degree than they are competitive. The Nickel Plate is mainly an east-and-west line, while the Wheeling is largely a north-and-south line. The former reaches none of the large industrial centers in northeastern Ohio except Cleveland. It uses the Wheeling to reach those centers and, in connection with the Pittsburgh & West Virginia, to obtain an entrance in the Pittsburgh territory."[29]

The Vans realized it would be a while before the ICC acted on this request. Therefore, as an intermediary step, they proposed to the ICC that the Wheeling shares owned by the Nickel Plate and by Alleghany be transferred to a voting trustee whom the commission would approve. On July 22, 1929, the ICC voted its approval of the plan. A week later, on August 1, E. N. Fancher, governor of the Federal Reserve Bank of Cleveland, accepted the appointment as trustee with authority to vote the Wheeling shares "for all purposes except for consolidation of the Wheeling" with either the Baltimore & Ohio, the New York Central, or the Nickel Plate, unless such an action was approved by the ICC. Thus, two and one-half years after the initial concerted attempt to prevent the Wheeling & Lake Erie from falling into the hands of those who wanted it for a fifth eastern trunk line, the Van Sweringen brothers had succeeded. It was true they could not vote the shares themselves—but neither could anyone else.[30]

The Van Sweringens' involvement in the consolidation issue continued into the 1930s. Further sessions of the four-party conferences were not conclusive. As a result, the Vans determined to act for themselves and present to the ICC "the straight question of what railroads could be grouped with . . . [theirs] as a system." On February 20, 1929, the Chesapeake & Ohio asked the commission to find in the public interest a unification plan that combined elements from plans rejected several years earlier. Specifically, the Vans sought permission to link five roads they already owned—the C. & O., Hocking Valley, Pere Marquette, Nickel Plate, and Erie (the components of the "greater Nickel Plate" unification plan of 1925)—with seven others, already or about to be acquired: the Wheeling & Lake Erie, the Chicago & Eastern Illinois, the Virginian, the Delaware, Lackawanna & Western, the Bessemer & Lake Erie, the Pittsburgh & Shawmut, and the Pittsburgh, Shawmut & Northern. The brothers also proposed that their system have a partial interest with the New York Central, Pennsylvania, and Baltimore & Ohio in several bridge or terminal roads. Including lines owned or leased and 880 miles of trackage rights, this would create a system of 13,148 miles of railroad in the eastern region. It represented a capital investment of approximately $2,500,000,000. From such a consolidated system the petitioners expected greater competition, transportation service of a higher standard, lessened congestion, more diversified and better balanced traffic, capital and operating economies, and the removal of "railroad properties in the eastern territory from the field of speculation, . . . the financial stabilization of those railroads and . . . the bringing into fruition the national policy." Unlike other proposals previously presented by the Vans to the ICC, this one included neither detailed financial terms nor a request for authority to acquire the roads. Rather, it simply argued for the establishment of an ideal Chesapeake & Ohio system; if the commission approved the basic outline, the Vans would return with the necessary specifics. The proposal still presumed that ultimately there would be four railroad systems in the eastern region. A Baltimore & Ohio "go-it-alone" plan, submitted at the same time, assumed the same. Neither action, however, dissuaded Leonor Loree and the Taplins from preparing their own "fifth system" plans for the commission's consideration.[31]

One of the major reasons for this outpouring of consolidation plans was the commission's newly reborn interest in attempting to meet the congressional mandate of 1920 and develop a plan for consolidating all American railroads into a limited number of systems. As Commissioner Porter noted in his dissent in the second Wheeling & Lake

Erie case, the ICC had actually sought to return that mandate to Congress. But in late December, 1929, a commission with several new faces, having accepted its responsibility, issued a sixty-eight page document detailing its plan for consolidating all railroads into twenty-one systems, *five* of which would be in the eastern region. While the commissioners were now willing to give the Vans the unification they had asked for in 1925, as well as several other roads requested in the plan submitted in February, they still would not approve the brothers' bid for the Virginian, the Chicago & Eastern Illinois, and the Wheeling & Lake Erie. Furthermore, the commission wanted to take away the C. & O. of Indiana and incorporate it into a fifth system that would also include the Wabash, Norfolk & Western, Seaboard Air Line, Lehigh Valley, Wheeling & Lake Erie, Pittsburgh & West Virginia, and Western Maryland railroads. The Vans acknowledged the announcement of this plan by acceding to the commission's request to withdraw the application they had submitted in February since it did not state specific terms and conditions upon which the commission could act. But beyond this, the brothers took little heed of the ICC's proposal. Other matters occupied their time.[32]

From the beginning of their involvement in the railroad business, the Van Sweringen brothers insisted that diversity of traffic be a cornerstone of their policies. While forming Alleghany in 1929, they became acutely aware of how coal-oriented their empire had become. To obtain a better balance they followed the advice of the head of their intelligence service, Col. Leonard P. Ayres, and looked in a new direction. As O. P. later explained:

> We had been studying for a couple of years in a general way the growth of the country and became convinced of the certainty of development of the Southwest, and concluded that if we were to have any more railroad investment we would prefer it in that location. A study of the best railroad investment there—the one which afforded the greatest opportunity for future growth, development, and expansion, and possessing the diversity of basic traffic that we were looking for—led clearly to the Missouri Pacific system.

He also stressed that "there was no thought of consolidating the Chesapeake & Ohio system of the East with the Missouri Pacific in the West, nor was our conception that of a transcontinental railroad system."[33]

The 7,500 miles of Missouri Pacific (MoPac) track, combined with the more than 2,000-mile Texas & Pacific and the equally extensive New Orleans, Texas & Mexico (both controlled by the MoPac), gave the Missouri Pacific system almost 12,000 miles of track in the southwestern United States; the MoPac also had a half-interest in the 2,500-mile Denver & Rio Grande Western. All of this trackage crisscrossed Missouri, Arkansas, Kansas, southeastern Nebraska, south and east Texas, Colorado, and central Utah, and connected St. Louis, the MoPac's base of operations—and one of the western extremities of the Vans' eastern railroad empire—with such cities as New Orleans, Omaha, Denver, El Paso, Brownsville, Laredo, Houston, and Galveston. Instead of coal, the road hauled oil and oil products, agricultural products, fruits, vegetables, lumber, and manufactures. *Business Week* called it "a railroad system of great strategic importance, . . . the leading freight carrier in the Southwest [and] the dominant carrier in and out of St. Louis." Col. Ayres saw the need for an overhaul of finances and operations, but still recommended the road for purchase. It was well built and well administered, and it made money for its stockholders.[34]

The MoPac had been part of the Jay Gould empire until it was placed in receivership in 1915. Subsequently, it fell under control of Kuhn, Loeb & Company, the bankers who took it out of receivership two years later and in whose hands it rested in 1929. Starting anonymously in January, 1929, the Vans embarked on their buying campaign. When established a month later, Alleghany Corporation served as the primary vehicle for these purchases. By April, 1930, almost $76,000,000 had been spent by Alleghany for over half of the million and a half shares needed for majority control.[35]

Not until then did the public become aware of the Vans' latest coup. When informed that they possessed the controlling shares of the MoPac, W. H. Williams, chairman of the road, would not acknowledge the changed ownership and refused to allow Alleghany to move its representatives onto the board of directors. He cited as the basis for his action a Missouri statute that required any corporation wishing to acquire "more than ten per cent of the capital stock issued by any railroad . . . existing under or by virtue of the law of this State" to receive approval from the Missouri Public Service Commission. Neither the Vans nor their lawyers had ever heard of the law, but they easily and quickly overcame this slight setback. The necessary application was made to the Public Service Commission, hearings were held, and on May 6, the commission approved the application. In a week's time, Kuhn, Loeb directors had been replaced by the Van Sweringen group and O. P. Van Sweringen himself elected chairman of the company.[36]

In April, 1930, *Business Week* reported another Van Sweringen purchase: "Railroad men are busy this week trying once again to guess what the Van Sweringens have up their sleeves. The famous brothers have just acquired from the Thomas F. Ryan Estate working control of the Chicago & Eastern Illinois" (C. & E.I.). This railroad's 939 miles of track branched out from Chicago in three directions, connecting that city with Evansville, Indiana, on the Ohio River, and with St. Louis and Thebes, Illinois, on the Mississippi. One-half of the road's traffic consisted of coal; forest, agricultural, animal, and petroleum products made up the rest. The C. & E.I. held out certain transportation advantages for the Vans' railroads. First, it provided a useful and direct connection with St. Louis and the Missouri Pacific for their eastern lines which reached Chicago. Second, the general routing of MoPac traffic from the Southwest to the Northeast could avoid, when necessary, the congestion at St. Louis by using the MoPac's connection with the C. & E.I. at Thebes; similarly, it could bypass the congestion at Chicago by using the C. & E.I.'s connections with the Nickel Plate in central Illinois at either Mode or Hustle. When the Vans decided to buy the road, its transportation benefits compensated for a history of financial weakness that included no dividends paid since 1912, low earnings, and an operating loss of $2,500,000 in 1930. Despite this, the Vans agreed to pay the heirs of Thomas Fortune Ryan $8,000,000 for 51 percent of the Chicago & Eastern Illinois.[37]

The well-to-do Chesapeake & Ohio paid for these shares—but it did not buy them. Since such a purchase would have required the ICC's approval, another method had to be discovered, one that would give the Vans control of the road without the sanction of the ICC. Such a device was found; it was called an "option." It worked as follows: On January 7, 1930, the Vans' brokers, Paine, Webber, paid $8,000,000 to the executors of the Ryan estate. The same day Paine, Webber signed a contract with the C. & O. giving that road an option to buy the C. & E.I. shares whenever it received ICC approval to purchase them. The C. & O. paid the brokerage house $5,000,000 for the privilege of obtaining this option and guaranteed payment of the remaining $3,000,000. Since Paine, Webber voted the stock according to the brothers' wishes, control of the Chicago & Eastern Illinois was actually theirs.[38]

The other participants in the four-party conferences were expending their energies too: the New York Central was busily acquiring a sizeable portion of Lackawanna stock; the Pennsylvania Railroad established the Pennroad Corporation, the counterpart of the Vans' Alleghany Corporation, and secured control of the Pittsburgh & West Virginia and the Detroit, Toledo & Ironton plus considerable blocs of stock in the New Haven, the Boston & Maine, and other railroads; the Baltimore & Ohio obtained the Buffalo, Rochester & Pittsburgh, worked out plans for securing the Buffalo & Susquehanna, and doubled its shares of stock in the Reading. But even with all of these involvements, the railroads had to respond to the commission's proposals of 1929. Several factors finally led the roads to begin meeting again—after a break of over a year and a half—in an attempt to present to the commission a united front behind a plan for four, not five trunk lines in the eastern region. First of all, the important fifth-system possibilities no longer existed. Loree's sale of Lehigh Valley and Delaware & Hudson stock to the Pennsylvania, and an initial rejection by an ICC examiner of his application to build a line through northern Pennsylvania from Pittsburgh to Easton, effectively eliminated him from the consolidation picture. The Wabash—the road about which the ICC had proposed to build its fifth system—could not obtain the necessary financial backing for such a project. The Taplins acknowledged defeat late in 1930 when the ICC denied the application of their Pittsburgh & West Virginia to acquire the Wheeling & Lake Erie and when the Baltimore & Ohio refused to sell them the Western Maryland.[39]

President Herbert Hoover also played an important role in bringing about the resumption of the four-party conferences. In October, 1930, transportation expert William Z. Ripley convinced the President that the fifth line proposed by the ICC the previous year could never become a reality and suggested that the commission might now be amenable to a four-system plan. Hoover persuaded the four railroads' presidents to meet again and hammer out a settlement of their differences. He pursued this course of action, he later explained, "in the hope of effecting the consolidation policies declared by Congress in 1920 and especially at this time as a contribution to the recovery of business by enlarging opportunity for employment and by increasing the financial stability of the railways. . . ." In other words, consolidation, with its promises of large savings, now looked like a method of salvation for an important segment of the American economy then reeling not only from the effects of the depression but also from the impact of new competitors in the transportation industry—automobiles, buses, trucks, and airplanes. The railroad managements came to the same realization, and within two months rivalries had been forgotten, differences buried, and a four-party plan agreed upon.[40]

On December 30, 1930, Hoover announced that the conferences were a success. A week later the ICC received a letter signed by Presidents W. W. Atterbury of the Pennsylvania, P. E. Crowley of the New York Central, Daniel Willard of the Baltimore & Ohio, and John J. Bernet, representing the Vans. It stated that a general four-system plan had been drawn up and that specific applications would be submitted to the commission asking it to discard the five-system proposal in favor of a four-party scheme. The principal change, or course, lay in the elimination of the commission's fifth system—the Wabash-Seaboard Air Line-Norfolk & Western combination—and its distribution among the four parties. The railroads submitted their four-system plan in detailed form to the ICC on October 3, 1931. Its proponents saw it as "preeminently the best solution of the problem of railroad consolidation in the Eastern territory, excluding New England, which can be effectuated." President Hoover hailed it as a "substantial contribution" to business recovery. Basically, the proposal called for the following distribution of railroads:

1. *To the Pennsylvania*: Norfolk & Western; Wabash; Toledo, Peoria & Western; Detroit, Toledo & Ironton
2. *To the Baltimore & Ohio*: Western Maryland; Ann Arbor; Delaware & Hudson; Monon; Lehigh & Hudson River; Reading; Central of New Jersey; Buffalo, Rochester & Pittsburgh; Buffalo & Susquehanna; Chicago & Alton
3. *To the New York Central*: New York, Ontario & Western; Pittsburgh & Lake Erie; Delaware, Lackawanna & Western; Ulster & Delaware
4. *To the Chesapeake & Ohio*: Pere Marquette; Nickel Plate; Erie; Hocking Valley; Lehigh Valley; Bessemer & Lake Erie; Chicago & Eastern Illinois; Wheeling & Lake Erie; Pittsburgh & West Virginia (western division); Pittsburgh & Shawmut; Pittsburgh, Shawmut & Northern; Detroit & Mackinac; Mainstee & Northeastern; new construction between Portland and Portage, N.Y.
5. *Joint Control by the four systems of*: Delaware & Hudson; Lehigh & New England; Montour; Pittsburgh, Chartiers & Youghiogheny; Monongahela; Elgin, Joliet & Eastern; Akron & Barberton; Akron, Canton & Youngstown
6. *Joint Control by the Pennsylvania and the Chesapeake & Ohio of*: The Virginian
7. *Joint Control by the Baltimore & Ohio and the Chesapeake & Ohio of*: Detroit & Toledo Shore Line.[41]

On January 6, 1932, ICC Chairman C. R. Porter opened hearings on the four railroads' request for a modification of the commission's consolidation plan of 1929. In four months of testimony, cross-examination, written briefs, and oral arguments, the proponents and opponents presented their respective cases for and against a four-party consolidation system for the eastern region. Presidents Atterbury, Bernet, Crowley, and Willard considered the fifth system as proposed by the commission three years earlier "improbable," "impracticable," and "undesirable." The B. & O.'s Daniel Willard expected the substitute proposal to produce "strong, . . . efficient, . . . well-balanced . . . systems [that would] also be well balanced with each other." He predicted the four-system plan would succeed not only because it was "the best practicable solution for consolidation in the Eastern district" but also because it had the support of the presidents of the four existing systems, who believed "that under present trying conditions even greater benefits and advantages are possible from it than perhaps were at first appreciated."

President John J. Bernet of the Chesapeake & Ohio described in detail the proposal as it applied to the Van Sweringens' lines:

> The Chesapeake & Ohio-Nickel Plate System as proposed in the application would operate 14,630 miles, including proposed trackage rights, new construction and other railroads allocated to it, but excluding 337 miles in Canada and also excluding its interest in the joint railroads. The proposed system would be a strong system both physically and financially. It would have a minimum of four main tracks and a maximum of eight main tracks between New York and Buffalo. Between the extremities of Lake Erie, the Erie, Nickel Plate, Pere Marquette, and Wheeling & Lake Erie would be substantially equivalent to a four-track railroad. West of Toledo and Detroit, the Erie, Nickel Plate and Pere Marquette would have four main tracks to Chicago. In addition to this main stem between New York and Chicago, it would have the main line of the Chesapeake & Ohio between Hampton Roads and Chicago and Toledo, including a continuous double-track railroad from West Virginia and Kentucky coal fields to both Chicago and Toledo. It would have reasonably direct and efficient routes between all of the principal cities and gateways in Eastern territory except routes to and from Philadelphia and Baltimore.
>
> The proposed system would serve the North Atlantic ports of New York and Hampton Roads; the Lake Erie ports of Buffalo, Conneaut, Cleveland, Lorain, Huron, Sandusky, and Toledo; the Ohio River crossings at Cincinnati, Louisville and Evansville; and

the Mississippi River crossings at St. Louis and Thebes. It would also serve the western gateways at Chicago, Peoria and St. Louis and the New England gateways at Mechanicsville, Maybrook and Harlem River. It would have car ferries operating across Lake Michigan to the ports of Milwaukee, Manitowoc and Kewaunee. The proposed system would reach and serve 60 out of a total of 87 cities having a population of fifty thousand or more in Eastern Territory (excluding New England).

The investment in road and equipment of the railroads comprising the proposed system was about two billion one hundred million dollars at the close of the year 1930 and their combined net railway operating income for the year 1930 was 3.68 per cent on that investment. The corresponding percentage was 5.58 per cent in 1929 and 5.49 per cent in 1928. In each of the three years its return on investment compared favorably with those of the other three proposed systems.[42]

Others supported the plan. Ben B. Cain, vice-president and general counsel of the American Short Line Railroad Association, called the four-system plan "the best, if not the only practical means of solving the so-called weak road problem in the east." Gerrit Fort, chairman of the Maritime Association of the Boston Chamber of Commerce, testified on behalf of eighteen New England commercial organizations that "the plan would create four well-articulated and reasonably balanced systems, capable of rendering efficient service, and that it is important for the interest of New England that it be approved as promptly as possible."

Opposition, however, was considerable. While New England businessmen liked the proposal, five of the six governors of the New England states charged that the four-system plan "would tend to diminish competition and to close existing channels of trade and commerce." They protested "any invasion of New England by the trunk lines . . . through acquisition of [such] bridge lines" as the Delaware & Hudson, the New York, Ontario & Western, the Lehigh & Hudson River, and the Lehigh and New England. Representatives of Virginia and West Virginia forecast reduced competition, increased rates, and decreased tax revenues for their states as results of the plan. The City of Syracuse (New York) saw as "disastrous" the likelihood of it becoming a "one-railroad city," dependent on only the New York Central. A "Fifth Eastern Trunk Line Association, Inc." supported the ICC's original Wabash-Seaboard Air · Line-Norfolk & Western grouping, while "vigorous opposition" to the four-party plan also came from many of the railroads scheduled to be allocated to the four trunk lines. Winslow S. Pierce, chairman of the Wabash, declared that "no dismemberment and no absorption of the Wabash system is admissible either under the terms of the transportation act or independently as an economic proposition." The Delaware & Hudson and the Elgin, Joliet & Eastern, which the four lines proposed to control jointly, wanted to continue to operate as independent lines; the Monon asked that it be alloted to the Atlantic Coast Line and Southern systems.[43]

On July 21, 1932, the ICC made public its decision approving, with modifications, the four-system plan for the consolidation of the eastern railroads. The commission accepted the arguments of the plan's proponents as to the impracticability of the fifth system proposed in 1929. It noted that "no steps have been taken by any one with the object of carrying into effect system No. 7" (the fifth system), and that both the Wabash and the Seaboard Air Line, "which form in large part the backbone of that system," were in receivership. Furthermore, the commissioners now discovered that of the 57,000 miles of track in the eastern territory, the Pennsylvania, New York Central, Baltimore & Ohio, and Van Sweringens already controlled about 44,000 miles. Nearly half of the remaining trackage consisted of short lines and New England bridge lines. As they admitted, "This leaves less than 7,000 miles of railways, most of which so lacks coordination that to build out of these remaining properties a fifth system which would have the necessary physical and financial strength to serve the public efficiently and economically in competition with the other four systems already wholly or partly in being is impossible." Therefore,

We believe that the public interest will be best served by grouping the railways in eastern territory, excluding New England, into four systems, each having adequate main stems between the Atlantic seaboard and the Middle West, reaching a majority of the large producing and consuming centers of the territory, having the necessary physical and financial strength to serve the public efficiently and economically and to coordinate their services with other modern means of transportation, and which will be so constructed as to preserve healthful competition and maintain, as far as practicable, the existing routes and channels of trade and commerce. We are of opinion that the four systems proposed by the applicants, modified in the respects hereinafter noted, will achieve those objectives.

The modifications, designed to meet a variety of objections, were minimal: as requested, the Monon would be assigned to joint control of the Southern and the Atlantic Coast lines; the New York, Ontario & Western remained with the New Haven instead of going to the New York Central; the Delaware & Hudson stayed independent; and the Pennsylvania had to divest itself of all stock owned in New England roads.[44]

None of these modifications affected the Vans' Chesapeake & Ohio-Nickel Plate system. However, two others did. The commissioners heeded the coal owners from Virginia, West Virginia, Kentucky, and Tennessee who feared the loss of competitive freight rates if the coal-carrying Norfolk & Western *and* the Virginian should be absorbed by their rivals, the Pennsylvania and the C. & O. Therefore, while the commissioners permitted the Pennsylvania to acquire the Norfolk & Western, they awarded the Virginian to the New York Central. Another modification, however, compensated the Vans for this loss. The ICC accepted the arguments advanced by representatives of the City of Syracuse, who feared the effects of being dependent upon only one railway system. In order to assure that "competition will be fully preserved and existing routes and channels of trade and commerce maintained to the extent required by the public interest," the commissioners provided Syracuse with its second train system. They alloted the Vans the prosperous branch of the Lackawanna extending from Chenango Forks, New York, through Syracuse and Oswego, together with trackage rights to the latter system over the Lackawanna between Binghamton and Chenango Forks.[45]

The *New York Times* reported that "railroad circles hailed the plan as the most helpful factor in that industry in years" and noted the stock markets had reacted favorably to the announcement, with railroad stocks and bonds leading other issues in advances. The *Times* itself called it "the most far-reaching decision ever handed down by the Commission," one that "will give a sense of permanency and assurance to the railways generally and should certainly enable them to take advantage of the revival in trade which will in due course come." The Cleveland *Plain Dealer* wrote that "If . . . consolidation will show the way to economy and efficiency, no further time should be lost in completing the mergers which have been the subject of negotiation for a decade." But the overall reaction lacked enthusiasm, and the optimism was guarded. *Railway Age* did not find the decision particularly dramatic:

> In other words the commission, after having promulgated a plan which has resulted in very little voluntary unification in accordance with its allocations, has now consented to revamp its allocations in such a way as to fit, with some exceptions, the practical situation already existing as the result of affiliations built up by the railroads themselves during the period between the publication of the commission's tentative plan in 1921 and the promulgation of its "final" plan in 1929.

While railroad securities rallied for a short time immediately after the commission's acceptance of the four-party plan, the year as a whole saw them improving at a rate no faster than that of industrial and utility stocks. As Russell A. Weisman, a financial writer for the *Plain Dealer*, commented, "Consolidation is finally approved at a time when the economies it theoretically entails are more badly needed than ever before, but when the financial difficulty which makes consolidation desirable makes it also tremendously difficult." A *New York Times* editorial cautioned: "Under existing circumstances too much ought not to be expected from this proposal." Both echoed sentiments expressed by Commissioner Joseph B. Eastman in a blistering dissent from the majority's decision:

> The people of this country are either fighting to bar the wolf from the door or they are struggling inside the threshold to keep his fangs

from their throats. They have little time or money to spend on railroad consolidation plans. . . . As for the parts of the plan which remain to be accomplished . . . , no steps can now be taken which require substantial expenditures of cash. Applicants have no present means of obtaining capital funds in any large amount except from the Government. It is not certain that all of these four systems will be financially able to hang together.[46]

Since any plan adopted by the commission depended on the voluntary willingness and ability of the railroads to make it work, the most important reaction had to be that of the four railroads themselves. The Pennsylvania was annoyed that it lost a half-interest in the Virginian and its New England roads, and the Central was upset about the Chenango Forks Line arrangement. Even so, at a meeting in New York on September 23, 1932, the rail executives composed their differences and subsequently announced their acceptance of the ICC's plan. The commission took note of this in its *Annual Report* for 1932, commenting that the presidents "intend to proceed with consolidations in eastern territory . . . in general accord with our modified plan." A year later, O. P. Van Sweringen would make the following statement: "We are still expecting to get these railroads together, physically and financially speaking, in spite of the many difficulties we have encountered." But the predictions of Weisman and Eastman ultimately proved correct. A later assessment concluded: "With the economic life of the country slowed to a standstill, there was no chance that the Commission's revised plan would have any immediate effect. The Transportation Act contained no provision for carrying out the Commission's plan, and . . . the . . . eastern powers [did not have] the resources at hand to acquire any of the new properties assigned to them." The Van Sweringens had high hopes for the future. But those hopes would soon be dashed, for the empire they had constructed had already started to crumble.[47]

VIII

Death of an Empire

In an editorial entitled "Stock Market and Railways," *Railway Age* commented on November 2, 1929:

> Fundamentally, general business conditions are sound. . . . It would seem, therefore, that any recession in business that will occur will be comparatively small and brief, and that the railways can reasonably prepare for handling a normal volume of traffic, and anticipate that, by continuing to effect economies in operation, they will be able to gain financial results satisfactorily comparable to those recently secured.

The Van Sweringens subscribed to the same philosophy: business as usual. But in 1929 their empire, the value of which had reached over $3,000,000,000, was so closely tied to the maintenance of stock values that even the slightest tremor in the market could threaten the entire structure. For the two brothers the years after 1929 would be marked not by "business as usual" but by crisis after crisis, culminating in their collapse and that of their empire as well.[1]

That empire, based primarily on railroads, also had significant non-railroad components. During the late 1920s and early 1930s, the Vans purchased over $30,000,000 worth of stock in such companies as Midland Steel Products, Hupp Motors, Glidden Paints, Goodyear Tire and Rubber, National Lead, White Motor, Electric Auto Lite, Otis Steel, Lehigh Valley Coal, United Corporation, and Standard Brands Corporation. While such investments seem to have been made simply to make money in the stock market, other acquisitions in this period had more definite purposes. Vaness spent about $7,500,000 in 1929 to obtain the Higbee Company, an established Cleveland department store which would occupy one part of the Terminal Tower complex. Vaness also bought 6,760 shares of the Midland Bank Company, a Cleveland bank dominated by friends of the Vans, for $1,521,800. The brothers did not need the friendship of another Cleveland bank; they did need a tenant for another building in the Terminal Tower complex—and in 1930 the Midland Bank moved into the Midland Bank Building. Metropolitan Utilities, a newly organized Van Sweringen company, secured control of the Cleveland Railway Company, the operator of the city's trolleys, for slightly more than $3,000,000. By combining under the umbrella of Metropolitan Utilities the Cleveland Railway and their other traction holdings—Cleveland Interurban Railroad, Cleveland & Youngstown Railroad, Cleveland Traction Terminals, and Tractions Stores (lessee of the concessions area)—the Vans hoped to coordinate all of Cleveland's traction operations. Finally, on January 11, 1930, the Vans organized a holding company of businesses primarily involved in the production and distribution of anthracite coal. This new corporation, called the Pittston Company, took over the Erie Railroad's coal mining properties, the Hillside Coal & Iron Company and the Pennsylvania Coal Company, and linked them with another acquisition, the United States Distributing Corporation, a holding company which controlled fourteen other businesses connected with the trucking, warehousing, and distribution of ice, coal, and building materials.[2]

In mid-1929 the Vans conceived the idea of forming a new holding company for all of their Cleveland real-estate (urban and suburban) and traction interests. As usual, they went to the Morgan for assistance, but this time the bank denied their request. George Whitney, a partner in the bank, later explained: "We told them that we had never had anything to do with real estate, and that therefore we were not interested." So the Vans turned to the Guaranty Company for help. But Guaranty's reluctance to support a large-scale real-estate venture in the midst of a period of stock-market uncertainty meant that the Van Sweringen Corporation (V. S. Corp.), when finally created in April, 1930, was a much smaller, somewhat different, creature than first anticipated. Specifically, it did not include the Vans' traction or suburban real-estate interests. In order to keep its initial costs low and to maintain its control in the Vans' own hands, the corporation obtained its assets by exchanges of stock: Vaness received 1,124,800 shares for its stock in the Cleveland Terminals Building Company, the owner of the Public Square development, while the Vans' General Securities Corporation secured 620,000 shares in exchange for 500,000 shares of Alleghany Corporation it was holding. The brothers provided the latter assets to make the issue of the corporation's $30,000,000 worth of Guaranty-underwritten 5 percent notes more attractive to the investors who were going to provide the corporation with the new capital it wanted. Both Guaranty and the Van Sweringens assumed a rosy future for Alleghany.[3]

Two aspects of the agreement between the Vans and Guaranty would soon cause serious problems for the brothers. First, the 500,000 shares of Alleghany were considered "segregated assets," that is, the V. S. Corp. could not "mortgage, pledge, sell, transfer or otherwise dispose of" any of these shares "until such time as at least $15,000,000 aggregate principal amount of the [5 percent] notes shall have been retired and cancelled or called for redemption and payment duly provided for." An even more restrictive clause stipulated that the Vans would *personally* maintain a fixed ratio between the "segregated assets" and the notes outstanding. Specifically, if the market value of the Alleghany shares dropped to below one-half of the face value of the outstanding notes, the Vans had to deliver enough salable securities to reestablish the minimum ratio. As a later assessment commented:

It was a dangerous contract. The Van Sweringens were tying themselves more closely than ever to the market value of Alleghany. Before the contract was made a decline in the market price of Alleghany merely decreased the Van Sweringen assets; with the new arrangement it increased their debts as well. For every dollar Alleghany declined in value the Van Sweringen fortune fell by approximately $1,150,000—the proprietarial companies still owned 1,150,000 shares—and at the same time the brothers' own personal liability increased by $500,000—the number of Alleghany shares in the segregated assets account. The brothers were, therefore, doubly menaced by any slip in the market.[4]

The great bull market of 1925-1929 had carried the value of Van Sweringen stocks higher and higher: C. & O. soared from 89 to 279, Pere Marquette from 61 to 260, Erie from 26 to 93, Nickel Plate from 118 to 192. When the market broke, the value of those same stocks plummeted too: by September, 1930, C. & O. had fallen to 196, Pere Marquette to 130, Erie to 42, Nickel Plate to 105. And the Vans felt the impact of the Crash most acutely because of Vaness' account at Paine, Webber and V. S. Corp.'s "segregated assets" commitment.[5]

By 1930 Vaness' debt to Paine, Webber reached $35,000,000, and the brokerage firm now demanded payment. Initially, the V. S. Corp. helped to relieve this pressure on Vaness by transferring almost $20,000,000 to a subsidiary, the Cleveland Terminals Building Company, which subsequently paid $7,500,000 to Vaness for the Higbee Company shares it was holding. The Building Company also assisted in the Vaness relief effort by purchasing many of the blocs of industrial shares Vaness had acquired through Paine, Webber. These actions provided Vaness with enough cash to reduce its debt to the brokerage firm to $17,000,000. But by October, 1930, the continuing drop in the market had cut the value of the collateral securing those debts even more. With Paine, Webber requiring a margin of 25 percent over the face value of a debt, an account of $17,000,000 needed collateral worth $21,250,000. Yet the declining market made Vaness' collateral worth only $19,860,000. Vaness did not have additional securities which could be pledged as collateral, nor, given current prices, would it have made sense to sell any securities in the market. The Building Company came to the rescue again by assuming an additional $13,515,000 of Vaness debts to Paine, Webber; this reduced the amount Vaness owed to about $4,500,000. The amount of collateral behind Vaness' remaining debts to Paine, Webber stood at approximately $8,000,000, enough to meet the brokerage firm's margin requirement as long as the market fell no further.[6]

Every drop in the price of Alleghany also made the "segregated assets" agreement more and more onerous for the Vans. The brothers first enlisted Vaness, when it had money, and then the Building Company, to buy and sell Alleghany shares in order to bolster the price. But, as a later commentator noted, "such buying was . . . disastrously futile, a classic case of good money being thrown after bad. However authentic Hercules' feat in disposing of the monster, Hydra, it was slight labor compared with that the brothers had set for themselves and their newest publicly financed company." For despite these efforts, Alleghany, which had sold at a high of 56½ in 1929, had sunk to a low of 10¼ by October, 1930. As a result, the deficiency of the "segregated assets" account stood at $5,775,000.[7]

On October 23, 1930, the day on which the stock market again broke severely and Alleghany dropped to 10¼, O. P. Van Sweringen was summoned to a meeting in New York with representatives of J. P. Morgan & Company and the Guaranty Company "who were familiar with the predicament in which Mr. Van Sweringen would find himself because of the decline in securities." M. J. joined his brother in New York for a discussion of their various debts, which were considerable: Cleveland Terminals Building Company owed Paine, Webber $16,000,-000 and its parent, V. S. Corp., $2,500,000; Vaness still owned Paine, Webber $3,500,000; in a little over a week, V. S. Corp. would have to make an interest payment on its 6 percent notes. With the fall of Alleghany stock, something had to be done about the "segregated assets" account. The future looked bleak. All agreed, however, that neither the Van Sweringen empire, nor an important brokerage firm to which it owed money, could be allowed to collapse. The consequences, both real and psychological, of such failures to the movement to promote recovery would be monstrous. A later commentator suggested the Vans had learned early in their career the advantage debt brought: "O. P. in 1916 had shown his precocity by declaring, according to hearsay, that he thought owing and owning equally effective for purposes of insuring one's position in the world. After a time, as he saw, one's creditors would not dare to risk one's bankruptcy; a high building cannot be allowed to topple." But the public refinancing of these debts, the method employed so often in the past, could not be attempted in October, 1930. A loan was needed. It would not be a small one; $40,000,000 had to be obtained.[8]

Within a week, the terms and conditions were set. A New York banking syndicate that included J. P. Morgan & Company, Guaranty Trust Company, George Baker, Jr., Chase National Bank, Bankers Trust Company, and National City Bank, loaned Vaness $16,000,000 and Cleveland Terminals Building Company (its note endorsed by Vaness) $23,500,000. Interest on the loan, which matured on May 1, 1935, was set at 6 percent. The Vans personally guaranteed payment of the notes. Collateral consisted of nearly every salable security available to the brothers. Paine, Webber received approximately $16,000,000 from the Building Company and $3,500,000 from Vaness; the Building Company repaid V S. Corp. $2,500,000 and, for $5,000,000, acquired 500,000 shares of Alleghany common, enabling V. S. Corp. to make its interest payment on time; Vaness bought and delivered to V. S. Corp. $10,000,000 in United States Government notes, thereby eliminating the deficiency created by the drop in value of Alleghany and releasing the brothers from the "segregated assets" account commitment. This transaction, while it mortgaged the Vans and much of their empire, relieved some of the pressures that had threatened them for nearly a year. It carried them through another year before they were confronted with additional calamities.[9]

If 1930 had been a difficult year for the Van Sweringens, 1931 was worse. Ironically, the first few months of the year were peaceful: on May 1 the V. S. Corp. noteholders and the banking syndicate received their interest payments. When the brothers and their bankers arranged the loan of the previous year, they assumed that the worst was over and that economic recovery was on the way. In the fall of 1931 it became apparent that this assumption was false. The effects of the still worsening crisis could be seen on the Vans' most important railroads:

	Year	Gross Revenue	Net
C. & O.	1929	$150,667,975	$36,496,819
	1930	137,230,375	34,107,017
	1931	119,552,170	26,696,484
Erie	1929	$129,230,437	$11,677,740
	1930	108,996,611	4,171,149
	1931	90,153,601	901,093 (deficit)
Pere Marquette	1929	$ 48,468,439	$ 7,458,460
	1930	37,216,378	2,015,016
	1931	27,344,681	1,863,081 (deficit)
Missouri	1929	$139,807,915	$12,217,763
Pacific	1930	120,187,689	6,713,611
	1931	95,268,193	1,395,754
Nickel Plate	1929	$ 56,385,457	$ 7,390,042
	1930	46,533,186	4,396,744
	1931	36,551,359	210,413 (deficit)

As railroad income fell, the market value of Van Sweringen railroad issues tumbled: in 1931 Nickel Plate fell to 2½, Erie to 5, Missouri Pacific to 6⅝, Chesapeake & Ohio to 23⅜, and Pere Marquette to 4. All of this devastated Alleghany Corporation: its preferred plunged from 100 in 1930 to 2 in 1931, while the common went from 30 to 1⅛ in the same period. The primary objectives now were to rescue the Vans' holding companies and find the money to pay interest on their loans and notes. Efforts to save the railroads themselves would have to wait until later days.[10]

Van Sweringen Corporation, with an interest payment on its 6 percent notes due on November 1, 1931, brought on the immediate problem. Neither its Alleghany stock nor its real-estate assets provided sufficient income to make the payment. V. S. Corp. and its subsidiary, the Cleveland Terminals Building Company, were losing money; between them, they had less than $260,000 in free cash. Vaness had no money either. By the fall of 1931 New York bankers realized the loans of the previous year had not accomplished their goals. A Morgan employee wrote:

> With the changed situation now existing, the cash receipts will not be sufficient to pay overhead expenses, carrying charges and interest, and we have told the Van Sweringens that we see no point to our advancing additional money merely to pay ourselves interest. They have agreed to this and recognize that we are, in effect, the owners of all of their properties and that we shall have to determine policies as to what properties are to be protected, they to help in whatever way possible in carrying out our policies by virtue of their familiarity with the business and the assets, particularly the real estate.[11]

Fortune called the solution reached by the bankers and the Vans the "smartest deal in depression history." Because the action taken eliminated the Van Sweringen Corporation as a source of financial discomfort for everyone involved, namely, the bankers and the Vans, *Fortune* had assessed the situation correctly. On October 29, V. S. Corp. announced that the proceeds of the $10,000,000 in United States Government notes placed in its "segregated assets" account the previous year would be used to purchase the 6 percent notes then outstanding for $500 in cash and 20 shares of V. S. Corp. common. It was stipulated that when $15,000,000 of the notes had been turned in, they would be retired and cancelled; anything left in the "segregated assets" account after the December 1 deadline was to be returned to Vaness for the purchase and retirement of additional notes. Since these $1,000 notes had fallen in value to $340, most noteholders accepted the offer. The interest on the notes was paid, and all but $1,213,000 were retired. The "segregated assets" agreement stipulated that if half the note issue was retired the Vans' personal obligation would end; this maneuver, therefore, meant that the commitment ceased and the brothers had freed themselves from the burdensome notes and all they entailed.[12]

The next step was to save Alleghany. As a holding company with its income based on the income of railroads, Alleghany watched its income slide as the value of, and income from, those assets fell. This created problems, particularly in relation to its collateral trust bonds and its debts to Paine, Webber.

Alleghany's three bond issues—$24,532,000 in 5s of 1950, $21,938,000 in 5s of 1949, and $31,466,000 in 5s of 1944—had been constructed on a collateral trust basis, supplemented by an agreement which required that at four specific times during a year the cash and securities held as collateral be worth more than 150 percent of the outstanding bonds issued. If Alleghany could not maintain the value of the collateral, the trustees of the bonds (Guaranty Trust of New York) would "be entitled (1) to . . . receive all dividends on, and to vote . . . the pledged securities, and (2) to . . . receive all interest upon all bonds, securities or indebtedness pledged under this indenture and any and all other income of the trust estate. . . . " By September, 1931, the value of the collateral behind Alleghany's bonds had fallen sufficiently to bring the trust covenant into effect. Guaranty Trust now collected the income from Alleghany's assets; fortunately for the Vans, Guaranty rarely if ever interfered with their direction of their own companies.[13]

Alleghany's account at Paine, Webber was facing problems similar to those Vaness had encountered. Although the holding company had successfully reduced its Paine, Webber debt from $10,600,000 to $5,701,000 during the period September, 1931–January, 1932, the market value of the collateral securities in this margin account had also dropped during these months from $12,345,708 to $5,049,645, representing a decrease from a positive margin of 16.5 percent to a negative margin of 11.43 percent. Faced with this deficiency, the brokerage firm demanded Alleghany pay its indebtedness. Alleghany could not do so unless it sold some of its assets. But depressed market prices made a public sale unlikely—and the Vans refused to sell any of their own stock to outsiders, since they were still trying to retain control of an empire that was already no longer theirs. Neither Vaness, nor V.S. Corp., nor the Building Company had the necessary funds. But the Chesapeake & Ohio Railroad, relatively affluent because it continued to haul coal and pay dividends, did. Therefore, the C. & O. was drafted to obtain Alleghany's holdings of Pere Marquette (46,200 shares), Erie

(215,000 shares), and Nickel Plate (167,300 shares). Although the market value of those stocks on February 1, 1932, stood at $3,739,775, the railroad paid $5,573,675 . . . just about enough to cover the debt owed Paine, Webber. This arrangement created two knotty problems for the Vans. First, how would the C. & O., with only $4,400,000 of free cash in its treasury, pay for the shares? Second, what would be done about the ICC? The solution reached took care of both neatly.[14]

Paying for the stock turned out to be relatively easy. The C. & O. sold $4,000,000 worth of two-year, 6 percent notes to Paine, Webber; with the proceeds of that sale the railroad bought the blocs of stock from Alleghany; Alleghany then turned over $3,950,000 to its brokers, the C. & O. agreeing to pay the balance due. Obviously this circular maneuver merely substituted the C. & O.'s excellent credit for Alleghany's not-so-excellent credit, but it ended the crisis at Paine, Webber.[15]

The methods employed also concealed the transaction from the less than watchful eyes of the ICC. The issuance of *short-term* obligations eliminated the necessity of securing ICC approval of the note sale. But the acquisition by the C. & O. of sizeable blocs of stock in the Erie and Nickel Plate railroads raised the specter of having to secure ICC approval of a merger. Although the commission's "final" consolidation plan of 1929 grouped the roads together, the Vans had no interest in going thorough a year of ICC hearings when an immediate solution was demanded. Nor did the prospect of having to reveal the inflated prices which the C. & O. paid appeal to them. Under the circumstances the brothers again utilized a technique they had employed two years earlier in the acquisition of the Chicago & Eastern Illinois—a purchase in the form of an option. Only slightly more than $500,000 of the $5,500,000 paid by the C. & O. to Alleghany was for an outright purchase of stock, that of the 46,200 shares of Pere Marquette, a transaction already sanctioned by the ICC; the rest of the money went to Alleghany for a down payment and an option to buy the Nickel Plate and Erie shares. The contract between the C. & O. and Alleghany specifically stipulated that "the seller serves and shall have full power and authority to exercise all voting, consenting, and/or similar rights in respect of the optioned shares." The agreement also specified that "it is not intended hereby to give the buyer any control over the optioned stocks in violation of any law, and the buyer shall not have such control, anything herein to the contrary notwithstanding." The entire maneuver represented a simple rearrangement of the assets held by the Vans in various parts of their corporate empire; it did not threaten their control of their railroads.[16]

While the financial wells in New York made money available for the salvation of the Vans' holding companies, these same reservoirs ran dry when the brothers solicited help for their operating railroads. They then turned to the federal government for assistance; aid from Washington became available in January, 1932, when Congress established the Reconstruction Finance Corporation to provide loans to corporations in distress, particularly railroads. As O. P. noted, he and his brother were "on the [RFC's] doorstep waiting for them to open." From 1932 to 1934, the RFC loaned Van Sweringen railroads over $75,000,000:

Missouri Pacific	$23,134,800
Nickel Plate	18,200,000
Erie	16,582,000
Denver & Rio Grande Western	8,081,000
Chicago & Eastern Illinois	5,916,500
Pere Marquette	3,000,000
Texas & Pacific	700,000

Of this $75,000,000, nearly $20,000,000 went to repay bank loans; the rest went for wages, interest, equipment, taxes, and other obligations and corporate expenses. The Van Sweringen lines became one of the RFCs best customers.[17]

In addition to the Reconstruction Finance Corporation, another federal agency provided funds for several Van Sweringen railroads. Harold Ickes' Public Works Administration, in an attempt to stimulate employment, alloted $36,097,000 in loans, out of almost $200,000,000 available, to the C. & O., Chicago & Eastern Illinois, Erie, and Nickel Plate railroads for the purchase of equipment and supplies, including over 10,000 freight and 150 passenger cars and more than 30,000 tons of rails.[18]

The Vans' Shaker Heights home on South Park Boulevard.

Oris Paxton Van Sweringen (1879-1936)

Mantis James Van Sweringen (1881-1935)

Daisy Hill

These loans did not save two Van Sweringen railroads from bankruptcy. The Missouri Pacific's operating revenues fell by half, from $139,807,000 in 1929 to $69,920,000 in 1932; long-term indebtedness, and a policy of paying dividends despite the drop in revenue, exhausted the road's treasury. On March 31, 1933, citing an inability to meet $40,589,330 worth of bond maturities, interest, and taxes, the MoPac became the first railroad to file for reorganization under the new federal bankruptcy act. Under this statute, the road now had an opportunity to reorganize its financial structure under a trusteeship instead of waiting to be forced into eventual bankruptcy. When finally written, the plan would be submitted to the ICC and to the courts for approval; also, at least two-thirds of each of the different classes of creditors had to accept it. Three weeks later, the Chicago & Eastern Illinois took the same step. For this road, the loss of coal-carrying business from unionized mines, the competition of trucks, and the generally depressed business conditions meant a drop in bituminous coal handled from 7,168,247 tons in 1926 to 2,916,236 in 1932; freight revenues fell in the same period from $21,414,226 to $9,819,161. On April 18, 1933, the C. & E.I. knew it would be unable to pay $1,568,010 in interest, taxes, and obligations due May 1; it filed for bankruptcy. Judge C. B. Faris in St. Louis approved the MoPac petition and directed the existing management to continue to operate the property as trustees for the creditors and stockholders; Judge John P. Barnes did the same for the C. & E.I. in Chicago.[19]

The bankruptcy of the MoPac was much more serious than that of the C. & E.I. Alleghany Corporation had invested almost $90,000,000—nearly half of its funds—in that road. Even worse, one of Alleghany's bond issues—the 5 percent bonds due to mature in 1950—depended on income from its MoPac assets. In October, 1933, and again in April, 1934, Alleghany borrowed $5,550,000 from J. P. Morgan & Company to provide the necessary funds for these interest payments. This type of borrowing could not be resorted to forever. A long-term solution had to be found, and the brothers devised one. On March 15, 1934, Alleghany announced its proposal to holders of the 5 percent bonds due in 1950. It provided for the issue of a newly invented prior-preferred stock to compensate for the interest due on the bonds during the next five years. The stock would be worth $50 a share (the amount to which it was entitled if a liquidation took place), would pay $2.50 a year, and could be converted into ten shares of common.

The federal bankruptcy act used by the MoPac and the C. & E.I. also assisted Alleghany in meeting problems relating to the 5 percent bonds due in 1950. If two-thirds of the holders of those bonds agreed to the Vans' funding proposal, the new bankruptcy act could be enlisted to require *all* of the bondholders to accept it; this would eliminate problems that might come from a recalcitrant minority. At the end of November, when over 70 percent of the bondholders had assented, Alleghany filed a petition in United States District Court in Baltimore requesting confirmation of its plan of reorganization. On December 29, 1934, Judge Calvin Chesnut approved the petition, noting that the postponement of the payment of 5 percent interest on the bonds for five years might give the Missouri Pacific time to recover, since "the very best hope of ultimate payment of the 1950 Bondholders is to preserve the situation intact and to give the Alleghany Corporation an opportunity to see if it can work out its problems largely through the Missouri Pacific. . . ." When the bondholders received their 122,660 shares of the new preferred and the Morgan its 22,000 shares (as payment for the interest loans of October, 1933, and April, 1934), this "mild case of bankruptcy" eliminated the necessity of making interest payments on these particular bonds for five years.[20]

The one bright spot for the Van Sweringen empire centered around the Chesapeake Corporation, the holding company one step below Alleghany through which the Vans controlled the C. & O. In 1930 the railroad brought out a new issue of stock. In July of that year, to finance the purchase of the over 250,000 shares of new stock needed to maintain the desired percentage of control, Chesapeake Corporation had borrowed $32,500,000 at 4½ percent from a banking syndicate headed by J. P. Morgan & Company. It proved impossible to repay this loan when it came due three months later. This did not worry the bankers, because the C. & O. was still making money. They contented themselves with renewing the loan at interest payments now computed at 5½ percent. But by April, 1932, the collateral behind the loan—250,000 shares of C. & O. common and 27,500 shares of Pere Marquette common—had fallen in value and the Morgan bank felt compelled to obtain the Vans' assurance that "the assets of the corporation would not be diminished by the distribution of dividends if they—the participating banks—objected."[21]

In April, 1933, when the loan had been reduced to $30,500,000, the decision was made to liquidate it entirely. This was accomplished in two steps. In a market that saw C. & O. common rise from 35⅜ to 46¾ in the period of May 17 to July 6, the sale of 240,000 shares of C. & O. stock brought in more than $9,550,000 and cut the loan principal to slightly less than $21,000,000. Further sales through February, 1934, reduced the loan to $18,000,000. To eliminate the obligation completely, the Vans negotiated the issue of $18,000,000 worth of 5 percent, ten-year convertible Chesapeake Corporation bonds. The collateral for the new issue would be 1,000,000 shares of C. & O. common. When offered to the public on December 21, 1934, the bonds sold very well, bringing the Chesapeake Corporation $17,705,000. Combined with $490,750 from the company's treasury, this gave Chesapeake the necessary funds to pay off the bankers entirely.[22]

While the bankers made money on the Chesapeake loan, they lost much more on another venture. In discussions held between the Vans and their New York creditors during the early months of 1935, it became apparent that Vaness and the Cleveland Terminals Building Company would not be able to repay $50,000,000 in principal and accumulated interest due on May 1 from the loans made in 1930. The bankers made it clear that in the event of a default they would have no choice but to foreclose and sell the collateral securing the loans. They could not have expected to recoup the entire amount: at current market prices, the Alleghany shares alone would bring in only slightly more than $3,000,000.[23]

On May 1, 1935, the Vans and their two companies formally notified J. P. Morgan & Company of their inability to meet their obligations maturing that day. Four and one-half months later the New York banks announced their intention of selling at a public auction the collateral behind the two loans. The brothers issued a statement in which they gave their consent to the sale and reported that they "have completed arrangements to bid for the collateral at the sale and have also arranged for new capital to carry on the enterprises." The capital referred to was to come from two important Midwest industrialists, George A. Ball and George A. Tomlinson, who had agreed to back the Vans in this venture. As one chronicler later wrote, "The plan by which the Van Sweringens were to work their salvation"—and reacquire control of corporations having a book value of approximately $3,000,000,000—"equalled anything in their past as an exercise in financial-legal expertness."

On September 28 the Midamerica Corporation was incorporated. This new holding company had broad powers, but its real purpose was to purchase the collateral being auctioned in New York. From an authorized 250,000 shares of no-par non-voting preferred and 150,000 shares of no-par voting common, the first issue consisted of only 20,000 shares of preferred and 15,000 of common, for which Ball and Tomlinson agreed to pay $2,015,000. But the two industrialists did not want to control the stock they had just bought, nor did they want to operate the companies that would be owned by Midamerica if it was successful at the auction. In fact, one week before Midamerica's formal incorporation, Ball and Tomlinson had written to the brothers:

> These companies, in the main, prospered up to the time of the depression. We believe that under the *same* control, direction, and management they will again prosper if the present improvement in business conditions shall continue, as we believe it will. If we did not so believe, we should not be interested in acquiring these securities, in whole or in part, under any circumstances. As it is, we should be interested if, but *only* if, we could be assured that you will participate actively in their direction and management.

In order to bring this about, the industrialists gave the Vans a ten-year option to buy 8,250 shares of the voting common, deposited in escrow, at cost plus 5 percent interest per year, during which time of "such option you will have the sole and exclusive right to vote and represent such deposited common shares." This meant that if Midamerica succeeded at the auction, the Vans would once more have "sole and exclusive" control of their companies without having had to expend one penny for it. *The Wall Street Journal* was optimistic about the prospects: "At present, with confident backers, prestige, and assets of their own, it would seem likely that they might retain control of their rail empire. They have weathered earlier storms and come through them seemingly none the worse off."[24]

The sale was held on September 30, 1935, in the auction rooms of Adrian H. Muller & Son at 18 Vesey Street in lower Manhattan. Known as the "securities graveyard," these rooms, which faced the cemetery of St. Paul's Chapel, served as the recognized clearinghouse for defaulted securities. Some four hundred people squeezed into the dingy, yellow chamber. They included George M. Whitney, the "tall, smartly-dressed and very bored looking" partner in J. P. Morgan & Company, and F. A. O. Schwarz, a "tense" lawyer from Davis, Polk, Wardwell, Gardiner & Reed, there to bid for the Morgan. A "pale, white-haired man" explained to bystanders: "I lost plenty in Alleghany. I'm here to see the obsequies." In the most inconspicuous corner of the auction room sat O. P. Van Sweringen, "grave, sometimes resting his head on his hand or donning spectacles to scrutinize memoranda."

At 3:30 P.M. the auctioneer began reading the list of securities for sale. It became obvious that the only bidders for the parcel carrying control of Alleghany would be the Morgan interests and Midamerica; rumors that Leonor F. Loree or the Rockefellers would bid never materialized. The Morgan put in a "protective" bid of $2,802,101. The auctioneer asked for a higher bid. Col. Leonard P. Ayres, bidding on behalf of Midamerica Corporation, called out: "Two million, eight hundred and three thousand." The auctioneer intoned: "Going once . . . Going twice . . . Last call. . . . The bid stands at $2,803,-000." This, combined with another $318,000 spent for 33,859 shares of Pittson Company, gave back to the Vans, through Midamerica, most of their empire. Specifically, they received the following:

	Shares or Amount
Alleghany Corp. common stock	2,064,492
Alleghany Corp. 5½% pfd. stock, $30 warrants	25,000
Alleghany Corp. 5½% pfd. stock, $40 warrants	5,600
Alleghany Corp. 5½% pfd. stock, ex-warrants	3,950
Alleghany Corp. 20-year 5s, 1950 C/D	$456,000.00
Cleveland Railway Co. common stock	40,393
Cleveland Terminals Bldg. Co., 2nd mortgage bonds	$1,200,000.00
Higbee Co. common stock	100,000
Higbee Co. 6% subordinated notes	$2,595,398.85
Higbee Co. 6% subordinated notes	$258,506.94
Participation in Higbee Co. $523,043.51 note	$69,673.71
Huron-Fourth Co. common stock	250
Long Lake Co. common stock	196
Long Lake Co. 6% demand notes	$817,460.36
Metropolitan Utilities, Inc., 6% demand notes	$278,204.84
Pittston Co. common stock	33,859
Terminal Bldg. Co. common stock	17,000
Terminal Bldg. Co. 6% demand notes	$207,176.60
Terminal Bldg. Co. 6% demand notes	$170,430.29
Van Sweringen Co. common stock	122,000
Van Sweringen Co. 6% demand notes	$6,261,697.59
Van Sweringen Corp. common stock	1,244,580
Van Sweringen Corp. 5-year 6% notes	$13,787,000.00
Van Sweringen Corp. 6% demand notes	$554,103.00
Van Sweringen Corp. 6% subordinated notes	$2,595,398.85

The *New York Times* called it "the greatest auction sale of securities in Wall Street history." When it was over, O. P.'s face, pale until the end, reddened. His friends turned to congratulate him; he smiled. George Whitney, representing the bankers who lost 90% of their investment, came over and shook O. P.'s hand and then placed his arm around him. O. P. said to those near him: "I'm sorry it had to be done this way. I'd rather have paid the bills."[25]

The *Times* also saw in the sale "an instructive object lesson in shifting values, a sidelight on human delusion and a picture of results which will often follow 'company pyramiding.' " The *Plain Dealer* reacted more positively:

From the Cleveland point of view the result of the auction is entirely favorable. The Van Sweringens will again have a free hand in the management of the multiple affairs long associated with their name and with continued improvement in the rail and general business situation should be able to work their way out of the difficulties they encountered shortly after the stock market break in 1929. . . . Clevelanders who have watched the Van Sweringens over all the years now feel assured that with control of their properties back in their own hands the program will command the necessary support and will move forward as the economic situation improves.[26]

Indeed, the Vans' triumph brought them over a critical hurdle in the fight to preserve their corporate empire and regain the position they held before the Crash. But much remained to be done: such problems as the reorganizations of the Missouri Pacific and other railroads, their faltering real-estate operations, and the other debts due banks in New York and Cleveland—all had to be solved. The solutions reached would have to be O. P.'s alone, for only a few months after the auction, M. J. Van Sweringen died at the age of fifty-four. Suffering from high blood pressure, he entered Hanna House of Lakeside Hospital in August, 1935. Influenza weakened his condition, and he could not join his brother in New York for the auction. He died on December 12, 1935, of heart disease. The simple funeral at Daisy Hill, the brothers' country estate in Hunting Valley, lasted less than half an hour. The Rev. Charles H. Meyers of Detroit, formerly of the Plymouth Church in Shaker Heights, conducted the service, which included a brief prayer, the reading of the Twenty-third Psalm, and a short eulogy. To those who came to express their sympathies O. P. could only say: "I've always been able to see a way, but to this there is no answer." M. J.'s estate, which he left to O. P., was worth $3,067 plus several hundred thousand dollars in insurance.[27]

The Vans had agreed that in the event of either's death the survivor would carry on. After M. J. died, O. P. tried, although his brother's presence remained strong. Each morning O. P. entered M. J.'s office in the Terminal Tower and switched on his desk lamp. Each evening he returned and shut the light off. O. P. used work to help him

forget his brother's death, plunging into various business problems
with abandon. Unfortunately, his misfortunes increased. During the
waning months of 1935, Missouri Pacific bondholders objected to the
plan developed for the reorganization of the road, and the ICC began an
investigation into Midamerica's control of the Van Sweringen
railroads. In February, 1936, the Van Sweringen Company and several
of its subsidiaries filed for bankruptcy. In May the Vans' old rival Frank
E. Taplin succeeded in obtaining minority representation on the board
of the Wheeling & Lake Erie. In October the Cleveland Terminals
Building Company and the Van Sweringen Corporation went bankrupt. The only bright spot, and one that gave O. P. a measure of hope,
centered around improving business conditions and the related
increase in railroad revenues. In particular, the value of securities
pledged as collateral behind two of the Alleghany bond issues had risen
to more than 150% of the value of those bonds. As a result Guaranty
Trust Company returned to O. P. control of that collateral, notably the
Chesapeake Corporation and its holdings in the C. & O.[28]

     O. P. did not live long enough to benefit from this turn of events.
On Sunday, November 22, 1936, a private car of the Nickel Plate left the
Cleveland Union Terminal. Accompanying O. P. on this business trip to
New York was William H. Wenneman, his personal secretary. A minor
collision at 4:00 a.m. in the Scranton yards damaged the car sufficiently
to require transfer to another car. The train finally left Scranton at
8:00 a.m. O. P. ate breakfast and, complaining of fatigue, went back to
sleep. Shortly after noon, as the train entered Hoboken, Wenneman
went to awaken his fifty-seven-year-old employer and found him dead of
a heart attack. In less than a year the Vans were joined in death.[29] They
now rest, side by side, in Lake View Cemetery. Their common headstone
bears this inscription:

Van Sweringen

Oris Paxton   Mantis James

1879–1936   1881–1935

"Brothers"

Conclusion

W<small>HO WERE</small> O. P. <small>AND</small> M. J. V<small>AN</small> S<small>WERINGEN</small>? Relatively little is known of their personal lives. This was not an accident. Their public relations man once received a summons to appear in the boss's office. "You've been working as our public relations man now for three months," said O. P., "and there has not been a single story about us in the newspapers." "Well, sir," the man began to respond, "you see. . ." "Splendid work," interrupted O. P. "Keep it up." The Vans remained familiar figures only in the board rooms and offices of companies with which they were associated. They had little interest in Cleveland society, and although they held memberships in all of the "right" clubs—Union, Chagrin Valley Hunt, Hermit, Cleveland Athletic, Shaker Heights Country, Canterbury Golf—they rarely appeared in them. They had no hobbies, avoided physical exercise, and disdained ostentation. At varying times, the brothers were noted for their "industry," "thrift," "low-key manner," "generosity," "modesty," and "simplicity in manner, food, dress, and pleasures."

Their only real pleasure—aside from an ascetic devotion to work and each other—was derived from "Daisy Hill," their country estate fifteen miles east of the Terminal Tower, in Hunting Valley.

Developed over a seven-year period at an estimated cost of $2,000,000, the estate included a main house, stables, nursery, greenhouse, man-made lake, and twenty-two garages. The main house contained fifty-four rooms—but O. P. and M. J. shared just one of the bedrooms; they slept in twin beds. A "Dickens Room" held many first or limited editions of that author's works, and scattered throughout the mansion were Dresden and Spode china, expensive antiques, and American paintings. Occasionally, the Vans entertained at Daisy Hill, and often they held business meetings there. Constant visitors were Benjamin L. Jenks, president of the Van Sweringen Company, and his wife Louise. The couple lived only a hundred yards away and often breakfasted with the brothers. Louise Jenks—who was also known as "Daisy"—often served as their hostess, advisor, and confidante.[1]

　　How does one assess the careers of O. P. and M. J. Van Sweringen? During the 1920s and 1930s countless newspapers and magazines tried in articles about these two fascinating brothers. Coming from the poorest of backgrounds, they found themselves in 1930 on the front page of the *New York Times* being cited in Ambassador James W. Gerard's famous list of sixty-four men "who rule the United States." This national prominence derived from their ownership of a railroad empire consisting of 30,000 miles of track and other equipment worth $3,000,000,000, the largest such grouping in the United States. While Senator Burton K. Wheeler's investigation in the late 1930s of railroads and holding companies called the purchase of the Missouri Pacific "the essential Van Sweringen blunder," the investigators also concluded that the Vans' system of railroads in the eastern part of the country—"a more reasonable composition of lines than that proposed by the Interstate Commerce Commission as a fifth eastern system in its 1929 plan"—had "financial strength and considerable operating logic as justification." Despite the Depression, the *Plain Dealer* commented, "The amazing fact is that [O. P.] held all his railroad properties intact . . . and almost all of his real estate. No other business man who had pyramided holdings as large as his in 1929 brought them so completely through." To which the Wheeler Committee would add: "The Van Sweringens had, perhaps, built more solidly than they knew in creating a power unit that survived them and was susceptible of being transferred from person to person, carrying with it a vast degree of prestige and authority."[2]

As leaders of the railroad world, the Vans took the initiative in the congressionally mandated movement to consolidate American railroads into a limited number of systems. In 1932, when the ICC finally accepted the brothers' suggestions for consolidation in the eastern region, the railroads found themselves financially unable to complete the mergers. Robert R. Young, who secured control of the Vans' railroads from George Ball in April, 1937, tried again in 1945 to join the C. & O., Nickel Plate, Pere Marquette, and Wheeling & Lake Erie, but opposition from stockholders forced him to abandon the idea. In the mid-1970s, fifty years after the Vans' first consolidation plan, a study sponsored jointly by the Council of Economic Advisors, the White House Office of Science and Technology, and the National Commission on Productivity recommended that "the nation's 38 largest railroads be consolidated into four to seven transcontinental systems as a means of revitalizing . . . a troubled industry." In retrospect, the 1920s represents a missed opportunity for the still urgently needed reorganization of the American railroad system.[3]

When the Vans died in the mid-1930s their position as America's preeminent railroaders had sunk considerably. A personal fortune estimated at more than $120,000,000 had become "70 millions of personal debts and a tangle of financial-legal debris" that was to take years to untangle. Where had they gone wrong? They had built a reputation as respectable, modest, hard-working, efficient businessmen with a knack for making railroads financially successful, for dreaming grand designs, and for convincing thousands of investors, large and small, to provide them the wherewithal to make those dreams a reality. In fact, their success in the 1920s derived, in part, from their ability to meet the needs and desires of many Americans by providing opportunities to make fortunes in a rising stock market.[4]

Can the Vans be blamed for the loss of those fortunes simply because they foresaw neither the Crash of 1929 nor the subsequent Depression? They were not alone in this regard, and they lost as much if not more than most of their investors. Indeed, as investors in their own companies, their insistence on acquiring 51 percent of the stock in a company in order to insure control—the Wheeler Committee called it "overinvestment"—made their own downfall that much more certain. Men with less pride or less hope in the future would have dumped their holdings to salvage as much as possible. Not O. P. and M. J. Van Sweringen. Eternally optimistic and convinced that recovery was just around the corner (not unlike most Americans in 1929), the Vans held on. As the Wheeler Committee noted, "Proof of the Van Sweringens' good faith is the extent to which they left their own financial position dependent on Alleghany and its common shares. Promoters setting out to ruin a company and its investors by wasting its assets are not likely to invest the bulk of their fortune in the company."[5]

Through it all, did they violate the law? They found legal loopholes to avoid paying taxes, a practice adopted by millions then and now. In April, 1934, the Cuyahoga County Grand Jury indicted O. P. Van Sweringen, Joseph R. Nutt, and Wilbur M. Baldwin (the latter two, respectively, chairman and president of Cleveland's Union Trust Company) for the alleged "window dressing" of a financial statement issued by the bank in 1931. The grand jury charged O. P. with being party to the sale and repurchase of securities which enabled the bank to produce a better financial statement than its actual condition warranted—by showing more assets and more deposits than it actually had. The indictment was still pending more than two years later when O. P. died. The brothers easily escaped the not-so-watchful eye of the Interstate Commerce Commission. *Railway Age* criticized their use of holding company financing as "a lawful evasion, but nevertheless an evasion" of the law which made the ICC responsible for regulating the issuance of railway secruities. *Fortune* agreed but also insisted, "The fact is that, while you may condemn the laws, no one has ever been able to impugn the legality of the holding company as practiced *chez* Van Sweringen. The brothers still enjoy the status of honest businessmen." And as the Wheeler Committee admitted: "The public at large . . . had no complaints against such dodges as these."[6]

What critics of the Van Sweringens did demand, however, were new laws to prevent a repetition of what they considered to be questionable activities. The Senate's investigation into stock-exchange practices—an inquiry which focused in part on the Vans' methods of financing—led to the passage of several statutes designed, as the committee's chief counsel Ferdinand Pecora later wrote, "to cope with the abuses it had revealed." Pecora cited the Banking Act of 1933, the Securities Act of 1933, and the Securities Exchange Act of 1934. Probably the most important piece of legislation in the area of holding company regulation was the Railroad Emergency Act of 1933, which brought railroad holding companies under the ICC's control. Ironically, this act might be cited as another Van Sweringen achievement. As the Wheeler Committee noted, "Indeed, the spectacle of the Van Sweringen system was one of the chief factors leading to the passage of the bill regulating public holding companies."[7]

The successes (and failures) which brought the Vans national attention have been forgotten; those on the local level cannot be. There were other things, the *Plain Dealer* editorialized at the time of O. P.'s death, "which most Clevelanders will remember about the Vans, rather than the brothers' adventures in railroad building. These are the monuments the two boys from Wooster leave behind to keep their memory green for long years to come." They made Cleveland the base of operations for their vast railroad empire and gave the city a model suburb, Shaker Heights, and a model shopping center, Shaker Square. With the Terminal Tower complex—still housing the surviving remnant of their empire, namely, the C. & O.—they gave Cleveland's downtown a new focus. The national acclaim they brought the city did much to reinstill in Clevelanders a sense of pride in their hometown.[8]

The Vans demonstrated their devotion to their city in a variety of other ways. In 1927 they joined a syndicate which purchased the Cleveland Indians. They tried to buy the *Plain Dealer* for $10,000,000; when those negotiations failed, O. P. became a substantial stockholder in the Cleveland *Times*. M. J. supported the Western Reserve Historical Society both with financial aid and, as the trustees of the Society noted at his death, "with suggestions and work in any way that would increase the usefulness of this institution in this community." Both O. P.

The Van Sweringen Pyramid (1934)

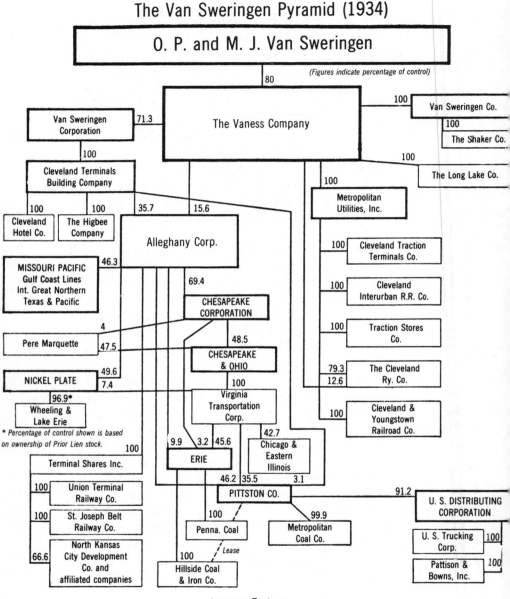

O. P. and M. J. Van Sweringen

(Figures indicate percentage of control)

80 — The Vaness Company

71.3 — Van Sweringen Corporation

100 — Van Sweringen Co.

100 — The Shaker Co.

100 — Cleveland Terminals Building Company

100 — The Long Lake Co.

100 — Metropolitan Utilities, Inc.

100 — Cleveland Hotel Co.

100 — The Higbee Company

35.7 15.6 — Alleghany Corp.

100 — Cleveland Traction Terminals Co.

100 — Cleveland Interurban R.R. Co.

MISSOURI PACIFIC Gulf Coast Lines Int. Great Northern Texas & Pacific — 46.3

69.4

CHESAPEAKE CORPORATION

100 — Traction Stores Co.

Pere Marquette — 4 / 47.5

48.5

CHESAPEAKE & OHIO

79.3 12.6 — The Cleveland Ry. Co.

NICKEL PLATE — 49.6 / 7.4

100 — Virginia Transportation Corp.

100 — Cleveland & Youngstown Railroad Co.

96.9* — Wheeling & Lake Erie

42.7

* Percentage of control shown is based on ownership of Prior Lien stock.

100 — Terminal Shares Inc.

9.9 3.2 45.6 — **ERIE**

Chicago & Eastern Illinois

100 — Union Terminal Railway Co.

46.2 35.5 3.1

100 — St. Joseph Belt Railway Co.

PITTSTON CO. — 91.2 — **U. S. DISTRIBUTING CORPORATION**

66.6 — North Kansas City Development Co. and affiliated companies

100 — Penna. Coal

99.9 — Metropolitan Coal Co.

U. S. Trucking Corp. — 100

Lease

100 — Hillside Coal & Iron Co.

Pattison & Bowns, Inc. — 100

SOURCE: *Fortune*

The Van Sweringen Pyramid, Revised (1936)

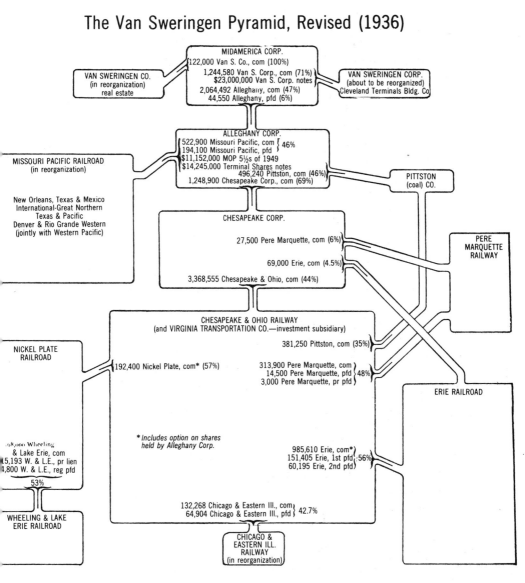

MIDAMERICA CORP.
122,000 Van S. Co., com (100%)
1,244,580 Van S. Corp., com (71%)
$23,000,000 Van S. Corp. notes
2,064,492 Alleghany, com (47%)
44,550 Alleghany, pfd (6%)

VAN SWERINGEN CO.
(in reorganization)
real estate

VAN SWERINGEN CORP.
(about to be reorganized)
Cleveland Terminals Bldg. Co

ALLEGHANY CORP.
522,900 Missouri Pacific, com ⎰ 46%
194,100 Missouri Pacific, pfd ⎱
$11,152,000 MOP 5½s of 1949
$14,245,000 Terminal Shares notes
496,240 Pittston, com (46%)
1,248,900 Chesapeake Corp., com (69%)

MISSOURI PACIFIC RAILROAD
(in reorganization)

New Orleans, Texas & Mexico
International-Great Northern
Texas & Pacific
Denver & Rio Grande Western
(jointly with Western Pacific)

PITTSTON
(coal) CO.

CHESAPEAKE CORP.
27,500 Pere Marquette, com (6%)
69,000 Erie, com (4.5%)
3,368,555 Chesapeake & Ohio, com (44%)

**PERE
MARQUETTE
RAILWAY**

CHESAPEAKE & OHIO RAILWAY
(and VIRGINIA TRANSPORTATION CO.—investment subsidiary)
381,250 Pittston, com (35%)

**NICKEL PLATE
RAILROAD**

192,400 Nickel Plate, com* (57%)

313,900 Pere Marquette, com ⎱
14,500 Pere Marquette, pfd ⎰48%
3,000 Pere Marquette, pr pfd ⎰

ERIE RAILROAD

*Includes option on shares
held by Alleghany Corp.

985,610 Erie, com*⎱
151,405 Erie, 1st pfd⎰56%
60,195 Erie, 2nd pfd⎰

.08,000 Wheeling
& Lake Erie, com
5,193 W. & L.E., pr lien
,800 W. & L.E., reg pfd
53%

132,268 Chicago & Eastern Ill., com ⎱ 42.7%
64,904 Chicago & Eastern Ill., pfd ⎰

**WHEELING & LAKE
ERIE RAILROAD**

**CHICAGO &
EASTERN ILL.
RAILWAY**
(in reorganization)

SOURCE: *Fortune*

and M. J. helped to underwrite the Society's genealogical collection, thereby making "the Society in this field . . . among the leaders in America." The Vans also displayed a commitment to the city's future with numerous plans for increased rapid-transit service for Cleveland and its suburbs. These included projected surface lines to Linndale, Rocky River, Warrensville Center, and Collinwood, as well as subways under West 25th Street (to Brookpark), Euclid-Mayfield, and St. Clair. The only route that ever came close to being built during the brothers' lifetimes was the East Cleveland Line, for which bridges and stairways were constructed and a line of track put down. The Cleveland Transit System, the result of Cleveland's purchase in April, 1942, from Metropolitan Utilities of the Cleveland Railway Company's streetcar and bus system, completed the project, and the rapid between Windermere and the airport follows the route proposed by the Vans.[9]

Over the years, Clevelanders have provided their own assessments of the Vans and of their contributions to the city. Newton D. Baker described for the Interstate Commerce Commission how most Clevelanders felt about their famous citizens in 1925:

> I can say with confidence to this Commission that if they will search where Mr. Van Sweringen or either of them are known, for their reputation, they will find it to be what I assert their character to be, men who in 20 years of large and varied operations, have conferred benefits upon the city in which they live, who have had multiple transactions with every sort of interest and men, and your Honors, with a search warrant could not find a person who believes that they have ever done an unrighteous thing or left an injury in the trail of their operations.

Ten years later, when Clevelanders had lost jobs and savings because of the Van Sweringen collapse, opinions changed. John W. Raper, columnist for the Cleveland *Press*, addressed the City Club in 1935. He spoke about the Vans:

> Yes, we are anti-Van. We're anti-both Vans. . . . Who in Cleveland is not anti-Van these days?
> May I not present to you the two unkissed cherubs? There

they sit in the Tower, the wonderful tower reaching up into the clouds—the highest thing in Cleveland, except the pile of defaulted bonds they built; that wonderful tower in whose top there burns a powerful light, its bright rays going far across the boundaries of the city, far out into the country. There in the Tower top it burns, night after night, in memory of the unknown bondholder. And there they sit, the unkissed cherubs, symbols of sublimity of virginity in masculinity. Pure in their private lives. But it can hardly be said that in their financial relations with the public they practiced continence.

Time, however, seems to have healed the wounds. Thirty years after the brothers' deaths, George Condon, a popular Cleveland historian and journalist, ended the debate: "Of all the men and women to walk the Cleveland scene over the past 170 years, O. P. and M. J. Van Sweringen did more to alter the face of the city than any other private citizens, individually or in combination. They left a deep imprint that shows no signs of eroding. They were the builders of modern Cleveland."[10]

Notes to the Text

I. HOW IT ALL BEGAN

1. H. H. Swearingen, *Family Register of Gerret van Sweringen*, 2nd ed. (Washington, 1894), pp. 1-5, 17-18, 26-27.

2. The family name went through several changes. According to Swearingen, "the orthography of the name as written by Gerret was 'van Sweringen.' The dropping of the prefix van and the interpolation of the a was probably done during the lifetime of Thomas. He grew up in an English-speaking community, and it was therefore as natural for him to insert the a as it was for him to drop the van. That he did drop the van is shown by the fact that Van was a given name for one of his sons . . ." (*Family Register of Gerret van Sweringen*, Preface). By 1832, however, the a had been permanently discarded by this branch of the line, while a capitalized *Van* had been appended. James Tower Sweringen dropped the *Van* at an early age; according to *The Cleveland Directory* (The Cleveland Directory Co., 1902-1904), his children brought it back in 1902 or 1903. Actually, their father may have earlier used the *Van* himself. There is a letter from Mantis to his father, dated April 15, 1887, which states: "Some one sent us a Penn. paper and there was a peace [*sic*] in it about you. It said, 'that James T. Van Sweringen was visiting relatives in Mifflintown' " (Virginia Taylor Hampton Collection, Western Reserve Historical Society, hereafter cited as VTHC).

3. *The Sun-Press* (Cleveland Heights, Ohio), October 26, 1961, p. 2-C; E. H. Hauenstein, "No Signs Left of Modest Homes Where Van Sweringens Lived When Brothers Who Became Famous Were Little Boys," Wooster *Daily Record*, October 8, 1952, p. 11.

160

4. Hauenstein, "No Signs Left," Wooster *Daily Record*; Geneva (Ohio) *Times*, January 20, 1886, quoted in letter from Alice M. Silliman, Librarian, Geneva Public Library, to Virginia Taylor Hampton, in VTHC; (Virginia) Taylor Hampton, "Cleveland's Fabulous Vans—Boyhood of Two Shy Brothers," *Cleveland News*, August 2, 1955.

5. Hauenstein, "No Signs Left," Wooster *Daily Record*; Silliman to Hampton, VTHC; various issues of *The Cleveland Directory* for the years 1890-1900.

6. Louise D. Jenks, *O.P. and M.J.* (privately printed, 1940), pp. 6, 7-11; John B. Oviatt, "My Early Acquaintance with Van Sweringens," manuscript (n.d.), VTHC; Hampton, "Cleveland's Fabulous Vans—Boyhood of Two Shy Brothers."

7. Hampton, "Cleveland's Fabulous Vans—Boyhood of Two Shy Brothers"; Jenks, *O. P. and M. J.*, pp. 8-9; Oviatt, "My Early Acquaintance with Van Sweringens"; *The Cleveland Directory* for 1901.

8. Hampton, "Cleveland's Fabulous Vans—Lured by Shaker's Farms," *Cleveland News*, August 3, 1955.

9. *The Cleveland Directory* for 1903; Hampton, "Cleveland's Fabulous Vans—Lured by Shaker's Farms"; Oviatt, "My Early Acquaintance with Van Sweringens"; Eugene Rachlis and John E. Marqusee, *The Land Lords* (New York, 1963), p. 69.

10. League of Women Voters, comps., *Government at Work in the City of Shaker Heights* (Shaker Heights, Ohio, 1961), p. 3; The Van Sweringen Company, *The Heritage of the Shakers* (Cleveland, 1923), p. 5; Mary Lou Conlin, *The North Union Story: A Shaker Society, 1822-1889* (Shaker Heights, Ohio, 1961), pp. 1, 4.

11. Alice Felt Tyler, *Freedom's Ferment: Phases of American Social History from the Colonial Period to the Outbreak of the Civil War* (Minneapolis, 1944), pp. 146-155; Conlin, *North Union Story*, p. 5.

12. Conlin, *North Union Story*, p. 5; Caroline B. Piercy, *The Valley of God's Pleasure: A Saga of the North Union Community* (New York, 1951), p. 119.

13. Piercy, *Valley of God's Pleasure*, p. 240; U.S. Congress, Senate, Committee on Interstate Commerce, *The Van Sweringen Corporate System: A Study in Holding Company Financing*, Report No. 714, 77th Cong., 1st Sess., 1941, p. 8 (one of the reports issued by Senator Burton K. Wheeler and his committee after investigating holding companies in the late 1930s; hereafter cited as *VSCS*); Hampton, "Cleveland's Fabulous Vans—Lured by Shaker's Farms." Avery's comment regarding the derivation of the name "Shaker Heights" appears in a letter he wrote to Charles A. Post dated October 7, 1935, a copy of which is in the Western Reserve Historical Society collection. Other individuals involved with The Shaker Heights Land Company in the early 1890s were T. Avery Lamb, Laurence Lamb, Luther Allen, Bird Housum, and Stewart H. Chisholm.

14. Rachlis and Marqusee, *The Land Lords*, p. 68; Cleveland *Plain Dealer* (hereafter cited as *PD*), December 13, 1935, p. 9.

15. *VSCS*, p. 8; Hampton, "Cleveland's Fabulous Vans—Lured by Shaker's Farms."

16. Hampton, "Cleveland's Fabulous Vans—Lured by Shaker's Farms."

17. I. T. Frary, "Suburban Landscape Planning in Cleveland," *Architectural Record*, Vol. 43, No. 4 (April, 1918), 372; *VSCS*, p. 8; Peter Bellamy, "Van Sweringens Put Shaker, Cleveland on the Right Track, Then Rode the Rails to Disaster," *PD*, October 25, 1961, pp. 19-20; Hampton, "Cleveland's Fabulous Vans—Lured by Shaker's Farms."

18. Hampton, "Cleveland's Fabulous Vans—Lured by Shaker's Farms"; Fred C. Kelly, "Interesting People: Two Young Men Who Are Real Estate Marvels," *The American Magazine*, Vol. 83, No. 3 (March, 1917), 50-51; *Heritage of the Shakers*, p. 48.

19. Several sources have been given for the origins of Shaker Heights' street names. Ernest H. Lynn has written: "The streets in Shaker were to a large extent named by H. C. Gallimore, an officer of the F. A. Pease Engineering Company. . . . Mr. Gallimore, an inveterate reader of English stories, found in these books the names of most of the streets in the suburb" ("Shaker Village," in Arthur A. Beduhn, ed., *Shaker Heights Then and Now* [Shaker Heights, Ohio, 1938], p. 26). In the Shaker Heights 50th Anniversary Issue of *The Sun-Press* it is stated that "a British postal directory was the source of street names" (October 26, 1961, p. 1-C). Caroline B. Piercy, in her unpublished notes for a projected "History of Shaker Heights," suggests the following: "The names of the streets were selected from towns in New England and in England, for the most part, since this section was part of the 'Western Reserve,' a settlement stemming out of Connecticut. Care was used to insure that the name was not then in use, although certain suburbs have since copied many of these names. Any names susceptible of puns, or such that the spelling was not phonetic with the pronunciation or those which denoted a setting or local[e] different from the street in mind were eliminated" (included in a bound volume of Taylor Hampton's series of articles on the Van Sweringens in the Shaker Historical Museum, Shaker Heights, Ohio).

20. "Outlook for an Empire," *Architectural Forum*, Vol. 64, No. 3 (March, 1936), 202-205; Rachlis and Marqusee, *The Land Lords*, p. 71; Lynn, "Shaker Village," pp. 26-27; Hampton, "Cleveland's Fabulous Vans—Lured by Shaker's Farms"; Alfred Pittman, "Builders of Business," *System: The Magazine of Business*, Vol. 36 (December, 1919), 1090; Piercy manuscript.

21. Piercy manuscript; The Van Sweringen Company, *Peaceful Shaker Village* (Cleveland, 1927); Kelly, "Interesting People," 50-51; John W. Love, "The Van Sweringens," *The American Review of Reviews*, Vol. 70 (November, 1924), 501.

22. William G. Rose, *Cleveland: The Making of a City* (Cleveland, 1950), p. 744; Frary, "Suburban Landscape Planning in Cleveland," 374; "Outlook for an Empire," 202-205; *Heritage of the Shakers*, pp. 6-7; Piercy manuscript.

23. Hampton, "Cleveland's Fabulous Vans—Triumph in Shaker," *Cleveland News*, August 11, 1955; Lynn, "Shaker Village," pp. 27-28.

24. Lynn, "Shaker Village," p. 25; Otto Miller, Jr., *A History of the Growth and Development of the Van Sweringen Railway System* (Bachelor's thesis, Harvard University, 1924; privately published), pp. 1-2; John A. Zangerle, "Shaker Village Land Values Show Rise of 7,200% in 23 Years," Cleveland *News-Leader*, November 25, 1923, Dramatic Section, p. 8; "Outlook for an Empire," 202-205.

25. Lynn, "Shaker Village," pp. 25-26; Rose, *Cleveland*, pp. 1092-1093; Piercy manuscript; *The Sun-Press*, October 26, 1961.

26. Kelly, "Interesting People," 50-51; Lynn, "Shaker Village," p. 28; Piercy manuscript; Rachlis and Marqusee, *The Land Lords*, p. 76; *Heritage of the Shakers*, p. 41; Rose, *Cleveland*, p. 828; Hampton, "Cleveland's Fabulous Vans—Triumph in Shaker"; *PD*, November 1, 1924, pp. 1, 18.

27. Piercy manuscript; Hampton, "Cleveland's Fabulous Vans—Triumph in Shaker"; "Miscellaneous Material on Shaker Heights," folder of assorted materials in Western Reserve Historical Society collection.

28. Rothermere is quoted in Hampton, "Cleveland's Fabulous Vans—Triumph in Shaker"; Karl N. Llewellyn, "Cleveland Whirlpool," *Today*, Vol. 1, No. 8 (December 16, 1933), 3; Frederick Lewis Allen, *The Lords of Creation* (New York, 1935), p. 294.

II. THE VANS BUY A RAILROAD

1. *The Sun-Press*, October 26, 1961, p. 4-C; O. P. Van Sweringen, "How to Protect Yourself When Buying a Home," *The American Magazine*, Vol. 85, No. 6 (June, 1916), 122.

2. Rachlis and Marqusee, *The Land Lords*, pp. 69-70; Hampton, "Cleveland's Fabulous Vans—Lured by Shaker's Farms"; Kenneth S. P. Morse, *Cleveland Streetcars* (published by author, Baltimore, c. 1955), p. 26.

3. O. P. Van Sweringen's comment is found in U.S. Interstate Commerce Commission, Finance Docket 1237, *The Cleveland Passenger Terminal Case*, Vol. 3, pp. 677-698. The complete records of this case, heard in 1921, are available at the Interstate Commerce Commission, Washington, D.C. A portion is reprinted in Harry Christiansen, *Northern Ohio's Interurbans and Rapid Transit Railway*, 3rd revised printing (Cleveland, 1966), pp. 105-109.

4. George E. Condon, *Cleveland: The Best Kept Secret* (Garden City, 1967), p. 187; F.D.1237, *Cleveland Passenger Terminal Case*, Vol. 3, pp. 677-698; Rachlis and Marqusee, *The Land Lords*, p. 73; The Van Sweringen Company, *The Story of the Rapid Transit* (Cleveland, 1920), *passim*. O. P. seemed to feel that the reason for Stanley's rejection of the Vans' proposal in 1907 had something to do with the traction controversy. When he testified before the ICC in 1921, he said: "I recall the Johnson fight was part of the difficulty in negotiating extensions" (F.D.1237, *Cleveland Passenger Terminal Case*, Vol. 3,

p. 925). Several years after, Herbert Corey agreed with this interpretation: "Perhaps—who knows?—Tom Johnson was partially responsible. . . . He was preaching three-cent fare for Cleveland and the investors in street railroad property saw their security threatened. Stanley would not tempt further attack by extension" (Herbert Corey, "They Turned a City Around," *Nation's Business*, Vol. 17, No. 13 [December, 1929], 32).

5.   Rachlis and Marqusee, *The Land Lords*, pp. 73-74; Corey, "They Turned a City Around," p. 32; U.S. Interstate Commerce Commission, Finance Docket 4671, *Nickel Plate Unification Case*, Vol. 7, p. 2678. (F.D.4671, available at the ICC in Washington, D.C., contains twenty-six cartons of testimony, letters, and exhibits relating to the case.)

6.   *The Story of the Rapid Transit*, n.p.; *VSCS*, p. 9; "Plans for the Cleveland & Youngstown Railroad," *Electric Railway Journal* (hereafter cited as *ERJ*), Vol. 38, No. 19 (November 4, 1911), 1006; *Cleveland News*, October 24, 1911, pp. 1, 8; editorial, "An Important Project," *PD*, October 25, 1911, p. 6; *PD*, May 7, 1912, p. 14.

7.   *VSCS*, p. 9.

8.   F.D.1237, *Cleveland Passenger Terminal Case*, Vol. 3, pp. 677-698; Edward Hungerford, *Men and Iron: The History of the New York Central* (New York, 1938), p. 410; *VSCS*, p. 9.

9.   John A. Rehor, *The Nickel Plate Story* (Milwaukee, 1965), p. 62; Rose, *Cleveland*, pp. 296, 600.

10.   U.S. Bureau of the Census, *Thirteenth United States Census (1910)*, Vol. 9, p. 976; *VSCS*, pp. 10, 179-181.

11.   F.D.1237, *Cleveland Passenger Terminal Case*, Vol. 3, pp. 677-698; *VSCS*, p. 10.

12.   *VSCS*, p. 10.

13.   Cleveland *City Record* (1915) for July 14, pp. 746, 749-750, September 1, p. 907, September 8, p. 933, and November 15, p. 1199; *PD*, July 13, 1915, pp. 1-2; "New Franchise Granted in Cleveland," *ERJ*, Vol. 46, No. 4 (July 24, 1915), 161-162. For a discussion of the New York Central agreement to build a lakefront depot, see chapter 3.

14.   "Work Begun on Cleveland & Youngstown Line," *ERJ*, Vol. 41, No. 22 (May 31, 1913), 978; "New Rapid Transit Line in Cleveland," *ERJ*, Vol. 56, No. 5, (July 31, 1920), 204; *The Story of the Rapid Transit*; *PD*, July 7, 1916, p. 1.

15.   F.D.1237, *Cleveland Passenger Terminal Case*, Vol. 3, pp. 677-698; *PD*, July 7, 1916, p. 1; F.D.4671, *Nickel Plate Unification Case*, Vol. 7, pp. 2677-2688; Rehor, *Nickel Plate Story*, p. 52.

16.   *VSCS*, p. 17; Rehor, *Nickel Plate Story*, p. 40; "Bachelors of Railroading," *Fortune*, Vol. 9, No. 3 (March, 1934), 62. According to Rehor, there were several reasons why the Central did not make use of the Nickel Plate's facilities in Cleveland: "During the 34 years the Nickel Plate languished under New York Central control, great pains were taken to create the impression that

the road was independently operated and to a large degree it actually was. Considerable sums had been spent for improvements and for new equipment, but the road's growth and capacity had been subtly restricted through continued use of obsolete facilities and standards. By contrast, the capacity of the Lake Shore had been greatly expanded over the years and it was as fine a railroad as existed anywhere. The industrial growth of the territory the two roads served had continued unabated, but this benefit had accrued almost entirely to the Lake Shore. Little or no attempt had been made to locate new industries on the Nickel Plate and prime industrial sites were allowed to become residential neighborhoods. As a result the road was almost totally dependent on traffic received from its connections. By 1916 the Nickel Plate had fallen into almost total obscurity" (p. 59).

17. *VSCS*, pp. 18-19; *PD*, July 7, 1916, p. 1; Rehor, *Nickel Plate Story*, p. 65.

18. *VSCS*, pp. 18-19; *PD*, July 7, 1916, p. 1; *New York Times*, July 7, 1916, p. 18.

19. *VSCS*, p. 20.

20. "In America, at least, the holding company is used primarily for one or more of four purposes. 1. To combine two or more hitherto independent companies under a centralized management or control. 2. To combine two or more companies, not only under a centralized control, but also under a unified financial structure. 3. To recapitalize the financial structure of one or more enterprises through a substitution of the securities of the holding company for the securities of the subsidiary companies. 4. To pyramid the voting control so as to give the organizers of the holding company control over the subsidiaries with a minimum amount of investment" (James C. Bonbright and Gardiner C. Means, *The Holding Company: Its Public Significance and Its Regulation* [New York, 1932], p. 12). The Vans specialized in numbers 3 and 4.

21. *VSCS*, pp. 22-23; U.S. Congress, House of Representatives, Committee on Interstate and Foreign Commerce, *Regulation of Stock Ownership in Railroads*, Report No. 2789, 71st Cong., 3rd Sess., 1931, p. 840 (hereafter cited as the *Splawn Report*, after the committee's special counsel, Walter M. W. Splawn). According to the Wheeler Committee Report, "The exclusive voting power was vested in the common stock unless a default in the payment of any quarterly dividend on the preferred stock continued for a period of 6 months. In such an event the holders of preferred stock were entitled to elect a majority of the directors" (*VSCS*, p. 22). This became standard practice for the Vans; as long as they kept paying dividends, no one seemed to mind.

22. *PD*, July 8, 1916, p. 6; *Cleveland News*, July 8, 1916, p. 8; Llewellyn, "Cleveland Whirlpool," 4; John T. Flynn, "The Betrayal of Cleveland," *Harper's Monthly Magazine*, Vol. 168 (January, 1934), 143-144.

23. Taylor Hampton, *The Nickel Plate Road* (Cleveland, 1947), pp. 224-225.

24. "Bachelors of Railroading," *Fortune*, 62-63; *PD*, December 13, 1935, p. 9; Rehor, *Nickel Plate Story*, p. 67.

25. "Bachelors of Railroading," *Fortune*, 63–64; Hampton, *Nickel Plate Road*, pp. 225–226; Rehor, *Nickel Plate Story*, pp. 68–70, 75; Miller, *History of the . . . Van Sweringen Railway System*, pp. 5–6; Joseph M. Goldsmith, "Who Are the Van Sweringens?" *The Magazine of Wall Street*, Vol. 31, No. 8 (February 17, 1923), 695–696; Sherman Gwinn, "Who Said the Days of Railroad Giants is Over?" *The American Magazine*, Vol. 106 (July, 1928), 25.

26. "Bachelors of Railroading," *Fortune*, 62; Bonbright and Means, *The Holding Company*, pp. 253, 262; Gwinn, "Who Said the Days of Railroad Giants is Over?" *American Magazine*, 25.

27. "New Rapid Transit Line in Cleveland," *ERJ*, 204–207; *The Story of the Rapid Transit*; Christiansen, *Northern Ohio's Interurbans*, pp. 113, 115.

28. "New Rapid Transit Line in Cleveland," *ERJ*, 205.

III.   A TOWERING ACHIEVEMENT

1. Rose, *Cleveland*, pp. 338–339; *Cleveland Leader*, November 12, 1866, p. 4.

2. Condon, *Cleveland*, pp. 189–190. Cleveland's population in 1860 was 43,417; by 1890, this figure had risen to 261,353—not a ten-fold increase, but enough to make the Union Depot out of date.

3. Edwin Childs Baxter, "The Grouping of Public Buildings in Cleveland," *The American Monthly Review of Reviews*, Vol. 31, No. 5 (May, 1905), 561–562; Frederic C. Howe, "The Cleveland Group Plan," *Charities and the Commons*, Vol. 19 (February 1, 1908), 1548; Robert Whitten, "City Planning in Cleveland," *Arts and Archaeology*, Vol. 16, Nos. 4–5 (October-November 1923), 144–145; Rose, *Cleveland*, pp. 629–630.

4. Daniel H. Burnham, John M. Carrère, and Arnold W. Brunner, *Report of the Group Plan of the Public Buildings of the City of Cleveland, Ohio* (Cleveland, 1903), n.p.; Rose, *Cleveland,* pp. 629–630; Baxter, "Grouping of Public Buildings," *American Review of Reviews*, 564.

5. Baxter, "Grouping of Public Buildings," *American Review of Reviews*, 562–564.

6. Testimony of Newton D. Baker, F.D. 1237, *The Cleveland Passenger Terminal Case*, Vol. 1, pp. 41–43; C. H. Cramer, *Open Shelves and Open Minds* (Cleveland, 1972), p. 142; *Cleveland v. Cleveland, C. C. & St. L. Ry.*, Ohio Decisions, Vol. 19 (Cuyahoga Common Pleas), pp. 372–395. This was the key decision in the "Bath Street" case. It was handed down by Judge J. Vickery on February 18, 1909, and was upheld on appeal.

7. *VSCS*, p. 249; testimony of Newton D. Baker, F.D. 1237, *Cleveland Passenger Terminal Case*, Vol. 1, pp. 47–48.

8. *Minutes of Meeting on Union Depot Matter, Held in Mayor Baker's Office on August 12, 1915* (transcript available in Municipal Reference Library, Cleveland Public Library); Rose, *Cleveland*, p. 734; *PD*, September 1, 1915, p. 8; *VSCS*, p. 249.

9. *VSCS*, pp. 9, 14; *PD*, October 24, 1911, p. 1; *ERJ*, Vol. 38, No. 19 (November 4, 1911), 1006; *Cleveland News*, May 7, 1912, pp. 1, 10; *Railway Review*, Vol. 57, No. 25 (December 18, 1915), 781; *PD*, July 7, 1916, p. 1; testimony of John L. Cannon, *In Re Initiated Ordinance No. 47814*, transcript of proceedings of first meeting held by Main Cleveland City Council Committee, September 11, 1918 (Manuscript, Ben B. Wickham Collection of Van Sweringen Miscellany, Western Reserve Historical Society), p. 7; testimony of O. P. Van Sweringen, F.D. 1237, *Cleveland Passenger Terminal Case*, Vol. 3, pp. 679-681. It was expected that the Lake Shore, the Southwestern, the Northern Ohio, the Gates Mills, and the Chagrin Falls, as well as the Cleveland & Youngstown—all interurbans—would use the terminal (testimony of O. P. Van Sweringen, *In Re Initiated Ordinance No. 47814*, October 16, 1918, p. 853). It was also expected that Cleveland's East Side trolleys (those on St. Clair, Superior, Wade Park, Payne, Euclid, Cedar, Central, Scovill, Broadway, and Woodland) which turned at or near Public Square, and the city's West Side trolleys (those on Detroit, Lorain, Pearl, and Clark) would also use the terminal (testimony of Newton D. Baker, F.D. 1237, *Cleveland Passenger Terminal Case*, Vol. 1, pp. 54-57).

10. Testimony of John L. Cannon, *In Re Initiated Ordinance No. 47814*, September 11, 1918, pp. 7-8; testimony of O. P. Van Sweringen, F.D. 1237, *Cleveland Passenger Terminal Case*, Vol. 3, pp. 686-688.

11. K. Austin Kerr, *American Railroad Politics, 1914-1920: Rates, Wages, and Efficiency* (Pittsburgh, 1968), pp. 39-40; testimony of O. P. Van Sweringen, *In Re Initiated Ordinance No. 47814*, September 13, 1918, pp. 87-89, 117-118, 122-123, October 23, 1918, pp. 235-236; *VSCS*, p. 31.

12. "New Plan for a Union Station at Cleveland, Ohio," *Railway Age* (hereafter cited as *RA*), Vol. 66, No. 12 (March 21, 1919), 756; "Comparison of Railroad Terminal Projects at Cleveland," *Engineering News-Record*, Vol. 82, No. 5 (January 30, 1919), 240-243; "Cleveland Public Square Authorized," *ibid.*, Vol. 87, No. 25 (December 22, 1921), 1021; "Bachelors of Railroading," *Fortune*, 164, 166; *VSCS*, p. 32.

13. *VSCS*, pp. 32, 36-37; testimony of O. P. Van Sweringen, F.D. 1237, *Cleveland Passenger Terminal Case*, Vol. 3, pp. 690-692.

14. Cleveland *City Record*, November 13, 1918, 876-888 (full text of ordinance).

15. *PD*, January 1, 1919, p. 19, January 2, 1919, pp. 6, 12, January 3, 1919, p. 1; *Cleveland News*, January 1, 1919, p. 16; *Certification of Board of Elections as to Vote For and Against Ordinance No. 47814*, reprinted in The Cleveland Union Terminals Company, *Legislation of the City of Cleveland and Documents Pertaining Thereto and Applications to and Orders of the Interstate Commerce Commission All in Connection with the Union Passenger Terminal of The Cleveland Union Terminals Company, Cleveland, Ohio* (Cleveland, 1930).

16. *VSCS*, pp. 33, 250-251.

17. *Ibid.*, pp. 35, 197; *Cleveland Press*, November 26, 1919, p. 2; *Cleveland News*, December 2, 1919, pp. 1-2; Section 96-1 of Ordinance No. 47814; *City*

Record, December 17, 1919, 1137. An "emergency ordinance" was needed because a regular ordinance would not take effect for forty days and any changes in the Ordinance of 1919 had to be made before January 6, 1920, or it would die automatically.

18. *City Record*, December 31, 1919, 1174; testimony of Peter Witt, F.D. 1237, *Cleveland Passenger Terminal Case*, Vol. 1, pp. 452-454; *PD*, December 30, 1919, p. 1.

19. *PD*, January 1, 1920, p. 2; *City Record*, Vol. 6, No. 314 (December 31, 1919), 1193-1195. Peter Witt insisted throughout the ICC hearings on the Terminal that Mayor Davis had misled the council. "I doubted whether Mayor Davis had authority to speak for the railroads," he testified, "and after I wrote to the Commission for the privilege of being permitted to appear here, I wrote to Daniel A. Willard, the President of the Baltimore & Ohio; Frederick Underwood, the President of the Erie Railroad, and Mr. Duncan, the President of the Wheeling & Lake Erie" asking if they had authorized Mayor Davis "to say for this company that this company would make use of the proposed depot when built." Witt received two replies, he said. Duncan wrote, in part, that "I was not present at any of the meetings referred to and do not know what occurred. I think Mayor Davis' statement must have been misinterpreted, because I am sure I did not authorize him to speak for the Wheeling & Lake Erie Railway Company or to say that it would make use of the proposed depot when built." C.W. Galloway of B. & O. responded that "we are not willing at this moment to make any definite promise to use the station until we can have some clearer idea as to what its use will involve." Witt received no reply from the Erie (testimony of Peter Witt, F.D. 1237, *Cleveland Passenger Terminal Case*, Vol. 1, p. 458). While all of Cleveland believed that all of the passenger trains coming into the city would use the depot (all, that is, except Witt and a few others), Mayor Davis never actually stated that he had firm pledges from the railroads to join the project.

20. U.S. Interstate Commerce Commission, *Cleveland Passenger Terminal Case*, Vol. 70, *ICC Reports* (1921), p. 342; A. R. Hatton to E. I. Lewis, June 15, 1921, and W. S. FitzGerald to E. E. Clark, March 16, 1921, in F. D. 1237, *Cleveland Passenger Terminal Case*, Vol. 1A (a bound volume of correspondence).

21. Carl Wittke, "Peter Witt, Tribune of the People," *Ohio State Archaeological and Historical Quarterly*, Vol. 58, No. 4 (October 1949), 363, 366, 375-376; *PD*, April 20, 1921, p. 6, August 3, 1921, p. 6, August 16, 1921, p. 2, August 20, 1921, pp. 1, 6; testimony of Newton D. Baker, F.D. 1237, *Cleveland Passenger Terminal Case*, Vol. 1, p. 57.

22. The ICC decisions can be found in Vol. 70, *ICC Reports*. They are reprinted in the collection of *Legislation . . . and Documents* cited in n.15 above, pp. 287-300 and 312-328; *VSCS*, pp. 45-46.

23. *PD*, August 16, 1921, p. 1, September 21, 1921, p. 1, September 22, 1921, pp. 1, 4; *Legislation . . . and Documents*, p. 311; W. A. Scullen, Administrator of the Catholic Diocese of Cleveland, to Joseph B. Eastman, August 30, 1921, Eastman Papers, Amherst College Library. Letters and resolutions supporting

the Depot on the Square, as cited in the text, are all bound in the correspondence volume of F.D. 1237, *Cleveland Passenger Terminal Case*, Vol. 1A.

24. *PD*, September 22, 1921, p. 4, September 23, 1921, pp. 1, 3.

25. *Ibid.*, September 23, 1921, p. 1.

26. *Ibid.*, September 22, 1921, p. 1.

27. *Legislation . . . and Documents*, pp. 314-316, 327-328; Claude M. Fuess, *Joseph B. Eastman: Servant of the People* (New York, 1952), p. 169.

28. *VSCS*, pp. 35-44, 48-54.

29. Taylor Hampton, "Cleveland's Fabulous Vans—They Remodel Downtown," *Cleveland News*, August 5, 1955; Condon, *Cleveland*, p. 191; The Terminal Tower Company, *The Terminal Tower* (Cleveland, 1963), pp. 5-7.

30. Condon, *Cleveland*, p. 192; The Cleveland Union Terminals Company & The Cleveland Terminals Building Company, *The Union Station: A Description of the New Passenger Facilities and Surrounding Improvements* (Cleveland, 1930), *passim*; "New Station's Facilities Finest in the World," *PD* (Union Terminal Section), June 29, 1930, p. 9; "Cleveland Union Station Project Far Advanced," *RA*, Vol. 85, No. 26 (December 29, 1928), 1287-1293; Rose, *Cleveland*, pp. 885-886; Henry-Russell Hitchcock, Jr., "Traffic and Building Art: New York City and Cleveland Contrasted," *Architectural Record*, Vol. 67, No. 6 (June, 1930), 557.

31. Hampton, "Cleveland's Fabulous Vans—They Remodel Downtown."

32. John F. Stover, *The Life and Decline of the American Railroad* (New York, 1970), pp. 200, 223; Harry Christiansen, "Railpax to End Dream of Former Era," *PD*, March 25, 1971, p. 12-A.

33. *PD*, June 28, 1930, p. 1.

IV. BACK TO RAILROADS

1. "Nickel Plate Averages 44.1 Miles Per Car Per Day," *RA*, Vol. 74, No. 5 (February 3, 1923), 341-343.

2. *VSCS*, pp. 55-56; "O. P. Van Sweringen before I. C. C.," *RA*, Vol. 78, No. 27 (June 6, 1925), 1380-1381.

3. William N. Leonard, *Railroad Consolidation under the Transportation Act of 1920* (New York, 1946), p. 57; *VSCS*, pp. 56-57; Merle Fainsod and Lincoln Gordon, *Government and the American Economy* (New York, 1948), pp. 265-266; I. L. Sharfman, *The Interstate Commerce Commission* (New York, 1931), Part 1, pp. 185-186. For the history of the origins of the Transportation Act of 1920, see Kerr, *American Railroad Politics, 1914-1920,* and Albro Martin, *Enterprise Denied: Origins of the Decline of American Railroads, 1897-1917* (New York, 1971).

4. Fainsod and Gordon, *Government and the American Economy*, pp. 265-266; Leonard, *Railroad Consolidation*, p. 64; *VSCS*, pp. 58-63.

5. *VSCS*, p. 62.

6. "O. P. Van Sweringen before I. C. C.," *RA*, 1381; U.S. Congress, Senate, *Hearings Before the Committee on Banking and Currency*, 73rd Cong., 1st Sess., 1933, *Stock Exchange Practices* (hereafter cited as *SEP*), Part 2, p. 564 (known as the Pecora Committee Hearings); Leonard, *Railroad Consolidation*, pp. 66–68; "Bachelors of Railroading," *Fortune*, 63–65; *VSCS*, pp. 58–64.

7. "O. P. Van Sweringen before I. C. C.," *RA*, 1381.

8. Gwinn, "Who Said the Days of Railroad Giants is Over?" *The American Magazine*, 25; Hampton, *The Nickel Plate Road*, pp. 230–231; *PD*, March 9, 1922, pp. 1, 4; Goldsmith, "Who Are the Van Sweringens?" *The Magazine of Wall Street*, 696.

9. For additional information about the financial history of the Clover Leaf and the negotiations for its purchase by the Vans, see Rehor, *Nickel Plate Story*, pp. 79–83 and 168–169, and Hampton, *Nickel Plate Road*, pp. 256-257.

10. *VSCS*, pp. 77–81; *PD*, March 9, 1922, pp. 1, 4; "Clover Leaf Acquired," *RA*, Vol. 72, No. 11 (March 18, 1922), 725.

11. *PD*, April 28, 1922, pp. 1, 2; Rehor, *Nickel Plate Story*, pp. 82–83; "The New Ohio Railroad Kings," *Literary Digest*, Vol. 76 (January 20, 1923), 12–13; Love, "The Van Sweringens," *American Review of Reviews*, 502; Goldsmith, "Who Are the Van Sweringens?" *Magazine of Wall Street*, 696, 755–756; "O. P. Van Sweringen before I. C. C.," *RA*, 1381.

12. Rehor, *Nickel Plate Story*, pp. 82–83; *VSCS*, pp. 71–73, 309; "Van Sweringen Interests Buy Control," *RA*, Vol. 72, No. 18, (May 6, 1922), 1091.

13. *PD*, April 28, 1922, pp. 1-2.

14. *SEP*, Part 2, pp. 600–602; *VSCS*, p. 65.

15. *VSCS*, pp. 65–67.

16. *Splawn Report*, pp. 1108–1109; *VSCS*, pp. 67–70.

17. *VSCS*, pp. 73–74.

18. *Splawn Report*, p. 846; *VSCS*, pp. 80–81.

19. *Splawn Report*, pp. 844–845; *VSCS*, pp. 74–75. According to *VSCS*, "Mr. Nutt, as president of the Union Trust Company, and Mr. Nutt as director and shareholder in Vaness, were in agreement that the Lake Erie & Western deal was a good one and Vaness a company with proper credit for carrying it through" (p. 75). Mr. Nutt, no doubt, would have said the same about the Clover Leaf!

20. *VSCS*, p. 81.

21. *Ibid.*, pp. 83–84; Miller, *History of the . . . Van Sweringen Railway System*, pp. 13-14.

22. *PD*, December 29, 1922, p. 1, May 16, 1923, p. 11.

23. *VSCS*, pp. 84–86. The preferred stock would enjoy priority with respect to dividends and in the event of liquidation, but the usual voting rights were removed except under certain "special and narrow" conditions. This device of non-voting preferred had been used by the Vans in the formation of the Nickel

Plate Securities, Western, and Vaness companies and it was one they would continue to use, despite much criticism, in the future.

24. *Ibid.*, pp. 84-87; "Asks Authority for Consolidation," *RA*, Vol. 74, No. 21 (April 28, 1923), 1077.

25. "Brief on Nickel Plate Consolidation," *RA*, Vol. 74, No. 26 (June 2, 1923), 1327-1328; "Legal Questions in S. P. and Nickel Plate Cases," *RA*, Vol. 74, No. 27 (June 9, 1923), 1382-1384; "Oral Argument on Nickel Plate Consolidation," *RA*, Vol. 74, No. 28 (June 16, 1923), 1472; *VSCS*, pp. 86-89. The Eastman dissent can be found in U.S. Interstate Commerce Commission, *Operation of Lines and Issue of Capital Stock by The New York, Chicago & St. Louis Railroad Company*, Vol. 79, *ICC Reports* (1923), pp. 581-595, which includes the majority decision as well.

26. From the majority decision, Vol. 79, *ICC Reports*, pp. 581-595. According to *VSCS*, "*Snyder vs. the New York, Chicago & St. Louis R. R. Co.*, 118 Ohio St. 72, 1928, 160 N. E. 615, affirmed per curiam, 278 U. S. 578, 1929, however, upheld the view of the majority in the instant case that the consolidation section of the Transportation Act of 1920 was permissive and not mandatory. Inasmuch as this point was never reviewed by the Supreme Court of the United States, it might be said that the construction of the majority in 79 I. C. C., p. 581, is the prevailing and approved doctrine" (p. 89).

27. *VSCS*, pp. 89-92; *PD*, December 29, 1922, p. 4. A summarized breakdown of the Vans' debt in July, 1923, looks something like this:

Nickel Plate	$8,577,760.23
Clover Leaf	4,387,548.02
L.E. & W.	5,470,347.99
	$18,435,656.24

Added to this was $2,607,095.13 of new Nickel Plate stock purchased from August to October, 1923, while negotiations were going on with the investment syndicate to keep the price of the security up. Grand total: $21,042,751.37 (*VSCS*, pp. 91-92).

28. *VSCS*, pp. 92-95, 97-100.

29. "Consolidation of the Nickel Plate," *RA*, Vol. 75, No. 3 (July 21, 1923), 131; *PD*, June 9, 1923, p. 2; "The New Ohio Railroad Kings," *Literary Digest*, 13; "Nickel Plate Averages 44.1 Miles Per Car Per Day," *RA*, 342; Hampton, *Nickel Plate Road*, p. 340.

30. *VSCS*, p. 100; "The Van Sweringen Group," *RA*, Vol. 72, No. 18, (May 6, 1922), 1047; Goldsmith, "Who Are the Van Sweringens?" *Magazine of Wall Street*, 755-756; "The New Ohio Railroad Kings," *Literary Digest*, 13.

V. A GREATER NICKEL PLATE

1. Rehor, *Nickel Plate Story*, p. 171; "The New Ohio Railroad Kings," *Literary Digest*, 12-13.

2. Gwinn, "Who Said the Days of Railroad Giants is Over?" *The American Magazine*, 25; Miller, *History of the . . . Van Sweringen Railway System*, pp. 19-21; "Van Sweringens Acquire C. & O. Stock Interest," *RA*, Vol. 74, No. 2 (January 13, 1923), 193-194; Rehor, *Nickel Plate Story*, p. 171; "Chesapeake and Ohio Had Eventful Year in 1922," *RA*, Vol. 74, No. 6 (February 10, 1923), 387-389.

3. Charles W. Turner, *Chessie's Road* (Richmond, 1956), p. 172; *VSCS*, p. 101; Miller, *History of the . . . Van Sweringen Railway System*, pp. 19-20; "Van Sweringens Acquire C.&O. Stock Interest," *RA*, 193-194; "Chesapeake and Ohio Had Eventful Year in 1922," *RA*, 387-389.

4. *VSCS*, pp. 102-108 *passim*; *SEP*, p. 565; "Bachelors of Railroading," *Fortune*, 65. The Morgans had a similarly high opinion of the Van Sweringens. As George Whitney, a partner in J. P. Morgan & Company, testified before the Pecora Committee in 1933, "We first became acquainted with them as far back as 1916, and from 1920 on we had had a great faith in their aim of trying to build this railroad system. We believed they were excellent operators of railroads, and their records with the roads they have got now have certainly proven that" (*SEP*, p. 163).

5. "C. & O.—Nickel Plate," *RA* (editorial), Vol. 73, No. 27 (December 30, 1922), 1219; "Chesapeake and Ohio Had Eventful Year in 1922," *RA*, 387-389; *The Magazine of Wall Street*, Vol. 31, No. 9 (March 3, 1923), 830.

6. *PD*, January 16, 1923, p. 18; Miller, *History of the . . . Van Sweringen Railway System*, p. 19; Rehor, *Nickel Plate Story*, p. 171; *VSCS*, p. 113; "Van Sweringen Control Will Give C. & O. Much Needed Outlet," *RA*, Vol. 74, No. 4 (January 27, 1923), 296; "Chesapeake and Ohio Had Eventful Year in 1922," *RA*, 387-389.

7. *VSCS*, pp. 108-112.

8. "Van Sweringens Acquire C. & O. Stock Interest," *RA*, 193-194; *VSCS*, pp. 112-114; U.S. Interstate Commerce Commission, *Interlocking Directors—New York, Chicago & St. Louis and Chesapeake & Ohio*, Vol. 76, *ICC Reports* (1923), pp. 549-556.

9. *VSCS*, pp. 113, 137-140; "O. P. Van Sweringen before ICC," *RA*, 1382.

10. "Directors Approve Van Sweringen Merger Offer," *RA*, Vol. 77, No. 9 (August 30, 1924), 383; *VSCS*, pp. 115-118; Leonard, *Railroad Consolidation Under the Transportation Act of 1920*, p. 132.

11. Miller, *History of the . . . Van Sweringen Railway System*, p. 23; Edward Hungerford, *Men of Erie: A Story of Human Effort* (New York, 1946), p. 318; Rehor, *Nickel Plate Story*, p. 174; *VSCS*, p. 117.

12. *VSCS*, pp. 116-118, 396; *The Magazine of Wall Street*, Vol. 32, No. 11 (September 29, 1923), 994; "Directors Approve Van Sweringen Merger Offer," *RA*, 383.

13. *VSCS*, pp. 116-129 *passim*; *SEP*, pp. 565, 630. Ernest R. Graham of the Chicago architectural firm of Graham, Anderson, Probst and White told Clarence W. Barron, the publisher of *The Wall Street Journal*, the following story of the first meeting between the Vans and Baker:

When the Van Sweringens went to George F. Baker, he asked them two questions: "Do you work [*sic?*—should be "worry"?], and do you sleep well?" They are clean boys—they said they slept like tops and never worried. Baker said, "All right, I am with you" (quoted in Arthur Pound and Samuel Taylor Moore, eds., *They Told Barron* [New York, 1930], pp. 290–291).

14. Rehor, *Nickel Plate Story*, p. 124; Miller, *History of the . . . Van Sweringen Railway System*, p. 24; VSCS, pp. 131–133; Paul W. Ivey, "The Pere Marquette Railroad: An Historical Study of the Growth and Development of One of Michigan's Most Important Railway Systems" (Ph.D. dissertation, University of Michigan, 1919), pp. 163–166.

15. *SEP*, pp. 566, 651–652; VSCS, pp. 131–132, 134–136; "Bachelors of Railroading," *Fortune*, 160; "Directors Approve Van Sweringen Merger Offer," RA, 384.

16. VSCS, p. 113; Turner, *Chessie's Road*, pp. 173–174, 177, 184–187; Jim Alan Ross, "The Pioneer Erie," *Erie Railroad Magazine*, Vol. 47, No. 3 (May 1951—Centennial Issue), 9; Hungerford, *Men of Erie*, pp. 239–246 *passim*.

17. *New York Times*, June 25, 1924, p. 32. On the four-party conferences see the following: VSCS pp. 141–144; "Four Great Eastern Systems Proposed to I.C.C.," RA, Vol. 77, No. 16 (October 18, 1924), 683–684; "Pennsylvania Objects to Four-System Plan," RA, Vol. 77, No. 18 (November 1, 1924), 807–809.

18. VSCS, p. 145. The "Proposal by O. P. and M. J. Van Sweringen for the Unified Control and Operation of the Railroads of the New York, Chicago and St. Louis Railroad Company, the Chesapeake and Ohio Railway Company, the Hocking Valley Railway Company, Erie Railroad Company, Pere Marquette Railway Company" is reprinted in VSCS, pp. 411–419. As the following statistics (from VSCS, p. 145) indicate, the brothers' proposed system would compare favorably with the other major eastern trunk lines:

	Miles of Line Operated	Investment in Road and Equipment
Proposed system	9,213	$1,228,863,070
New York Central	12,093	1,878,762,969
Pennsylvania Railroad	11,379	2,246,661,561
Baltimore & Ohio	5,316	795,447,338

	Operating Revenue	Rate of Return on Book Investment
Proposed system	$340,364,051	4.823%
New York Central	588,171,010	5.748%
Pennsylvania Railroad	693,718,881	3.745%
Baltimore & Ohio	227,084,805	4.749%

19. Miller, *History of the . . . Van Sweringen Railway System*, pp. 25–26; Leonard, *Railroad Consolidation*, pp. 56–57; VSCS, p. 416.

20. Bonbright and Means, *The Holding Company*, p. 256; *VSCS*, pp. 151-153.

21. *VSCS*, pp. 146-149; "New York, Chicago & St. Louis—Plan Declared Operative," *RA*, Vol. 78, No. 6 (February 7, 1925), 393.

22. "Hearing on Nickel Plate Merger," *RA*, Vol. 78, No. 21 (April 25, 1925), 1037-1040; Rehor, *Nickel Plate Story*, p. 177; testimony of Emory R. Johnson, July 29, 1925, F.D.4671, *Nickel Plate Unification Case*, Vol. 14, pp. 4758-4762 *passim*; testimony of William J. Cunningham, June 25, 1925, F.D.4671, *Nickel Plate Unification Case*, Vol. 9, p. 3409; "Nickel Plate Hearing," *RA*, Vol. 78, No. 23 (May 9, 1925), 1158; "Hearing on Nickel Plate Unification," *RA*, Vol. 78, No. 24 (May 16, 1925), 1221. The Letters and resolutions are bound in Vols. 1A and 1B of F.D.4671, *Nickel Plate Unification Case*.

23. *PD*, March 3, 1926, p. 11; *VSCS*, pp. 156-160; Turner, *Chessie's Road*, pp. 190-195.

24. HONESTY to the ICC, n.d., received July 3, 1925, "Many Citizens of Virginia" to the ICC, February 26, 1926, John B. Thomas to Pres. Calvin Coolidge, May 10, 1925, all in Vol. 1B of F.D.4671, *Nickel Plate Unification Case*; "A Proposal to Hold Up Nickel Plate Decision," *RA*, Vol. 80, No. 8 (February 20, 1926), 491; Wheeler Resolution (S. Res. 148), U.S. *Congressional Record*, 69th Cong., 1st Sess., February 16, 1926, Vol. 67, Part 4, p. 4046.

25. *PD*, May 29, 1925, pp. 1, 5, 8; James L. Wright, "It Isn't Just Money to Him," *Nation's Business*, Vol. 13 (October, 1925), 28.

26. "O. P. Van Sweringen before I.C.C.," *RA*, 1380-1384; Wright, "It Isn't Just Money to Him," *Nation's Business*, 28; *PD*, March 3, 1926, p. 1.

27. The text of the decision is available in U.S. Interstate Commerce Commission, *Nickel Plate Unification*, Vol. 105, *ICC Reports* (1928). It is reprinted in "Nickel Plate Application Denied," *RA*, Vol. 80, No. 10 (March 6, 1926), 586-591 *passim*.

28. "Nickel Plate Application Denied," *RA*, 590. The Commissioners had some harsh words not only for the Vans' financial methods but also for the problem of "stockholder lethargy": "We believe it to be self-evident that the public interest requires that the entire body of stockholders of a railroad which is bonded in excess of one half of its investment, and not a powerful few, shall be responsible for its management. The lethargy of ordinary stockholders in exercising their power to control the management of these large corporations has often been commented on, but nevertheless the power should be in their hands to use as they see fit. It is inimical to the public interest to strip stockholders of their voting power, thus rendering it so much easier to control a great transportation system by a comparatively limited amount of investment."

29. *PD*, March 4, 1926, pp. 1-2, 5 (quoting *Philadelphia Public-Ledger* and *New York Times*).

30. Joseph B. Eastman to C. R. Hillyer, March 6, 1926, Eastman Papers, Amherst College Library; *Financial World*, Vol. 45, No. 10 (March 6, 1926);

"Consolidation Requisites Defined," *United States Investor*, Vol. 37, No. 10 (March 6, 1926), 80; *Wall Street Journal*, as quoted in the *Literary Digest*, Vol. 88 (March 13, 1926), 8-9; F. J. Lisman, "Comment on Nickel Plate Decision," *RA*, Vol. 80, No. 15 (March 13, 1926), 801-802; Benjamin Graham, "A Victory for the Small Stockholder," *Magazine of Wall Street*, Vol. 37 (March 27, 1926), 985.

31. M. H. Hutchinson to B. H. Meyer, March 4, 1926, M. F. Connors to Commissioner Frank McManamy, March 4, 1926, Davis R. Dewey to B. H. Meyer, March 6, 1926, W. Z. Ripley to B. H. Meyer, March 4, 1926, all in Vol. 1B of F.D.4671. The newspaper opinions are collected in an article in the *PD*, March 4, 1926, p. 5.

32. *PD*, March 3, 1926, p. 1.

33. *VSCS*, pp. 165-166; *PD*, March 3, 1926, p. 1; Rose, *Cleveland*, p. 839.

VI. THE C. & O. UNIFICATION CASE

1. As of February 28, 1926, these debts were as follows:

To Paine, Webber	$8,783,544.14	
To Hayden, Stone	4,053,448.97	
Total Brokerage Debts		$12,836,993.11
Continental & Commercial		
Nat'l. Bank of Chicago	822,095.00	
Union Trust Co.	850,000.00	
Guaranty Trust Co.	3,600,000.00	
Guardian Trust Co.	1,200,000.00	
Cleveland Trust Co.	500,000.00	
Chemical National Bank	1,000,000.00	
J. P. Morgan & Co.	6,000,000.00	
Total Bank Loans		$13,972,095.00
3 year 6% Collateral		
Trust Notes		7,030,000.00
	Total	$33,839,088.11

Source: *VSCS*, p. 166.

2. *VSCS*, pp. 455-459; Taylor Hampton, "Cleveland's Fabulous Vans—O. P.'s Generalship Saves Eastern Rail 'Empire,' " *Cleveland News*, August 16, 1955. The collateral demanded by the Morgan bank consisted of:

104,000	shares of Erie Railroad Co. common, at 28	$ 2,912,000
200,000	shares of C. & O. Ry. Co. common, at 129	25,800,000
110,000	shares of Nickel Plate common, at 160	17,600,000
30,000	shares of Pere Marquette common, at 84	2,520,000
		$48,832,000

Source: *VSCS*, p. 457.

3. ICC Decision, *RA*, March 6, 1926, p. 589; *VSCS*, p. 459.

4. *VSCS*, p. 465, which stated that "the theory was, evidently, that a wholly-owned holding company, subsidiary to a railroad company, could be freer

in its financial life than the common carrier which owned it. The railroads were expressly subject to the authority of the ICC as in acquiring stock control of another carrier, borrowing money, etc. The contention of the Van Sweringens, and other railroad managers, was that an indirect acquisition of railroad stock through a subsidiary holding company, or the borrowing of money by such a company, could be carried out without having to secure permission of the Commission." This position was not challenged by the ICC for several years. Only in the early 1930s did the commission assert its control over such wholly owned holding companies in a suit against the Pennsylvania Railroad and its subsidiary, the Pennsylvania Company.

5.   *VSCS,* pp. 462-470 *passim.* As noted in chapter 5, the Vans had acquired 200,008 shares in 1924, of which 50,000 shares had been turned over to George F. Baker and two of his associates. These shares had cost $7,748,510.98.

6.   ICC Decision, *RA,* March 6, 1926, 588-589; *VSCS,* pp. 462, 484; "Chesapeake & Ohio—New Directors," *RA,* Vol. 80, No. 20 (April 17, 1926), 1100.

7.   It should be remembered that to that date the brothers did not assert themselves in either the Pere Marquette or the Erie, except to secure the election of John J. Bernet as president of the latter road. Except for Bernet, they had no representatives on the board of directors of the Erie and none at all on the board of the Pere Marquette (R. W. Vincent, "Will the Nickel Plate Merger Ever Be?" *Magazine of Wall Street,* Vol. 39 [February 12, 1927], 700, 772).

8.   ICC Decision, *RA,* March 6, 1926, 590; "New York, Chicago & St. Louis—Merger Plan Discussed with Interstate Commerce Commissioner," *RA,* Vol. 80, No. 37 (June 19, 1926), 1942; *VSCS,* pp. 462-463; "C. & O. Hearing Concluded," *RA,* Vol. 82, No. 30 (June 25, 1927), 2011.

9.   *VSCS,* pp. 462-463; ICC Decision, *RA,* March 6, 1926, 590. In November, 1926, the C. & O. received ICC approval to purchase the Chesapeake & Hocking, the railroad incorporated the previous month to construct the 63-mile-long link between the C. & O. at Gregg, Ohio, with its subsidiary, the Hocking Valley, at Valley Crossing, Ohio. By September, 1927, when completed, this gave the C. & O. a continuous line of track from the tidewater at Newport News on Hampton Roads to Toledo on the Great Lakes ("Chesapeake & Ohio—Control of Chesapeake & Hocking Authorized," *RA,* Vol. 81, No. 22 [November 27, 1926], 1062; *SEP,* p. 566; "C. & O. Completes the Last Link in Line to Toledo," *RA,* Vol. 84, No. 13 [March 31, 1928], 730).

10.   U. S. Interstate Commerce Commission, *Proposed Control of Erie Railroad Company and Pere Marquette Railway Company by Chesapeake & Ohio Railway Company,* Vol. 138, *ICC Reports* (1928), pp. 522-523; "Van Sweringens Propose New Plan," *RA,* Vol. 82, No. 8 (February 19, 1927), 512; *VSCS,* p. 485.

11.   *VSCS,* pp. 469-470.

12.   *Ibid.,* pp. 471-473. One year later, on May 25, the Chesapeake Corporation "divested itself of the right to engage in transportation, and ended

its lawyers' worries that the Interstate Commerce Commission might have jurisdiction over its affairs" (*VSCS*, p. 471).

13. "Chesapeake Corporation—Organization and Sale of Bonds," *RA*, Vol. 82, No. 24 (May 14, 1927), 1479; *VSCS*, pp. 474, 478-480.

14. "Van Sweringens Propose New Plan," *RA*, 512; *VSCS*, p. 485.

15. For coverage of the ICC hearings on the Vans' application, see the following issues of *Railway Age*: "Van Sweringens Propose New Plan," Vol. 82, No. 8 (February 19, 1927), 512-514; "Hearings on C. & O. Merger Plan Begun," Vol. 82, No. 24 (May 14, 1927), 1440; "C. & O. Acquisition Plan Hearing," Vol. 82, No. 25 (May 21, 1927), 1497-1500; "Van Sweringen Urges Early Decision," Vol. 82, No. 28 (June 11, 1927), 1786-1788; "Van Sweringen Hearing Develops Controversies," Vol. 82, No. 29 (June 18, 1927), 1962-1964; "C. & O. Hearing Concluded," Vol. 82, No. 30 (June 25, 1927), 2009-2012. See also Vol. 138, *ICC Reports*, pp. 525-526.

16. The C. & O. Minority "Stockholders' Protective Committee" now consisted of George S. Kemp, Granville G. Valentine, J. Luther Moon, and Berkeley Williams, all of Richmond, Virginia, and Lindsey Hopkins of Atlanta, Georgia. In addition to the issues of *Railway Age* cited in note 15 above, further information on the minority committee may be gleaned from the following issues of that journal: "Chesapeake & Ohio—Minority Stockholders Allowed to Intervene in Acquisition Proceedings," Vol. 82, No. 15 (March 12, 1927), 918-919; "Erie—Attack by C. & O. Stockholders' Protective Committee," Vol. 82, No. 28 (June 11, 1927), 1922; "Chesapeake & Ohio—Files Brief on Merger," Vol. 83, No. 7 (August 13, 1927), 318; "Chesapeake & Ohio—Brief of Minority Stockholders Opposes Acquisition of Control of Erie and Pere Marquette," Vol. 83, No. 11 (September 10, 1927), 503; "Chesapeake & Ohio—Merger Application Argued before I.C.C.," Vol. 83, No. 19 (November 5, 1927), 912-913.

17. Vol. 138, *ICC Reports*, p. 528.

18. *Ibid.*, pp. 529-530. A later report noted: "The lack of a final plan for unification of the country's railroads made most of the commissioners reluctant to take a stand on specific consolidation proposals. Their attitude in general was to let sleeping dogs lie." (*VSCS*, p. 489).

19. Vol. 138, *ICC Reports*, pp. 531-533.

20. *Ibid.*, pp. 533-534; *VSCS*, p. 491.

21. Vol. 138, *ICC Reports*, pp. 541-545; *VSCS*, pp. 489, 493-494.

22. Vol. 138, *ICC Reports*, pp. 537-541; *VSCS*, pp. 491-493; *PD*, May 19, 1928, p. 9.

23. U. S. Interstate Commerce Commission, *Proposed Control of Erie Railroad Co. and Pere Marquette Railway Co. by Chesapeake & Ohio Railway Co.*, Vol. 150, *ICC Reports* (1929), pp. 751-762.

24. *VSCS*, pp. 525-526; "C. & O. Asks Change in I.C.C. Orders," *RA*, Vol. 85, No. 5 (August 4, 1928), 227-230; "George Cole Scott," *RA*, Vol. 85, No. 12

(September 22, 1928), 573; "Chesapeake & Ohio—Acquisition of Pere Marquette Stock," *RA*, Vol. 85, No. 22 (December 1, 1928), 114; "Chesapeake & Ohio—Hearing on Purchase of Pere Marquette Stock," *RA*, Vol. 85, No. 23 (December 8, 1928), 1163; "Chesapeake & Ohio—Asks Authority to Issue Stock at Par," *RA*, Vol. 85, No. 26 (December 29, 1928), 1323; "Chesapeake & Ohio—Stock Issue," *RA*, Vol. 86, No. 5 (February 22, 1929), 341.

25. "C. & O. May Issue Stock at Par," *RA*, Vol. 86, No. 15 (April 13, 1929), 841–843; *VSCS*, pp. 526–527.

26. Vol. 150, *ICC Reports*, pp. 760–761; Commissioners Taylor and McManamy supported Eastman in his dissent.

27. "Chesapeake & Ohio—Control of Pere Marquette," *RA*, Vol. 85, No. 6 (August 11, 1928), 287; *VSCS*, pp. 527–529; "Interstate Commerce Commission," *RA*, Vol. 86, No. 22 (June 1, 1929), 1301.

VII.   THE CONSOLIDATION PROBLEM, 1924–1932

1. U.S. Interstate Commerce Commission, *Interlocking Directors of Wheeling & Lake Erie and Trunk Lines*, Vol. 138, *ICC Reports* (1928), pp. 644, 646–647.

2. See chapter 4; *Interstate Commerce Commission v. Baltimore & Ohio Railroad Company*, Vol. 152, *ICC Reports* (1929), pp. 745–746; *VSCS*, pp. 141–144, 497; Leonard, *Railroad Consolidation*, pp. 135–139; George H. Burgess and Miles C. Kennedy, *Centennial History of the Pennsylvania Railroad Company* (Philadelphia, 1949), pp. 580–581. The Pennsylvania's objections centered around the proposed award of the Lehigh Valley to the New York Central. In a Central-controlled Lehigh Valley the Pennsylvania saw "a new direct route from New York to Pittsburgh and Chicago, cutting through the heart of the Pennsylvania's jealously guarded territory" (Leonard, *Railroad Consolidation*, pp. 137–139).

3. Of the Van Sweringens, Patrick Crowley of the New York Central, Daniel Willard of the B. & O., and Loree, the only college graduate (Rutgers, 1877) was Loree (*PD*, February 10, 1927, p. 9).

4. Leonard, *Railroad Consolidation*, p. 143; Rehor, *Nickel Plate Story*, p. 196; Burgess and Kennedy, *History of the Pennsylvania Railroad*, pp. 635–636.

5. *VSCS*, p. 498; Rehor, *Nickel Plate Story*, p. 196; "Wheeling & Lake Erie Changes Control," *RA*, Vol. 82, No. 7 (February 12, 1927), 459–460.

6. Leonard, *Railroad Consolidation*, p. 144.

7. *VSCS*, pp. 497–506.

8. *Ibid.*, pp. 497–506; Vol. 138, *ICC Reports*, pp. 652–653; Rehor, *Nickel Plate Story*, pp. 196, 198; "Wheeling and Lake Erie Changes Control," *RA*, 459–461; *PD*, February 10, 1927, p. 10. The alliance had completed its purchases in the open market of Wheeling & Lake Erie stock by January 26, paying 27½-30 during the first week of that month and 50-53 during the last days of the buying campaign. The Taplins, too, combed the market for free shares of Wheeling,

securing 31,000 shares between January 22 and January 25. This raised their total holdings in the road to over 50,000 shares. The withdrawal of most of the free Wheeling stock from the market by the alliance and the Taplins set the stage for excitement when, a week later, the first week of February, a near "corner" developed, causing the price of the stock to soar, albeit briefly, to 130. Within three days, however, it had fallen back to the range of 64-77. The entire incident, the subject of much comment and concern on Wall Street and in the New York newspapers, had been caused indirectly by the Vans, their allies, and the Taplins. But they all had concluded their purchases by the end of January and had no part in the "corner." (*VSCS*, pp. 504-506; *Commercial and Financial Chronicle*, Vol. 124 [February 12, 1927], 873-876; "Wheeling and Lake Erie Changes Control," *RA*, 459-461; Leonard, *Railroad Consolidation*, p. 145).

9. *VSCS*, p. 506; Vol. 138, *ICC Reports*, p. 650.

10. Under paragraph 12 of section 20a of the Transportation Act of 1920, the commission had to approve the appointment of a person wishing to serve as director of more than one road (Leonard, *Railroad Consolidation*, p. 145).

11. Vol. 138, *ICC Reports*, pp. 650-654; "I.C.C. Investigates W. & L.E. Stock Purchase," *RA*, Vol. 82, No. 30 (June 25, 1927), 1995-1996; "Right of Trunk Lines to Control W. & L.E. Questioned," *RA*, Vol. 83, No. 1 (July 2, 1927), 9; "Wheeling & Lake Erie—Representation of Trunk Lines on Directorate," *RA*, Vol 83, No. 11 (September 10, 1927), 503; "Wheeling & Lake Erie—Exceptions to Proposed Report in Directorship Case," *RA*, Vol. 83, No. 5 (December 17, 1927), 1235. A recent student of the ICC has commented on merger cases in the 1920s: "In the large group of cases where intervenors alleged that the acquisition of control would lessen competition, the issue appears more contrived than real. Whether the acquired lines were parallel or complementary to the acquiring line, the intervenors were obviously apprehensive that new and more efficient through routes would be created that would rival intervenors' through routes or bypass intervenors operating as connecting lines. Thus intervenors' charges of possible injury to the public by lessened competition were usually shams which attempted to prevent the promotion of consolidations that effected more efficient allocation of resources and more genuine competition" (Michael Conant, *Railroad Mergers and Abandonments* [Berkeley, 1964], pp. 52-53).

12. Vol. 138, *ICC Reports*, pp. 654-666; *VSCS*, pp. 506-508.

13. Vol. 138, *ICC Reports,* p. 655; Vol. 152, *ICC Reports*, p. 721; "I.C.C. Decisions on 'Merger' Plans," *RA*, Vol. 84, No. 21 (May 26, 1928), 1216.

14. *VSCS*, pp. 513-514; "Another Van Sweringen Railroad," *The Literary Digest*, Vol. 99 (November 3, 1928), 71-73; Thomas H. Gammack, "The Railroading Van Sweringens," *The Outlook and Independent*, Vol. 150 (November 7, 1928), 1136.

15. *VSCS*, pp. 514-515; "Van Sweringens Purchase 67 Per Cent of B. R. & P. Stock," *RA*, Vol. 85, No. 15 (October 13, 1928), 710.

16. *VSCS*, pp. 515-517. O. P. Van Sweringen told George Shriver of the impending announcement as the two entered the ICC Building in Washington

for discussions with Commissioner Porter on the matter of the four-party conferences. After the meeting, as he related in a memorandum of the meeting, Shriver suggested that the two speak to Mr. Crowley of the New York Central about the purchase, but O. P. snapped, "No, I want no conference with Crowley or anyone else, after Crowley failed to support me in the effort to have the conferences between the roads continued under the Commission." (This comment referred to a dispute at the end of one meeting caused by O. P.'s suggestion that Commissioner Porter be asked to sit in on the four-party conferences as something of an umpire. No one but the Vans liked the idea.) Further discussion that day between the two quickly broke down, and, as Shriver recalled, O. P. left saying "And if that is your attitude you can go to hell." This seems to be one of the rare instances in which the usually calm O. P. Van Sweringen lost his temper (*ibid.* pp. 516–517).

17.   Vol. 152, *ICC Reports*, p. 722.

18.   *Ibid.*, pp. 725–726, 731–732. Conant has commented on the ICC's definition of competition as used in the Wheeling case: "The Commission has stated that 'competition between carriers, within the purpose of section 5 of the act, exists wherever there is such possibility of election of routes as may have an influence upon service or rates.' Since rates were fixed by rate bureaus and service determined primarily by the route of the lines and the state of technology in operating equipment, this definition was rather chimerical" (Conant, *Railroad Mergers and Abandonments*, p. 52).

19.   Vol. 152, *ICC Reports*, pp. 733–734; "Wheeling & Lake Erie—Argument in Anti-Trust Case," *RA*, Vol. 85, No. 23 (December 8, 1928), 1164; "Briefs in W. & L.E. Anti-Trust Case," *RA*, Vol. 85, No. 12 (September 22, 1928), 547–548.

20.   Vol. 152, *ICC Reports*, pp. 735–736; *VSCS*, pp. 508–509.

21.   "Trunk Lines Ordered to Dispose of W. & L.E. Stock," *RA*, Vol. 86, No. 11 (March 16, 1929), 629–630; Vol. 152, *ICC Reports*, pp. 742–748; *VSCS*, pp. 509–510.

22.   Vol. 152, *ICC Reports*, p. 737.

23.   Joseph Borkin, in his biography *Robert R. Young, the Populist of Wall Street* (New York, 1969), makes the following comment about the formation of Alleghany: "According to what may be an apocryphal story, the adventurous but poorly educated Van Sweringens had intended to name their new holding company after the Allegheny Mountains but could only approximate the spelling. After all the legalities were completed, and the certificates printed, a horrified clerk in J. P. Morgan & Company discovered the misspelling—but too late" (p. 28).

24.   "Bachelors of Railroading," *Fortune*, 163; *VSCS*, p. 534; *SEP*, p. 567; "Alleghany Corporation—Organization by Van Sweringens," *RA*, Vol. 86, No. 5 (February 2, 1929), 341. The principal officers of Alleghany when formed were O. P. Van Sweringen, President, M. J. Van Sweringen, Vice-President, C. L. Bradley, Vice-President, D. S. Barrett, Treasurer, and John P. Murphy, Secretary (*VSCS*, p. 535).

25. *VSCS*, pp. 532-537. Some 4,000,000 shares of common and 750,000 shares of preferred were kept in the Alleghany treasury for future issuance. Of the $85,000,000 worth of secruities issued and marketed by the Morgan, the following types and amounts were sold:

$35,000,000 principal amount of 5% collateral trust bonds
   250,000 shares of $100 par value 5½% preferred stock
1,250,000 shares of no-par common stock at $20
   375,000 warrants to purchase one share of common stock
            attached to preferred stock, at $1 each

26. The Morgan did not distribute the 1,250,000 shares of Alleghany common publicly. The firm and its members kept approximately 350,000 shares; the Guaranty Company, a close ally of the Morgan bank, received 500,000 shares; Drexel & Company got 50,000; and most of the remaining 350,000 shares went to 225 friends of J. P. Morgan and Company. This group found themselves on what became known as the "Alleghany preferred list." For a dispassionate account of this cause *célèbre*, which has more to do with the Morgan than with the Van Sweringens, see *VSCS*, pp. 540-549. For a passionate account, see Ferdinand Pecora, *Wall Street Under Oath* (New York, 1939), pp. 27-34.

27. The acquisition by Alleghany of the various blocs of stock was not a simple one-to-one operation; rather, it involved the establishment of two new holding companies—Geneva Corporation and General Securities Corporation—and the shuffling back and forth between these new holding companies and Vaness and Chesapeake Corporation of the securities. All of these maneuvers were carried out in accord with a section of the Federal tax law "providing that gains or losses on exchanges of securities under certain conditions shall not be recognized for tax purposes." As a result, the Vans avoided paying an income tax on some $20,000,000 of profits resulting from the creation of Alleghany (see *VSCS*, pp. 549-555). O. P. said this was done in order "to avail of the income tax exemption provided by Congress in connection with corporate reorganizations." "In other words," *Fortune* commented in 1934, "like most American businessmen, they effected large business economies with the aid of laws that have since fallen into general disrepute" ("Bachelors of Railroading," *Fortune*, 163).

28. *VSCS*, pp. 510-511, 554-556; "Nickel Plate Seeks Control of W. & L.E.," *RA*, Vol. 86, No. 16 (April 20, 1929), 917-918; *Interstate Commerce Commission v. Baltimore & Ohio Railroad Company*, Vol. 156, *ICC Reports* (1929), pp. 607-616.

29. "Nickel Plate Seeks Control of W. & L.E.," *RA*, 917-918.

30. *VSCS*, pp. 510-511; Vol. 156, *ICC Reports*, pp. 608-609; "Trustee to Hold W. & L.E. Stock," *RA*, Vol. 87, No. 6 (August 10, 1929), 372.

31. O. P. Van Sweringen is quoted in Pierce H. Fulton, "Railroads Renew the 'Battle of the East,' " *The Magazine of Wall Street*, Vol. 43, No. 10 (March 9, 1929), 818-819, 888-890; "Van Sweringen System Proposed," *RA*, Vol. 86, No. 8 (February 23, 1929), 448-451; *VSCS*, pp. 579-581.

32. "Recent Developments in the Consolidation Situation," *RA*, Vol. 86, No. 9 (March 2, 1929), 515; "I.C.C. Consolidation Plan," *RA*, Vol. 87, No. 26

(December 28, 1929), 1469–1476; *In the Matter of Consolidation of the Railway Properties of the United States into a Limited Number of Systems*, Vol. 159, *ICC Reports* (1929), pp. 522–589; *VSCS*, pp. 582–583; "Chesapeake & Ohio—Unification Plan Withdrawn," *RA*, Vol. 88, No. 15 (April 12, 1930), 894.

33.   *SEP*, pp. 567–568; "Bachelors of Railroading," *Fortune*, 164.

34.   *VSCS*, pp. 557-559; "Van Sweringens Reach Out into Southwest," *Business Week*, March 19, 1930, 12-13; *SEP*, p. 568.

35.   *VSCS*, pp. 558–561; "Missouri Commission Hears Alleghany Request for M. P. Control," *RA*, Vol. 88, No. 17 (April 26, 1930), 988.

36.   *VSCS*, pp. 562–564. From mid-1929 until the end of 1931, Alleghany held a 20 per cent interest in the Kansas City Southern Railroad, which ran from Kansas City to Port Arthur, Texas. It was acquired, for almost $10,000,000, probably for ultimate inclusion in the MoPac; for the time being it was being kept "reasonably safe from competitors." It was sold late in 1931, at a considerable loss, to the Chicago Great Western, a Van Sweringen ally, when Alleghany needed money (*VSCS*, pp. 566–567).

37.   "The Van Sweringens Drive Another Golden Spike," *Business Week*, April 2, 1930, 8; "Chicago & Eastern Illinois Changes Executives," *RA*, Vol. 90, No. 2 (January 10, 1931), 155–156; *VSCS*, pp. 907–908.

38.   *VSCS*, pp. 908–910. The Wheeler Committee Report states that these devices "successfully concealed the acquisition from all but the insiders involved" (*VSCS*, p. 908). Yet on April 2, 1930, less than three months after the purchase had been made, *Business Week* published an article about it. The Vans were not blameless, however. See *VSCS*, pp. 909–911, on how they used subterfuge to keep the details of the deal secret.

39.   Leonard, *Railroad Consolidation*, pp. 199–201; "Wabash Asks Control of W. & L. E.," *RA*, Vol. 88, No. 19 (May 10, 1930), 1139–1140; "New 'Fifth System' Plan Proposed," *RA*, Vol. 88, No. 25 (June 21, 1930), 1475–1477; *VSCS*, pp. 1128–1129.

40.   *VSCS*, pp. 1131–1135; Harold F. Lane, "Four System Plan in East," *RA*, Vol. 90, No. 2 (January 10, 1931), 147–152; Stover, *The Life and Decline of the American Railroad*, pp. 127-157 *passim*.

41.   Lane, "Four System Plan," *RA*; "Four-System Plan Submitted to I.C.C.," *RA*, Vol. 91, No. 15 (October 10, 1931), 549–552; Leonard, *Railroad Consolidation*, pp. 202–203.

42.   Leonard, *Railroad Consolidation*, pp. 202-204; "Four-System Plan Hearings," *RA*, Vol. 92, No. 2 (January 9, 1932), 91-92; "Eastern Consolidation Hearings," *RA*, Vol. 92, No. 3 (January 16, 1932), 123–126, 134 (source for Bernet's statement).

43.   Leonard, *Railroad Consolidation*, pp. 203-204; "Association Formed to Support Fifth Eastern System," *RA*, Vol. 91, No. 23 (December 5, 1931), 882; "New England Governors Oppose Four-System Plan," *RA*, Vol. 91, No. 25 (December 19, 1931), 951; "Chicago, Indianapolis & Louisville—Allocation to

B. & O. System Opposed" and "Delaware & Hudson—Four-System Plan Opposed," *RA*, Vol. 91, No. 26 (December 26, 1931), 999; "Hearings on Four-System Plan Resumed," *RA*, Vol. 92, No. 8 (February 20, 1932), 342-343; "Four-System Plan Hearings Continued," *RA*, Vol. 92, No. 9 (February 27, 1932), 377-378; "Hearings on Four-System Plan Continue," *RA*, Vol. 92, No. 10 (March 5, 1932), 417-418; "Four-System Hearings Concluded," *RA*, Vol. 92, No. 11 (March 12, 1932), 433-434; "Briefs on Four-System Plan Filed with I.C.C.," *RA*, Vol. 92, No. 17 (April 13, 1932), 702, 706-707.

44. *In the Matter of Consolidation of the Railway Properties of the United States into a Limited Number of Systems,* Vol. 185, *ICC Reports* (1932), pp. 406-414.

45. Vol. 185, *ICC Reports*, pp. 414-421; Leonard, *Railroad Consolidation*, p. 204; *VSCS*, pp. 1135-1136.

46. *New York Times*, July 22, 1932, p. 1, July 23, 1932, pp. 1, 10; *PD*, July 22, 1932, p. 8, July 23, 1932, p. 6; "Four-System Plan Approved," *RA*, Vol. 93, No. 5 (July 30, 1932), 150; Leonard, *Railroad Consolidation*, pp. 205-206; for Eastman dissent, see Vol. 185, *ICC Reports*, pp. 422-451.

47. *New York Times*, September 24, 1932, pp. 1, 8; Interstate Commerce Commission, *Annual Report for 1932*, p. 32; The "later assessment" is in *VSCS*, p. 1137; *SEP*, p. 567.

VIII   DEATH OF AN EMPIRE

1. "Stock Market and Railways," *RA*, Vol. 87, No. 18 (November 2, 1929), 1041-1042; *VSCS*, p. 922.

2. *VSCS*, pp. 584-591, 861-870; "Van Sweringens Acquire Interest in New York Trucking Concern," *RA*, Vol. 28, No. 4 (January 25, 1930), 316-317.

3. *VSCS*, pp. 871-876, 883-885.

4. *Ibid.*, pp. 887-888.

5. "Bachelors of Railroading," *Fortune*, 160; *VSCS*, p. 922. The actual price for C. & O. in 1930 was 49; however, the stock had recently split 4 for 1. The price of 196 represents the adjusted equivalent.

6. *VSCS*, pp. 910-916, 924-928. The Building Company had already obtained $10,000,000 by mortgaging the Builders Exchange-Medical Arts, Garage, and Midland Bank group of buildings to the Prudential Insurance Company in June, 1930.

7. *Ibid.*, pp. 916-924.

8. *Ibid.*, pp. 930-935. The quotation about the Vans' predicament comes from a memorandum submitted to the Wheeler Committee by G. R. Herzog, assistant to the liquidator of the Union Trust Co., summarizing a conversation he had with O. P. in late 1933.

9. *Ibid.*, pp. 938-940. The collateral for the two loans was as follows:
(1) for Vaness' $16,000,000 loan: 550,000 shares of Alleghany Corp.

common stock; 10,000 shares of Cleveland Railway common stock certificates of deposit; 10,900 shares of Erie 2nd preferred; 1,000 shares of Missouri Pacific common; 11,439 shares of Electric Autolite; 5,000 shares of C. & O. common; 5,000 shares of Chesapeake Corp. common; 17,142 shares of Alleghany Corp. common; 5,000 shares of Otis Steel; 1,744,800 shares of Van Sweringen Corp.; 122,000 shares of Van Sweringen Co. common; 17,000 shares of Terminal Bldg. Co.; 250 shares of Huron Fourth Co.; 196 shares of Long Lake Co.; 1,350,000 shares of Alleghany Corp. warrants; 500 shares of Continental Illinois Bank & Trust Co.; 2,000 shares of Missouri Pacific common; 8,260 shares of Midland Bank; 32,000 shares of Cleveland Railway certificates of deposit; stock of United States Coal Co. as received; Note of the Van Sweringen Corp. for $10,000,000 subordinate to the $30,000,000 6 percent notes evidencing the advance of $10,000,000 to the guaranty fund

(2)   for Cleveland Terminals Building Company's $23,500,000 loan: 11,500 shares of Alleghany Corp. preferred with $30 warrants; 115,612 shares of Hupp Motor Co.; 5,075 shares of Inland Steel Co.; 35,000 shares of Lehigh Valley Coal Corp. common; 8,250 shares of Midland Steel Products 1st preferred; 2,175 shares of Midland Steel Products $2 stock; 17,287 shares of Midland Steel Products common; 213,667 shares of Otis Steel Co.; 33,859 shares of Pittston Co.; 62,314 shares of White Motor Co.; 1,122,950 shares of Alleghany Corp. common; 100,000 shares of Higbee Co. common; 500,000 shares of Alleghany Corp. common

10.   *VSCS*, pp. 959–961, 1065–1066.

11.   *Ibid.*, pp. 960–961.

12.   "Bachelors of Railroading," *Fortune*, 182; *VSCS*, pp. 976-979.

13.   *VSCS*, pp. 1063–1068.

14.   *Ibid.*, pp. 1068, 1073–1077.

15.   *Ibid.*, pp. 1079–1083.

16.   *Ibid.*, pp. 1083–1090.

17.   *SEP,*, Part 2, p. 766; *VSCS*, pp. 1101–1103; "Railway Loan Policies Discussed at White House," *RA*, Vol. 92, No. 13 (March 26, 1932), 525–526; "I.C.C. 'Coordinated' into Reluctant Relief," *RA*, Vol. 92, No. 14 (April 2, 1932), 565–566; "Chicago & Eastern Illinois—R. F. C. Loan" and "Erie-R. F. C. Loan," *RA*, Vol. 93, No. 18 (October 18, 1932), 626.

18.   "Public Works Administration Loans Bring Orders for Equipment and Employment," *RA*, Vol. 96, No. 6 (February 10, 1934), 235–236; "More P. W. A. Loan Contracts Signed," *RA*, Vol. 95, No. 7 (February 17, 1934), 273; "P. W. A. Loans," *RA*, Vol. 96, No. 11 (March 24, 1934), 454; "More Than Half of P. W. A. Railroad Loans Paid Out," *RA*, Vol. 97, No. 9 (September 1, 1934), 269-270.

19.   *VSCS*, pp. 1105-1112; "Bachelors of Railroading," *Fortune*, p. 170; "Missouri Pacific to Reorganize under New Law," *RA*, Vol. 94, No. 14 (April 8, 1933), 508, 514; "C. & E. I. To Reorganize under New Bankruptcy Law," *Ra*, Vol. 94, No. 17 (April 29, 1933), 624.

20. *VSCS*, pp. 1105, 1113-1116; Peter H. Noyes, "A Lesson for Van Sweringen Bond Holders," *The Nation*, Vol. 138, No. 3591 (May 2, 1934), 508-509.

21. *VSCS*, pp. 1117-1125. Based as they were on C. & O. dividends, Chesapeake Corporation dividends, which ranged between $4 and $5 million during the years 1929 through 1931, could have been used to pay off the loan. However, those Chesapeake dividends went to pay the interest on various Alleghany bonds. If those bonds lost this source of income and defaulted, the entire Van Sweringen structure could collapse. The bankers who made the $32,500,000 loan to Chesapeake had also invested $39,500,000 the same year in Vaness and Cleveland Terminals Building Company. They knew that any jolt to Chesapeake would affect Alleghany, and ultimately Vaness and the Terminals Building Company. Therefore, they had no great desire to press the issue.

22. *VSCS*, pp. 1117-1123.

23. *Ibid.*, pp. 1151-1155. From January through April, 1935, the price of Alleghany common ranged from ¾ to 1⅞.

24. *Ibid.*, pp. 1156, 1165-1167; "Morgan & Company to Sell Van Sweringen Collateral," *RA*, Vol. 99, No. 12 (September 21, 1935), 358, The *Wall Street Journal* is quoted in "An Empire on the Auction-Block," *Literary Digest*, Vol. 120, No. 12 (September 21, 1935), 36.

25. *New York Herald-Tribune*, October 1, 1935, as quoted in *VSCS*, pp. 1167-1170; *New York Times*, October 1, 1935, pp. 1, 8; *PD*, of $5,515,000 at the auction. This figure includes $1,582,000 that the stock exchange firm of Hallgarten & Co. paid for other salable items in the auction.

26. *New York Times*, October 2, 1935, p. 22; *PD*, October 1, 1935, p. 8.

27. *VSCS*, pp. 1170-1171, 1173; *PD*, October 1, 1935, p. 5; *PD*, December 13, 1935, pp. 1, 8; Taylor Hampton, "Cleveland's Fabulous Vans—Death Ends the Dreams," *Cleveland News*, August 19, 1955.

28. Taylor Hampton, "Cleveland's Fabulous Vans—Death Ends the Dreams;" *VSCS*, pp. 1171-1172; "Reorganization Plan Filed by the "Missouri Pacific," *RA*, Vol. 99, No. 5 (August 3, 1935), 163-164; "Missouri Pacific— Reorganization," *RA*, Vol. 100, No. 18 (May 2, 1936), 742; "MIssouri Pacific— Bondholders' Committee Reports," *RA*, Vol. 100, No. 24 (June 13, 1936), 965; "Control of Van Sweringen Roads Inquired Into by I.C.C.," *RA*, Vol. 100, No. 7 (February 15, 1936), 289.

29. *PD*, November 24, 1936, p. 1; Taylor Hampton, "Cleveland's Fabulous Vans—Death Ends the Dreams."

CONCLUSION

1. Condon, *Cleveland*, pp. 193-196; "Bachelors of Railroading," *Fortune*, p. 59; Taylor Hampton, "Cleveland's Fabulous Vans—What Were They Like?" *Cleveland News*, August 15, 1955, and "Cleveland's Fabulous Vans—Their Wonderful Daisy Hill," *Cleveland News*, August 12, 1955. For more on Daisy

Hill, see the series of articles by Grace Goulder, "The Story of Daisy Hill," in the *Plain Dealer Sunday Magazine*, September 25, October 2, 9, 16, 1966.

2. *New York Times*, August 21, 1930, p. 1; *VSCS*, pp. 1177, 1190, 1194; *PD*, November 24, 1936, pp. 1, 2.

3. Borkin, *Robert R. Young*, pp. 35, 68-69; *New York Times*, December 2, 1973, p. 42. For the modern history of the merger movement see Stover, *Life and Decline of the American Railroad*, pp. 280-286.

4. *VSCS*, pp. 1071, 1196-1197.

5. *Ibid.*, pp. 1179, 1183-1190, 1192-1195.

6. "The Van Sweringen Case," *RA*, Vol. 101, No. 25 (December 19, 1936), 899; *PD*, April 14, 1934, pp. 1, 5; *PD*, November 24, 1936, p. 2; "Bachelors of Railroading," *Fortune*, p. 59.

7. Pecora, *Wall Street Under Oath*, pp. 284-288; *VSCS*, pp. 1194-1195.

8. *PD*, November 24, 1936, pp. 1, 2.

9. Condon, *Cleveland*, pp. 275-276; "The Current State of Mr. Van Sweringen," *Fortune*, Vol. 14, No. 6 (December, 1936), 179; "Memorial to Mantis James Van Sweringen" by the Trustees of the Western Reserve Historical Society, December, 1935, in Western Reserve Historical Society Collection; Christiansen, *Northern Ohio's Interurbans and Rapid Transit Railways*, pp. 115-117; Hampton, "Cleveland's Fabulous Vans—Properties Paid Out," *Cleveland News*, August 22, 1955.

10. Testimony of Newton D. Baker, F. D. 4671, *Nickel Plate Unification Case*, Vol. 9, p. 3287; John W. Raper, *The Soviet Table, or The Rise of Civilization in Cleveland* (privately published, c. 1935), pp. 12-13; Condon, *Cleveland*, p. 183.

Bibliography

Unpublished Materials

Berger, Robert E. "Holding and Investment Company Ownership of Railroad Securities." Ph.D. dissertation, Columbia University, 1951.

Blake, Joseph G. "The Van Sweringen Developments in Cleveland." Senior thesis, Department of History, University of Notre Dame, 1968.

Joseph B. Eastman Papers. Amherst College Library.

Haberman, Ian S. "The Van Sweringens of Cleveland: The Biography of an Empire." Ph.D. dissertation, Case Western Reserve University, 1975.

Virginia Taylor Hampton Collection. Western Reserve Historical Society.

"Minutes of Meeting on Union Depot matter, held in Mayor Baker's office on August 12, 1915, at 11:30 A.M." Municipal Reference Library, Cleveland Public Library.

"Miscellaneous Material on Shaker Heights." Western Reserve Historical Society.

Piercy, Caroline B. "History of Shaker Heights." Shaker Historical Museum, Shaker Heights, Ohio, n.d.

Resseger, Edwin. "The Indelible Dream." Honors thesis, Brown University, c. 1964.

Wenneman, William H. "A Short History of the Nickel Plate Railroad." Western Reserve Historical Society.

Ben B. Wickham Collection of Van Sweringen Miscellany. Western Reserve Historical Society.

Peter Witt Papers. Western Reserve Historical Society.

Public Documents

Cleveland, Ohio. *The City Record.* 1915, 1918–1919.

187

————. *Proceedings of the City Council.* 1911-1912.

Cleveland v. *Cleveland, C. C. & St. L. Ry.* Ohio Decisions, Vol. 19, Cuyahoga Common Pleas, February 18, 1909.

U. S. Bureau of Statistics. *Interstate Commerce Commission Activities, 1887-1937.* Washington, D. C., 1937.

U. S. Bureau of the Census. *Thirteenth Census of the United States: 1910 Manufactures—Ohio.*

U. S. *Congressional Record.* Vol. 59, Part 4.

U. S. *Congressional Record.* Vol. 67, Part 4.

U. S. House of Representatives, Committee on Interstate and Foreign Commerce. *Regulation of Stock Ownership in Railroads.* Report No. 2789, 71st Cong., 3rd Sess., 1931. (This document is known as the Splawn Report.)

U. S. Interstate Commerce Commission. Finance Docket 1237: *Cleveland Passenger Terminal Case.*

————. *Cleveland Passenger Terminal Case.* Vol. 70, *ICC Reports* (1921).

————. *Interlocking Directors—New York, Chicago & St. Louis and Chesapeake & Ohio.* Vol. 76, *ICC Reports* (1923).

————. *Operation of Lines and Issue of Capital Stock by the New York, Chicago & St. Louis Railroad Company.* Vol. 79, *ICC Reports* (1923).

————. Finance Docket 4671: *Nickel Plate Unification.*

————. *Nickel Plate Unification.* Vol. 105, *ICC Reports* (1928).

————. *Proposed Control of Erie Railroad Company and Pere Marquette Railway Company by Chesapeake & Ohio Railway Company.* Vol. 138, *ICC Reports* (1928).

————. *Interlocking Directors of Wheeling & Lake Erie and Trunk Lines.* Vol. 138, *ICC Reports* (1928).

————. *Proposed Control of Erie Railroad Co. and Pere Marquette Railway Co. by Chesapeake & Ohio Railway Co.* Vol. 150, *ICC Reports* (1929).

————. *Interstate Commerce Commission v. Baltimore & Ohio Railroad Company.* Vol. 152, *ICC Reports* (1929).

————. *Interstate Commerce Commission v. Baltimore & Ohio Railroad Company.* Vol. 156, *ICC Reports* (1929).

————. *In the Matter of Consolidation of the Railway Properties of the United States into a Limited Number of Systems.* Vol. 159, *ICC Reports* (1929).

————. *In the Matter of Consolidation of the Railway Properties of the United States into a Limited Number of Systems.* Vol. 185, *ICC Reports* (1932).

_____. *Annual Report.* 1932.

U. S. Senate, Committee on Banking and Currency. *Stock Exchange Practices.* Hearings on Report No. 56, 73rd Cong., 1st Sess., 1933. (These are known as the Pecora Committee Hearings.)

U. S. Senate, Committee on Interstate Commerce. *Railroad Consolidation in the Eastern Region; Investigation of Railroads, Holding Companies, and Affiliated Companies.* Report No. 1182, 76th Cong., 3rd Sess., 1940. (This is known as the Wheeler Committee Report.)

_____. *The Van Sweringen Corporate System: A Study in Holding Company Financing.* Report No. 714, 77th Cong., 1st Sess., 1941. (This is a supplement to the Wheeler Committee Report.)

Books

Allen, Frederick Lewis. *The Lords of Creation.* New York: Harper & Brothers, 1935.

Bonbright, James C., and Means, Gardiner C. *The Holding Company: Its Public Significance and Its Regulation.* New York: McGraw-Hill Book Company, 1932.

Borkin, Joseph. *Robert R. Young, the Populist of Wall Street.* New York: Harper & Row, 1969.

Burgess, George H., and Kennedy, Miles C. *Centennial History of the Pennsylvania Railroad Company.* Philadelphia: The Pennsylvania Railroad Company, 1949.

Burnham, Daniel H., Carrère, John M., and Brunner, Arnold W. *Report of the Group Plan of the Public Buildings of the City of Cleveland, Ohio.* Cleveland, 1903.

Christiansen, Harry. *Northern Ohio's Inter-Urbans and Rapid Transit Railways.* 3rd rev. ed. Cleveland: Transit Data, 1966.

The Cleveland Directory. Cleveland: The Cleveland Directory Company, 1890-1925.

The Cleveland "Mall" Plan. Cleveland: Department of Information, 1927.

Conant, Michael. *Railroad Mergers and Abandonments.* Berkeley: University of California Press, 1964.

Condon, George E. *Cleveland: The Best Kept Secret.* Garden City, New York: Doubleday & Company, 1967.

Conlin, Mary Lou. *The North Union Story: A Shaker Society, 1822-1889.* Shaker Heights, Ohio: The Shaker Historical Society, 1961.

Cramer, C. H. *Open Shelves and Open Minds: The History of the Cleveland Public Library.* Cleveland: The Press of Case Western Reserve University, 1972.

Dictionary of American Biography. Vol. 21, Supplement One. New York: Charles Scribners' Sons, 1944.

Electric Railways of Northeastern Ohio. Bulletin 108. Chicago: Central Electric Railfans' Association, 1965.

Fainsod, Merle, and Gordon, Lincoln. *Government and the American Economy.* Rev. ed. New York: W. W. Norton & Company, 1948.

Fuess, Claude M. *Joseph B. Eastman: Servant of the People.* New York: Columbia University Press, 1952.

Gallion, Arthur B. *The Urban Pattern: City Planning and Design.* Princeton: D. Van Nostrand Company, 1950.

Glaab, Charles N., and Brown, A. Theodore. *A History of Urban America.* New York: The Macmillan Company, 1967.

Hampton, (Virginia) Taylor. *The Nickel Plate Road.* Cleveland: The World Publishing Company, 1947.

The Heritage of the Shakers. Cleveland: The Van Sweringen Company, 1923.

Hungerford, Edward. *Men and Iron: The History of the New York Central.* New York: Thomas Y. Crowell Company, 1938.

Hungerford, Edward. *Men of Erie: A Story of Human Effort.* New York: Random House, 1946.

Ivey, Paul W. *The Pere Marquette Railroad: An Historical Study of the Growth and Development of One of Michigan's Most Important Railway Systems.* Ann Arbor: University of Michigan, 1919.

Jenks, Louise D. *O. P. and M. J.* Cleveland (?): Privately printed, 1940.

Josephson, Matthew. *The Money Lords: The Great Finance Capitalists.* New York: Weybright & Talley, 1972.

Kerr, K. Austin. *American Railroad Politics, 1914-1920: Rates, Wages, and Efficiency.* Pittsburgh: University of Pittsburgh Press, 1968.

League of Women Voters of Shaker Heights, comp. *Government at Work in the City of Shaker Heights.* Published by the City of Shaker Heights, Ohio, 1961.

Legislation of the City of Cleveland and Documents Pertaining Thereto and Applications to and Orders of the Interstate Commerce Commission All in Connection with the Union Passenger Terminal of The Cleveland Union Terminals Company, Cleveland, Ohio. Cleveland: The Cleveland Union Terminals Company, 1930.

Leonard, William N. *Railroad Consolidation under the Transportation Act of 1920*. New York: Columbia University Press, 1946.

Lynn, Ernest H. "Shaker Village." In *Shaker Heights: Then and Now*, edited by Arthur A. Bedhun. Shaker Heights, Ohio: The Shaker Heights Board of Education, 1938.

Martin, Albro. *Enterprise Denied: Origins of the Decline of American Railroads, 1897-1917*. New York, Columbia University Press, 1971.

McDonald, Forrest. *Insull*. Chicago: University of Chicago Press, 1962.

McKelvey, Blake. *The Emergence of Metropolitan America, 1915-1966*. New Brunswick, New Jersey: Rutgers University Press, 1968.

Meeks, Carroll L. V. *The Railroad Station: An Architectural History*. New Haven: Yale University Press, 1956.

Miller, Otto, Jr. *A History of the Growth and Development of the Van Sweringen Railway System*. Cleveland: Privately published, 1924 (Bachelor's Degree thesis, Harvard University).

Morse, Kenneth S. P. *Cleveland Streetcars*. Baltimore: Published by the author, c. 1955.

National Cyclopaedia of American Biography. Current Volume A. New York: James T. White & Company, 1930.

Peaceful Shaker Village. Cleveland: The Van Sweringen Company, 1927.

Piercy, Caroline B. *The Valley of God's Pleasure: A Saga of the North Union Shaker Community*. New York: Stratford House, 1951.

Pound, Arthur, and Moore, Samuel Taylor, eds. *They Told Barron—Conversations and Revelations of an American Pepys in Wall Street. The Notes of the Late Clarence W. Barron*. New York: Harper & Brothers, 1930.

Rachlis, Eugene, and Marqusee, John F. *The Land Lords*. New York: Random House, 1963.

Raper, John W. *The Soviet Table, or the Rise of Civilization in Cleveland*. An address before the City Club of Cleveland. Privately printed, c. 1935.

Rehor, John A. *The Nickel Plate Story*. Milwaukee: Kalmbach Publishing Company, 1965.

Ripley, William Z. *Main Street and Wall Street*. Boston: Little, Brown & Company, 1927.

Rose, William G. *Cleveland: The Making of a City*. Cleveland: The World Publishing Company, 1950.

Sharfman, I. L. *The Interstate Commerce Commission: A Study in Administrative Law and Procedure*. New York: The Commonwealth Fund, 1935.

Sobel, Robert. *The Great Bull Market: Wall Street in the 1920s*. New York: W. W. Norton & Company, 1968.

Soule, George. *Prosperity Decade, From War to Depression: 1917–1929*. New York: Harper & Row, 1968 (originally published by Holt, Rinehart & Winston, 1947).

The Story of the Rapid Transit. Cleveland: The Van Sweringen Company, 1920.

Stover, John F. *The Life and Decline of the American Railroad*. New York: Oxford University Press, 1970.

Swearingen H. H. *Family Register of Gerret van Sweringen*. 2nd ed. Washington: Privately printed, 1894.

The Terminal Tower. Cleveland: The Terminal Tower Company, 1963.

Tunnard, Christopher, and Read, Henry Hope. *American Skyline: The Growth and Form of Our Cities and Towns*. Boston: Houghton Mifflin Company, 1955.

Turner, Charles W. *Chessie's Road*. Richmond: Garrett & Massie, 1956.

Tyler, Alice Felt. *Freedom's Ferment: Phases of American Social History from the Colonial Period to the Outbreak of the Civil War*. Minneapolis: University of Minnesota Press, 1944.

The Union Station: A Description of the New Passenger Facilities and Surrounding Improvements. Cleveland: The Cleveland Union Terminals Company and The Cleveland Terminals Building Company, 1930.

A Walk around Shaker Square. Cleveland: The Shaker Square Association, n.d.

White, Trentwell M. *Famous Leaders of Industry* (Third Series). *The Life Stories of Boys Who Have Succeeded*. Boston: L. C. Page & Company, 1931.

Articles, Newspapers, and Periodicals

"Another Van Sweringen Railroad." *The Literary Digest*, Vol. 99 (November 3, 1928), 71–73.

"Are the Van Sweringens Playing a Bogey Game?" *Current Opinion*, Vol. 74 (April 23, 1923), 415–417.

"Bachelors of Railroading." *Fortune*, Vol. 9, No. 3 (March, 1934), 59–67, 160–182.

Baxter, Edwin Childs. "The Grouping of Public Buildings in Cleveland," *The American Monthly Review of Reviews*, Vol. 31, No. 5 (May, 1905), 561-566.

Bird, Hobart S. "The Van Sweringens Turn Nickel Plate into Gold." *The Nation*, Vol. 122, No. 3167 (March 17, 1926), 277–279.

Business Week. 1929–1935.

Cleveland *Leader*.

The Cleveland News.

Cleveland *Plain Dealer.*

Cleveland Press.

The Commercial and Financial Chronicle, Vol. 124, Part 1 (February 12, 1927), 973-976.

"Consolidation Requisites Defined." *United States Investor,* Vol. 37, No. 10 (March 6, 1926).

Corey, Herbert. "They Turned a City Around." *Nation's Business,* Vol. 17, No. 13 (December, 1929), 31-33, 116-118.

"The Current State of Mr. Van Sweringen." *Fortune,* Vol. 14, No. 6 (December, 1936), 110-112, 179-190.

Davenport, Walter. "Oris and Mantis." *Liberty,* Vol. 1, No. 16 (August 23, 1924), 45-46.

"The Defeated Railway Merger." *The Nation,* Vol. 122 (March 17, 1926), 273-274.

Dodge, Daniel. "An Empire in Hock: The Story of the Van Sweringen Railroads." *The American Mercury,* Vol. 34 (February, 1935), 160-174.

Electric Railway Journal. 1911-1920.

"An Empire on the Auction-Block." *Literary Digest,* Vol. 120, No. 12 (September 21, 1935), 36.

Engineering News-Record. 1919-1921.

Flynn, John T. "The Betrayal of Cleveland." *Harper's Monthly Magazine,* Vol. 168 (January, 1934), 142-150.

Flynn, John T. "Will the Fifth Line Fight?" *World's Work,* Vol. 60 (March, 1931), 35-39.

Frary, I. T. "Suburban Landscape Planning in Cleveland." *The Architectural Record,* Vol. 43, No. 4 (April, 1918), 371-374.

Fulton, Pierce H. "Railroads Renew the 'Battle of the East.'" *The Magazine of Wall Street,* Vol. 43, No. 10 (March 9, 1929), 818-819, 888-890.

Gammack, Thomas H. "The Railroading Van Sweringens." *The Outlook and Independent,* Vol. 160 (November 7, 1928), 1136.

Gnaedinger, L. B. N., "The Men in the Railroad Mergers." *World's Work,* (June, 1930), 34-35.

Goldsmith, Joseph M. "Who Are the Van Sweringens?" *The Magazine of Wall Street,* Vol. 31, No. 8 (February 17, 1923), 695-696, 755-756.

Goulder, Grace. "The Story of Daisy Hill." *The Plain Dealer Sunday Magazine,* September 25, October 2, 9, 16, 1966.

Graham, Benjamin. "Are C. & O. Holders Unfairly Treated?" *The Magazine of Wall Street,* Vol. 35, No. 8 (February 14, 1925), 644-645, 708-710.

Graham, Benjamin. "A Victory for the Small Stockholder." *The Magazine of Wall Street*, Vol. 37 (March 27, 1926), 985-987, 1052.

Gregg, Albert S. "A Tower That Dominates All Cleveland." *World's Work*, Vol. 59, No. 2 (February, 1930), 54-56.

Griffen, Richard F. "The Revival of Railroad Romance." *New York Herald-Tribune Magazine*, July 27, 1924.

Gwinn, Sherman. "Who Said the Days of Railroading Giants is Over?" *The American Magazine*, Vol. 106 (July, 1928), 25, 129-133.

Hampton, (Virginia) Taylor. "Cleveland's Fabulous Vans." *Cleveland News*, August, 1955.

Hauenstein, E. H. "No Signs Left of Modest Homes Where Van Sweringens Lived When Brothers Who Became Famous Were Little Boys." Wooster *Daily Record*, October 8, 1952.

Hitchcock, Henry-Russell, Jr. "Traffic and Building Art: New York City and Cleveland Contrasted." *Architectural Record*, Vol. 67, No. 6 (June, 1930), 557.

Howe, Frederic C. "The Cleveland Group Plan." *Charities and The Commons*, Vol. 19 (February 1, 1908), 1548.

"How Not to Nickel Plate." *Literary Digest*, Vol. 88 (March 13, 1926), 8-9.

"The Interchangeable Van Sweringens." *The World's Work*, Vol. 49, No. 6 (April, 1925), 594-598.

Josephson, Matthew. "Mass Civilization and the Individual." *The Outlook and Independent*, Vol. 152, No. 6 (June 5, 1929), 207.

Kelly, Fred C. "Interesting People: Two Young Men Who Are Real Estate Marvels." *The American Magazine*, Vol. 83, No. 3 (March, 1917), 50-51.

Lawrence, David. "American Business and Business Men." *The Saturday Evening Post*, Vol. 202, No. 47 (May 24, 1930), 40.

Llewellyn, Karl N. "Cleveland Whirlpool." *Today*, Vol. 1, No. 8 (December 16, 1933), 3-5, 24.

Love, John W. "The Van Sweringens." *The American Review of Reviews*, Vol. 70 (November, 1924), 498-504.

The Magazine of Wall Street, Vol. 31, No. 9 (March 3, 1923), 830.

"The New Ohio Railroad Kings." *Literary Digest*, Vol. 76 (January 20, 1923), 12-13.

The New York Times.

"The Nickel Plate Decision." *The New Republic*, Vol. 46 (March 17, 1926), 87-88.

"Nickel Plate Merger." *The Traffic World*, Vol. 37, No. 10 (March 6, 1926), 609.

Noyes, Peter H. "A Lesson for Van Sweringen Bond-Holders." *The Nation*, Vol. 138, No. 3591 (May 2, 1934), 508–509.

"Outlook for an Empire." *The Architectural Forum*, Vol. 64, No. 3 (March, 1936), 202–205.

Pittman, Alfred. "Builders of Business." *System: The Magazine of Business*, Vol. 36 (December, 1919), 1090–1091.

Pollock, J. A. Jr. "Nickel Plate's Brilliant Future." *The Magazine of Wall Street*, Vol. 38 No. 12, (October 9, 1926), 1140–1141, 1170–1172.

Powers, Barnard. "Who's Behind the Van Sweringens?" *The Magazine of Wall Street*, Vol. 34, No. 6 (July 19, 1924), 433–435, 497–500.

"The Railroads." *The Financial World*, Vol. 45, No. 10 (March 6, 1926).

Railway Age. 1916–1936.

Railway Age Gazette. 1916–1918.

Railway Review. 1915, 1919.

"The Real Van Sweringens—Brothers, Bachelors, Builders." *The Business Week*, March 19, 1930, 36–37.

Ross, Jim Alan. "The Pioneer Erie." *Erie Railroad Magazine*, Vol. 47, No. 3, Centennial Issue (May 1951).

"Shaker Heights 50th Anniversary Issue." *The Sun-Press*, October 26, 1961.

Soule, George. "Railroad Consolidation: Where We Stand after the Van Sweringen Decision." *The New Republic*, Vol. 46 (March 31, 1926), 161–164.

Stevens, W. H. S. "Stockholders' Voting Rights and the Centralization of Voting Control." *Quarterly Journal of Economics*, Vol. 40, (May, 1926), 352–392.

Tucker, Ray T. "Teaming Up the Iron Horse: The Van Sweringens Show the Profits of Railroad Consolidation." *The Independent*, Vol. 115 (November 21, 1925), 577–578, 593–594.

Van Sweringen, O. P. "How to Protect Yourself When Buying a Home," *The American Magazine*, Vol. 85, No. 6 (June, 1916), 120–122.

"The Van Sweringens Drive Another Golden Spike." *Business Week*, April 2, 1930, 8.

"Van Sweringens Reach Out into Southwest." *Business Week*, March 19, 1930, 12–13.

Vincent, R. W. "Will the Nickel Plate Merger Ever Be?" *The Magazine of Wall Street*, Vol. 39 (February 12, 1927), 698–700, 772–774.

Waterman, Richard. "Joining Railroads Their Own Way." *The Nation's Business*, Vol. 12 (October, 1924), 52–56.

Whitten, Robert. "City Planning in Cleveland." *Art and Archaeology*, Vol. 16, Nos. 4–5 (October–November, 1923), 141–148.

Wittke, Carl. "Peter Witt, Tribune of the People." *Ohio State Archaeological and Historical Quarterly*, Vol. 58, No. 4 (October, 1949).

Wright, James L. "It Isn't Just Money to Him." *Nation's Business*, Vol. 13 (October, 1925), 28–29.

Zangerle, John A. "Shaker Village Land Values Show Rise of 7,200% in 23 Years." *Cleveland News-Leader*, November 25, 1923, Dramatic Section, p. 8.

Index